W9-CSE-065

SAP® Exchange Infrastructure for Developers

 **PRESS**

SAP PRESS is a joint initiative of SAP and Galileo Press. The know-how offered by SAP specialists combined with the expertise of the publishing house Galileo Press offers the reader expert books in the field. SAP PRESS features first-hand information and expert advice, and provides useful skills for professional decision-making.

SAP PRESS offers a variety of books on technical and business related topics for the SAP user. For further information, please visit our website: *www.sap-press.com.*

J. Stumpe, J. Orb
SAP Exchange Infrastructure
2005, 270 pp.
ISBN 978-1-59229-037-6

A. Rohr, T. Meigen, A. Fischer
SAP NetWeaver/.NET Interoperability
2007, app. 400 pp.
ISBN 978-1-59229-088-8

M. Helfen, M. Lauer, H. Trauthwein
Testing SAP Solutions
2007, app. 315 pp.
ISBN 978-1-59229-127-4

K. Verruijt, A. Roebers, A. de Heus
Job Scheduling for SAP
2006, 303 pp.
ISBN 978-1-59229-093-2

Valentin Nicolescu, Burkhardt Funk, Peter Niemeyer,
Matthias Heiler, Holger Wittges, Thomas Morandell,
Florian Visintin, Benedikt Kleine Stegemann

SAP® Exchange Infrastructure for Developers

Galileo Press

Bonn • Boston

ISBN   978-1-59229-118-2

1st edition 2007

Translation Lemoine International, Inc., Salt Lake City, UT
Editor Stefan Proksch
Copy Editor Chuck Toporek, Galileo Press, Inc., Boston, MA
Cover Design Silke Braun
Layout Design Vera Brauner
Production Iris Warkus
Typesetting SatzPro, Krefeld
Printed and bound in Germany

© 2007 by Galileo Press
SAP PRESS is an imprint of Galileo Press,
Boston (MA), USA
Bonn, Germany

German Edition first published 2006 by Galileo Press.

All rights reserved. Neither this publication nor any part of it may be copied or reproduced in any form or by any means or translated into another language, without the prior consent of Galileo Press, Rheinwerkallee 4, 53227 Bonn, Germany.

Galileo Press makes no warranties or representations with respect to the content hereof and specifically disclaims any implied warranties of merchantability or fitness for any particular purpose. Galileo Press assumes no responsibility for any errors that may appear in this publication.

All of the screenshots and graphics reproduced in this book are subject to copyright © SAP AG, Dietmar-Hopp-Allee 16, 69190 Walldorf, Germany.

SAP, the SAP logo, mySAP, mySAP.com, mySAP Business Suite, SAP NetWeaver, SAP R/3, SAP R/2, SAP B2B, SAPtronic, SAPscript, SAP BW, SAP CRM, SAP EarlyWatch, SAP ArchiveLink, SAP GUI, SAP Business Workflow, SAP Business Engineer, SAP Business Navigator, SAP Business Framework, SAP Business Information Warehouse, SAP interenterprise solutions, SAP APO, AcceleratedSAP, InterSAP, SAPoffice, SAPfind, SAPfile, SAPtime, SAPmail, SAP-access, SAP-EDI, R/3 Retail, Accelerated HR, Accelerated HiTech, Accelerated Consumer Products, ABAP, ABAP/4, ALE/WEB, BAPI, Business Framework, BW Explorer, Enjoy-SAP, mySAP.com e-business platform, mySAP Enterprise Portals, RIVA, SAPPHIRE, TeamSAP, Webflow and SAP PRESS are registered or unregistered trademarks of SAP AG, Walldorf, Germany.

All other products mentioned in this book are registered or unregistered trademarks of their respective companies.

Contents at a Glance

Contents

PART II PRACTICES AND EXERCISES

Foreword

The current discussion about *enterprise service-oriented architecture* (enterprise SOA) is firmly rooted in the idea of integrating specialist enterprise services to form flexible and modular solutions. In this context, integration platforms are used to connect and coordinate individual services on the technical level. Integration platforms thus play a central role in the modern enterprise landscape. Analyzing and learning about these platforms is therefore a key requirement in the design of modern software architectures.

Integration platforms come in many shapes and sizes, from comprehensive EAI solutions to lighter-weight offerings that currently tend to be known as *enterprise service bus* (ESB). The heterogeneity of these solutions alone prompts us to look at this topic in greater detail. Also, the sheer quantity of very specific requirements that arise from integrating processes within and across enterprises creates a significant barrier to entry that the user must first overcome.

This book is intended as a "leg-up" over this barrier. It is the result of a process of cross-pollination between theory and practice—theory in terms of its structured approach and didactic presentation of a complex topic; and practice in that it analyzes part of a piece of enterprise software that has become indispensable for most enterprises worldwide. The book invites the reader to explore new concepts by means of comprehensive examples. The focus is on practical issues in the areas of application of *SAP NetWeaver Exchange Infrastructure* (SAP XI), while the relevant underlying theory is explained to the degree that is necessary for the reader to understand the exercises.

Our hope is that this book will help many readers to get to grips with the topic of process and integration design on the basis of the SAP XI.

On that note, we wish you interesting and enlightening reading!

Prof. Dr. Helmut Krcmar
(Chair of Information Management,
Technische Universität München)

Dr. Wolfgang Fassnacht
(Senior Product Manager, SAP NetWeaver
Process Integration and Enterprise Services)

Preface

This book uses practical examples to provide you with an introduction to process-oriented integration using *SAP NetWeaver Exchange Infrastructure* (SAP XI).

Content

Integrating business processes within and across enterprise boundaries has played a central role in system landscape design for many years. While the focus was initially on the internal enterprise level, it has shifted, and is now on the implementation of process chains with external business partners. The increasing complexity of implementing these kinds of scenarios makes ever-higher demands of consultants and IT staff. "Group thinking" and "thinking outside the box" are just two approaches to overcome this challenge. An important factor in keeping up with this fast pace is engaging on a practical level with the latest state-of-the-art products in the field.

With Release 3.0 of SAP NetWeaver Exchange Infrastructure, SAP has created a product that, thanks to its extensive range of functions and easy-to-understand usability design, is particularly suitable for representing and implementing integration processes. The practical exercises in this book are intended to make you familiar with the functional processes, using this application and how it fits into SAP system landscapes as a basis.

Before focusing on the SAP product, **Chapter 1** takes a look at the approaches, architectures, and standards in the area of integration; this lays the groundwork for the exercises in Chapter 4 and 5. It also explains the significance of EAI platforms and takes an initial look at *business process management* (BPM).

Structure of the book

Chapter 2 describes how the SAP NetWeaver Exchange Infrastructure fits into the SAP product family and, in particular, clarifies its role within SAP NetWeaver. In doing so, the chapter uses simple examples to meaningfully describe the individual components of SAP XI and how they work on a fundamental level. These descriptions also introduce you to the concepts used by the components.

At this point, you are now equipped for the second, practical part of the book. To ensure that you can complete all the exercises in your SAP (training) landscape, **Chapter 3** takes you through all the necessary preparations step-by-step. It explains all the settings of the NetWeaver Exchange Infrastructure and the systems that are connected thru the NetWeaver Exchange Infrastructure in detail, so you can gain a better understanding of the technical processes in the practical exercises.

In **Chapter 4**, you carry out the first individual exercises using the prepared training landscape. This chapter focuses particularly on how to use SAP XI components and how to implement the processes. It also teaches you about the most important adapters and monitoring methods in this context. In the exercises, we have placed particular emphasis on making it easy for you to recreate and trace the origins of all objects. In doing so, none of the objects "fall out of the sky"; after all, you create most objects from scratch in your daily work. You will also examine the basics of business process management, a subject that is dealt with in greater detail in the case study.

Once you have become familiar with the underlying technologies of SAP XI, **Chapter 5** takes you through the process of implementing a complete sales process, from the customer inquiry to invoice creation. This scenario is based on the SARIDIS case study used in SAP training courses at educational institutions.

Chapter 6 provides you with ideas for expanding this case study you worked on in Chapter 5. It introduces you to the "beer distribution game," which can likewise be used as the basis of a case study. Finally, the chapter examines the significance of SAP XI in the context of *Enterprise Service-Oriented Architecture*, and gives you helpful hints on the future development of SAP NetWeaver Exchange Infrastructure.

Audience of this book

The authors of this book are active in the fields of both pedagogies and practice. Therefore, this book is suitable for a wider target readership than it may at first appear. With several years' experience of SAP training in third-level education contexts, we know about the practical demands made of consultants and graduates. At the same time, we are faced with the daily challenge of explaining complex issues in a clear, comprehensible manner.

As such, the target audience of this book is consultants, IT staff, and decision-makers who want an introduction to SAP XI. With this audience in mind, we have painstakingly chosen highly relevant and practical problems when describing concepts and selecting exercises, and have provided support and advice on how to implement SAP XI in your enterprise.

This book will also appeal to future practitioners who are preparing for "the real world" in various educational institutions, including university and technical college students. With these third- and even second-level students of information management and information technology in mind, we have tried to describe the fundamental concepts in a meaningful and memorable way, so they can understand the significance of the individual components and steps.

This wide target readership also means that this book is suitable for both the self-taught and for use in classroom settings with a student group and an instructor. The source code and examples were designed with a course size of 20 students and one instructor in mind.

To carry out the practical tasks in this book, you should already have some initial experience with SAP products and a basic understanding of how to use them. To better comprehend the exercises, you should also have some basic knowledge of ABAP programming. However, these are not absolute prerequisites, as all ABAP development work is open and available for use as a template. Knowledge of previous SAP integration mechanisms, such as IDocs, will also help you get the most from this book. **Prerequisites**

The goal of this book is to enable you to quickly and easily delve into the SAP NetWeaver Exchange Infrastructure and its functions. Our hope is that the information you find in this book is easy to understand, and the examples can be quickly adapted to your work in the real-world. Unfortunately, the complexity of the material doesn't always make it possible for us to present "finished" components and settings. Nonetheless, we have done so wherever possible. The book's companion Web sites—*http://www.sap-press.com* and *http://www. sap-press.de/1383*—contain templates for files, transports, sample code, and everything else to make it easier for you to work on the exercises. In addition to the exercises and the case study, you'll also find many other ideas at the end of the book that you can use to further develop the practical exercises and apply to other case studies and scenarios. **Notes on usage**

We make every effort to include an errata list of any errors that you or we may notice, as quickly and in as much detail as possible. Do not hesitate to let us know about any errors you notice, and feel free to suggest any improvements that could be made to the book for future editions. At the same time, keep in mind that this book represents the first step in this area for many readers, so we have kept the content as simple and as relevant to everyday practice as possible. This balancing act has meant that in many places we have not described the problems in as much depth as we otherwise could have. Nonetheless, we hope that other authors will take up where we leave off, possibly even in direct response to this book.

Acknowledgments There is no doubt that this book would not exist if many people had not at first encouraged us to work on this project, and then actually done what they promised to do—that is, take an active part in creating this work.

We would first like to thank our families and friends, who supported and encouraged us right through the conception and writing phases.

We also want to thank all the others who provided us with help and advice: Thomas Mattern, Wolfgang Fassnacht, Harald Nehring and Sven Gierse, who helped with the conception of this book; Sven Leukert, Claudia Weller and Thomas Volmering for reviewing the individual chapters; Heino Schrader and Professor Dr. Helmut Krcmar for providing access to the XI system; Dr. Amelia Maurizio and James Farrar in the SAP University Alliances program, for their support; Dr. Markus Friesen, Andreas Holz, Eckhard Schaumann and Michael Unterberger of SUN for providing and supporting great hardware; Matthias Mohr and Astrid Hoffmann for allowing us to use the SARIDIS case study; Joachim Biggel for his help with ABAP development; Patrick Bollinger who helped us with "teething problems"; and last but by no means least, Alexander Mors, Andre Bögelsack and Holger Jehle in the *SAP Hochschul Competence Center* at the Technische Universität München.

Valentin Nicolescu   Prof. Dr. Burkhardt Funk
Prof. Dr. Peter Niemeyer   Matthias Heiler
Dr. Holger Wittges   Thomas Morandell
Florian Visintin   Benedikt Kleine Stegemann
June 2006

PART I
Basics

This chapter explains why it is necessary to integrate information systems and the basic issues involved. It also discusses the main difficulties of integration and presents concepts for solving these problems.

1 Integrating Enterprise Information Systems

1.1 Basic Principles

The heterogeneity of modern application landscapes means that integrating enterprise information systems is one of the main tasks that face IT departments.

This chapter outlines the development of this subject area, and explains why integration is so important in this context. A practical example provides an overview of the problems that can arise in the integration process, as well as the concepts and technologies used to solve these problems. The chapter ends with a review of the components found in a typical integration platform, such as SAP NetWeaver.

1.1.1 Historical development

In the 1950s and 1960s, enterprise IT landscapes were dominated by mainframe computers and the monolithic application systems that ran on them. At the time, very few business processes were supported by IT, and thus, there was no clear need to integrate these individual solutions. However, as enterprise IT support became more common at the start of the 1970s, there was an increasing need to integrate enterprise applications, such as those used for materials management, human resources, and financial accounting. In the same period, the "Cologne" integration model of Grochla, and the reference models of Scheer and Mertens, led to the first concepts of integrated information processing.

Starting-point: Monolithic application systems

CIM and ERP   The subject of integration took on a more practical approach with the development of *computer-integrated manufacturing* (CIM). The primary benefit of CIM is that it automates data flow between different applications. For example, in the automobile industry, *bills of materials* (BOMs) could be generated in a *computer-aided design* (CAD) system and then automatically transferred to and used in materials management and *production planning and control systems* (PPS).

Since the mid-1980s, *enterprise resource planning (ERP) providers have been working toward the goal of providing pre-integrated applications.* This works very well, provided that only applications from a single provider (one "software generation") are used. However, practice has shown that although they use ERP systems, most companies still favor outdated, standalone applications, which, because of their complexity and importance for the business, are simply too expensive to replace with standard software. What's more, enterprises often take the *best-of-breed* approach; in other words, they simply choose the best product on the market in the case of each individual application. Both of these issues highlight the need to integrate IT systems.

Cross-enterprise   While the initial focus was on integrating internal enterprise applica-
integration   tion systems (*enterprise application integration* [see Conrad, et al., 2006]), cross-enterprise integration came onto the scene by the end of the 1970s (see Figure 1.1). Initially, the focus was on bilateral data exchange based on data carriers and proprietary formats. Semantic and industry-specific standards, such as SWIFT (banking), ODETTE (automotive) and RosettaNet (high-tech), were later added to these formats within the framework of *Electronic Data Interchange* (EDI). While these standards are still in use today, XML-based message formats have increased in importance. Using standards such as the *Resource Description Framework* (RDF), these formats can support the naming conventions of individual industries and, at the same time, be adapted to each individual case.

Today's electronic marketplaces and e-procurement platforms place the emphasis on specialist applications that enable process-oriented integration across enterprise boundaries. Widely-used standards, such as message formats and protocols, and infrastructure services, such as security, process engines, and monitoring, make this kind of integration cost-efficient, fast, and flexible to implement. Integration platforms—commercial or free—are being increasingly used for this purpose. SAP NetWeaver Exchange Infrastructure (XI) is one such platform.

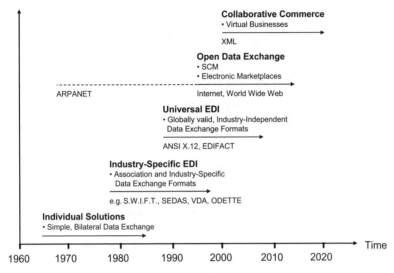

Figure 1.1 Historical Development of Cross-Enterprise Integration (Source: Scheckenbach, 1997)

1.1.2 Reasons for and goals of integrating IT systems

The technical reasons for integrating IT systems can be divided into the following three categories:

▶ **Platform differences**
This includes different programming languages, development and runtime environments, and various commercial components (such as databases).

▶ **Architecture differences**
This category includes different system and software architectures (for example, client/server architecture versus four-tier Web architecture) and different message modes (synchronous versus asynchronous).

▶ **Use of third-party and distributed services**
If enterprise services are distributed across multiple locations, or if an enterprise wants to use services of other enterprises (or both), these services are integrated using online interfaces or batch processing technologies.

Goals of
integration

According to studies by the Gartner Group and Forrester Research, Fortune 1000 companies spend $100 billion annually (i.e., around 35 percent of their IT budget) on integration work. The business goals of companies that make this high level of investment are as follows:

- To develop new products, reach new target customer groups, and incorporate more suppliers
- To achieve greater flexibility in the organization of processes and comprehensive process automation
- To reduce latency times in information delivery and information processing
- To reduce development costs

Also, a particular technical goal of any integration process is to reduce complexity and to enable existing software components and systems to be reused.

1.1.3 Characteristics of integration

According to Mertens, integration has four main characteristics: object, direction, scope, and degree of automation.

Integration object

Data, programs, functions, processes, and services are all *integration objects*. Data and programs refer to the technical elements that are to be integrated, while functions, processes, and services represent the business elements. For example, a service could be a credit-check of a potential customer. This service could itself be integrated into an order processing process which is linked to other services.

Integration
direction

As Figure 1.2 shows, *integration direction* differentiates between vertical and horizontal integration.

- *Vertical integration* supports decision-making within the framework of planning and control systems. The primary goal is to integrate data from different applications and data storage locations in the operational application systems. The various sales systems in a large mail order company (such as an online store, mail order, or call center) are good examples of vertical integration. Data from the individual sales systems is identified and aggregated to create cross-enterprise sales statistics. Sections 1.2 and 1.3 discuss the problems that can occur in this context, as well as their solutions.

▶ *Horizontal integration* connects the different stages of the value chain. For example, when the sales department receives a sales order, a staff member in that department forwards the order to the procurement department, then to the production department before the ordered goods are finally delivered.

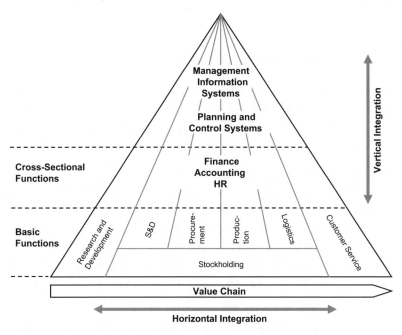

Figure 1.2 Horizontal and vertical integration within an enterprise (based on Mertens)

Integration scope also differentiates between cross-enterprise and intra-enterprise integration. Based on Mertens, the latter is divided into intra-department and cross-department integration, as before. An example of cross-department integration is a CRM system that accesses data and functions from the marketing, sales, product management, and customer service departments.

Integration scope

Regardless of whether human-machine interaction is required in the integration of IT systems, a distinction is drawn between fully-automated and partially-automated integration. Partially-automated integration requires functions to initiate and coordinate communication between human and machine. This can be done either by components that are developed in-house, components of an integration platform, or a specific *workflow management system* (WMS). Aside

Degree of automation and latency periods

from the *degree of automation*, the processing type and its associated latency period are also important integration characteristics. A distinction is drawn here between integration that takes place in real-time (such as credit card processing in an online store), and integration that takes place only a specific points in time (such as batch processing invoices).

1.2   Practical Integration Example

Example: Invoice verification process Now that you have learned about the reasons for and characteristics of integration in the previous section, this section uses the example of a core operational process—invoice verification—to illustrate the challenges that arise when integrating business processes.

Invoice verification process checks a number of things. For example, the customer should only pay for goods and services he has ordered and received, and he should only pay for them once. Also, in this age of the *Sarbanes-Oxley Act* (SOX), companies listed on the New York Stock Exchange (NYSE) are required by law to provide evidence of the goods and services they purchase. As such, it must be possible to audit the invoice verification and processing process, even for an archived invoice.

The invoice itself contains important information for auditing purposes, including:

▸ Details of the party who issued the invoice

▸ The goods or services for which it was issued

▸ Details about the party who ordered these goods or services

▸ When the goods or services were ordered

▸ The stock and/or serial numbers for the goods or services

The purchasing company must also maintain details of purchase orders, goods receipt confirmations, and previously paid invoices for future reference.

Multiple IT systems and applications This process usually involves multiple IT systems and applications. For example, orders and goods receipts are often executed in multiple, non-centralized ordering and goods receipt systems. Meanwhile, payments are processed in a centralized accounting system.

24

Therefore, it isn't always obvious which system contains the order. Also, the payment process may be handled by a *shared service center* for different regions, or the entire process may be outsourced to a *business process outsourcing* (BPO) provider. Both scenarios add another layer of complexity to the integration challenge. In the case of services, there usually isn't an application that fulfills a role similar to goods receipt. Instead, a workflow is triggered when the invoice is received, which causes the invoice to be released, rejected, or modified by the ordering party. In this case, a workflow can consist of multiple individual tasks (for example, if two employees need to approve an invoice before it can be paid, regardless of the amount).

The process steps shown in Figure 1.3 examine some of the real-world problems and tasks associated with integration from the viewpoint of the ordering company.

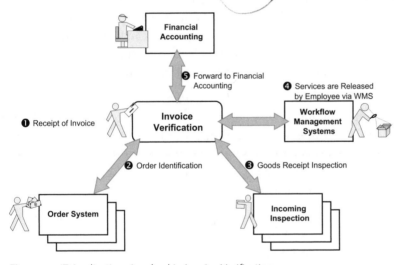

Figure 1.3 IT Applications Involved in Invoice Verification

Invoices can be received (see ❶) either in paper or electronic form. For the sake of compliance with statutory and legal requirements, electronic invoices must be digitally signed, and the digital signature must be checked at the invoice receipt stage (business and process complexity).

The actual invoice documents can contain either unstructured data (for example, a PDF document) or structured data (for example, EDIFACT, XML, or CSV). If the latter, it is possible — and indeed, preferable—to automatically import the data into the ordering company's IT system.

Except in cases where the ordering party has the market strength to specify binding requirements regarding invoice content and format to its suppliers (for example, to use a particular standard such as EDI-FACT), schema and data conflicts can arise between internal and external data display (see Conrad, 1997; Conrad, et al., 2006).

Schema conflicts

▶ A structural *schema conflict* exists if, for example, a supplier uses separate attributes to display the house number and street name, while the ordering party uses a single attribute that combines the two attributes. Similarly, the supplier may represent individual invoice items hierarchically, while the ordering company may combine these in a single order item.

▶ Aside from structural schema conflicts, various *description conflicts* can occur in integration. These can include scaling conflicts—due to different quantity and currency units—and data type conflicts. For example, a Postal or Zip Code may be displayed as a figure in one system and as a character string in another.

Data conflicts

▶ Unlike schema conflicts, *data conflicts* are content-based. In the context of integration, they can result from incorrect data and differing representations. A manual transfer error that occurs in the order processing process on the supplier's side can result in an incorrect order number, which then cannot be correctly assigned by the automatic invoice verification process.

In this case, a workflow is triggered that uses a similar analysis to provide the staff member with suggestions for which order is most likely to be the one in question on the invoice. Individual attributes can also be represented in different ways. For example, a contact person's gender can be coded as *male* or *female* on the supplier's side, while the ordering company may instead use a salutation, such as Mr. or Ms. The goal when solving these conflicts is to standardize incoming data in an internal format that can be interpreted by downstream applications.

Location transparency

The next step in invoice verification (see ❷) is to identify the order that belongs to the incoming invoice. For this, you must first identify the originating order system as there are multiple order systems at various locations. This is accomplished by using system-specific number ranges (such as 123–4711 for system 123). Because the actual invoice verification process doesn't contain information about the order systems and their technical location (a condition known as *location transparency*), a service is called that combines all the information about the landscape of the underlying order system; this service then calls the correct system. This functionality, known as *routing*, is implemented in the section on *recipient determination* in Chapter 4.

The incoming inspection (see ❸) is also executed in different applications at different locations. As before, a suitable encapsulation concept is used to establish location transparency from the viewpoint of the invoice verification process. If the incoming inspection systems were developed or purchased at different points in time, the interface technologies being used are also often different. For example, one system may process HTTP and Web service requests, while another may process only CORBA requests. As with location transparency, components that "hide" the technical complexity of the interfaces from the central process are required here. Also, for the incoming inspection to run smoothly, there are often communications restrictions on the network level (for example, firewalls or network address translators [NAT]) which must be considered.

Interface technologies

As described earlier, services rendered are verified (see ❹) by creating a workflow. Workflow management systems usually use *asynchronous communication*, which means that requests to the system (in this case, the request to initiate the workflow) won't wait for a response (after all, the ordering party first has to manually release the invoice). Instead, the called system notifies the calling party after the workflow task is completed. There are two prerequisites for this:

Communications types: Synchronous and asynchronous

▸ The network has to be available

▸ The calling party that is using the called system must have a callback system so it can respond to requests at any time.

In particular, the necessity of a callback system often causes problems because changes need to be made to the IT applications, as well as to the processes themselves. For example, if the IT application that supports the invoice verification process requires synchronous communication (this is sufficient for Steps ❷ and ❹ in Figure 1.3), an adapter is needed to receive incoming requests from the invoice verification process. This process formally responds synchronously to these events and forwards them asynchronously to the WMS. For the response from the WMS, the adapter makes the appropriate callback interface available. When the invoice is finally released, it is forwarded from the WMS to the financial accounting department (see Step ❺ in Figure 1.3).

Integration of the various IT systems in an enterprise is a prerequisite for an automated invoice verification process. The integration problems described in this section can obviously also occur in other integration scenarios, and integration platforms such as SAP XI provides corresponding functions (mapping) to solve these problems. This is discussed in greater detail in Section 1.4.

1.3　Integration Concepts and Technologies

Several concepts and technologies have been developed to solve integration problems described in Section 1.2. However, these aren't discussed in detail in this chapter; Appendix B provides a list for additional reading on this topic. Instead, we will describe the aspects of architectures, integration approaches, and technologies that are most important for using the SAP NetWeaver Exchange Infrastructure.

1.3.1　Architectures

Point-to-point integration

In the past, due to the lack of suitable concepts and technologies, integrating individual applications involved developing proprietary interfaces and directly connecting IT systems to each other. In practice, this still happens today when integrating a small number of applications. The primary benefit of this kind of *point-to-point integration* is that its implementation requires less time and effort than the introduction of a centralized integration solution.

However, because the number of required connections increases exponentially with the number of applications to be integrated, the level of complexity and the time and effort required for maintenance also quickly increases. Moreover, individual applications require information about the formats, interface technologies, and physical availability (for example, location and security mechanisms) of the other applications. If these properties change for one application, the other applications linked to it then have to be adapted accordingly.

These disadvantages can be overcome by introducing a centralized component.

▶ In a *hub-and-spoke architecture* (see Figure 1.4), the hub is the central integration platform. The applications to be integrated—the "spokes"—are connected to the hub either directly or via lightweight connectors.

Hub and spoke

The goal here is to make as few adaptations to the applications as possible during the integration process. Because the integration platform in hub-and-spoke architectures performs tasks such as routing and mapping, the applications need only limited information about the other applications with which they want to exchange information. The disadvantage of this architecture is that the central integration platform represents a *single point of failure* (SPOF) and a bottleneck in terms of message throughput.

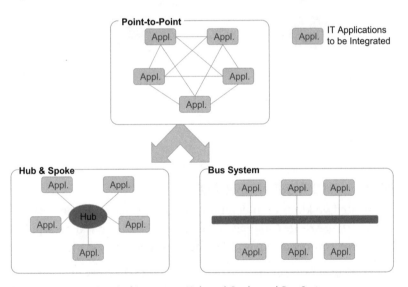

Figure 1.4 Integration Architectures—Hub-and-Spoke and Bus Systems

▶ This is where the *enterprise service bus* (ESB) concept comes in. Its purpose is to avoid both the "spaghetti" configuration of point-to-point integration and the single central component of the hub-and-spoke architecture. The ESB itself is not a self-contained component; rather, it consists of individual ESB services that are

Enterprise service bus

linked to each other in a message-oriented manner on the basis of Web services (see Figure 1.5).

Applications integrated with an ESB either already have a Web service interface or they use an appropriate wrapper. This approach has better scalability and availabiltiy than the hub-and-spoke architecture. However, on the minus side, it is more difficult to monitor and administrate the system. In this context, the SAP NetWeaver Exchange Infrastructure can be regarded as an ESB service used to create an ESB.

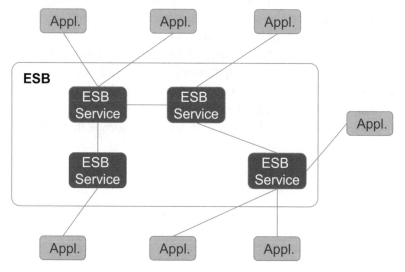

Figure 1.5 Enterprise Service Bus

1.3.2 Integration approaches

There are two kinds of integration approaches: data- and process-oriented. *Data-oriented approaches* focus on the technical viewpoint, while *process-oriented approaches* focus on the business viewpoint.

Data-oriented integration

Data-oriented integration is based on the various layers of a software system. In practice, integration is often based on *data storage*. With data storage, either the systems to be integrated jointly access a relational database, or the datasets are replicated or federated, or both. Database federation is done either physically or virtually. Physical federation involves bringing together the data, while virtual federation keeps the datasets physically separate and combines them virtually using multi-database languages such as SQL and MED.

Complex business applications typically don't have direct access to the datasets, as data integrity is ensured mainly by the connected application systems as well as by the database. Also, the required business information, such as the goods receipt confirmation in the invoice verification process described earlier, is not that easy to obtain by means of a simple database query. For this reason, application systems provide interfaces for *functional-level* integration (for example, BAPI and RFC).

For completeness, it's important to mention integration on the level of the presentation layer. In companies, this approach is used in the case of older applications that do not have direct access to the data storage (because of a proprietary database, for example) or its functions, but the company wants to integrate the functionality (e.g., in a portal). There are various tools for doing this. These tools include a terminal application with a user interface. Another application area of this integration approach is competition monitoring. Airlines, for example, can use this to monitor the booking levels of their competitors' flights to adjust their own prices.

Integration via presentation layer

Process-oriented integration uses the previously-mentioned functions on the technical level to link systems together, but concentrates on the business process. Integration platforms that support this approach (such as SAP XI) make it possible to model business processes, while also providing a suitable runtime environment. In the spirit of "separation of responsibilities," these tools keep the process logic separate from the individual applications. Configuration is independent of the business process design, so it is possible to exchange individual applications and flexibly use internal and external services (see Section 1.5).

Process-oriented integration

This concept is at the forefront of the current discussion about *service-oriented architectures* (SOA). The term "services" here refers to business-relevant, self-contained applications that can be used in various business processes. The literature (see Erl, 2006) describes numerous properties to such services, including:

Service-oriented architectures

▸ **Self-describing**
The service can be fully described on a formal level; that is, what operations are available and which data types can be exchanged. Formal self-description is the basis for the automatic generation of

proxies. Here, the word "Description" doesn't refer to the semantic description.

▶ **Locatable**
Potential consumers can locate and contact the service. There is a registry for this purpose that functions as the "Yellow Pages" of services and allows users to search for services.

▶ **Roughly structured**
Services are roughly structured when they return comprehensive data (for example, a sales order) in response to a service call instead of delivering individual attributes (such as an order quantity).

▶ **Loosely linked**
Services are said to be loosely linked when possible functional changes within the services have no effect on the available operations.

▶ **Independent**
Services are considered independent if they have no dependencies on other services; the availability of a service is not dependent on the availability and proper functioning of another service.

▶ **Reusable**
Reusability is one of the most important and longest-standing requirements in software technology. Its aim is to ensure that components are reused as often as possible without modification to the functional core and interfaces.

Service consumer, service provider, service registrar

There are three basic roles in service-oriented architectures:

▶ **Service consumer**
The service consumer first searches for a suitable services, implements the interfaces manually or automatically on the basis of the formal self-description, and then uses the service.

▶ **Service provider**
The service provider develops a service, makes it available as a Web service, and processes queries from service consumers on an ongoing basis.

▶ **Service registrar**
The service registrar provides registration services to service providers, and provides corresponding directory services to service consumers (such as service searches based on specific criteria).

The connection between these roles is shown in Figure 1.6. Section 6.3 explains the SAP view of a SOA in greater detail, as well as the significance of SAP XI in this context.

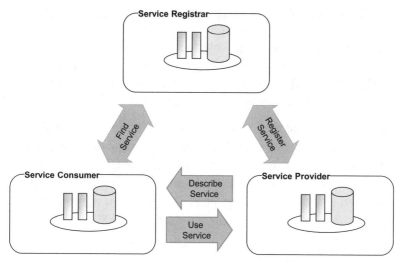

Figure 1.6 Roles in a Service-Oriented Architecture (SOA)

1.3.3 Technologies

Several integration technologies have been developed and used in recent decades, and it is beyond the scope of this book to describe them all in detail. Instead, the important technologies are reviewed in the context of SAP XI. Recommendations for further, more detailed reading on this topic are also presented.

Integration technologies can be generally divided into transport-oriented, object-oriented, message-oriented, and semantic standards.

▶ Transport-oriented standards are network-based protocols. SAP XI allows developers to build adapters that provide interfaces to the various standards. The current version of SAP XI enables external services and data to be integrated by means of HTTP, FTP, and SMTP. Section 4.1 in the practical part of this book demonstrates how to use the FTP adapter.

Transport-oriented standards

▶ There is a wide variety of object-oriented integration technologies. The most important are CORBA (see Aleksy, et al., 2005), RMI (see Grosso, 2001), and COM/DCOM. SAP XI currently does not provide adapters for these technologies, but it does enable

Object-oriented standards

commercial third-party products to be used and in-house adapters to be developed using the *Java Connector Architecture* (see Sharma, et al., 2002).

Message-oriented standards

▶ Message-oriented technologies have always been very important for integrating business applications. The reason for this is the necessity to use message communication in asynchronous use cases. There are various technologies and products (for example, WebSphere MQ by IBM) and general standards (such as Sun's Java Messaging Service); however, these are not described in this book.

Aside from technologies and standards, which are used to make the required infrastructure available for message exchange, the description and format of messages are also important; this is known as *semantic standards*. The SAP NetWeaver Exchange Infrastructure uses Web services (see Alonso, et al., 2004) for this purpose, in particular the *Web Service Description Language* (WSDL) and *Simple Object Access Protocol* (SOAP).

SOAP

SOAP is independent of transport protocol and communication mode (RPC vs. message-oriented), and uses XML for data display. Listing 1.1 shows an example of the structure of a SOAP message.

```
<?xml version='1.0' ?>
<env:Envelope
  xmlns:env="http://www.w3.org/2003/05/soap-envelope">
  <env:Header>
    <n:transaction xmlns:n="http://a.url.com/ns"
      env:mustUnderstand="true">
      <n:id>4711xyz</n:id>
    </n:transaction>
  </env:Header>
  <env:Body>
    <p:payment xmlns:p="http://bank.com/ns">
      <p:ccholder>Sandra Miller</p:ccholder>
      <p:ccnumber>4200000000000000</p:ccnumber>
      <p:valid>11.08</p:valid>
    </p:payment>
  </env:Body>
</env:Envelope>
```

Listing 1.1 Example of a SOAP Message

Every SOAP message consists of an envelope, an optional header inside the envelope, and the content, known as the body. The header contains meta-information about the message. It can contain session IDs and control the routing and encryption. The body contains application-specific data.

> **Note**
>
> SOAP is a W3C (*http://www.w3.org/TR/soap*) specification and is currently at version 1.2 (June 2003).

Syntactically, SOAP messages are described using WSDL. A WSDL document provides information about the more sophisticated data types used within a message, and the operations (functions) provided by a Web service. It also describes the formal properties of this service (for example, request-response vs. one-way) and the data types used. A WSDL document also specifies the link between (SOAP) messages and the transport protocol, and states the location of the service (URL). Proxy classes can be automatically generated using WSDL documents; these classes are then used as a basis for the server and for the client.

WSDL

SAP XI uses SOAP (or, more precisely, *SOAP with attachments*) for internal message communication. Section 4.3 in Part II of this book demonstrates some uses of external Web services in SAP XI. Conversely, interfaces defined in SAP XI can be provided externally as a Web service, including an automatically-generated WSDL document.

Various, mainly XML-based approaches have been developed for including Web services in business processes. The *Business Process Execution Language for Web Services* (BPEL or BPEL4WS; see Juric, et al., 2006) is a standard of the OASIS Group (*http://www.oasis-open.org*). BPEL is supported by several large software providers and is the basis of the SAP XI Business Process Engine. This Engine graphically displays executable processes and saves them as BPEL documents.

BPEL

BPEL documents specify which Web services can be called in a business process, in what order they can be called, whether these calls are synchronous or asynchronous, and which prerequisites have to be met before they can be called.

BPEL also provides variable declaration so that the status of business processes can be saved. The basic structured activities for specifying process logic that you are familiar with from programming languages are also available in BPEL: loops, conditions, sequences, and exceptions. BPEL processes can be called directly from within SAP XI, and can also be made available externally as a Web service. Section 4.4 describes how to use the Business Process Engine and BPEL.

1.4   EAI Platforms and Their Significance in Enterprises

When IT systems are integrated in practice, comprehensive integration platforms are often used instead of in-house software. Such platforms provide solutions to the problems discussed in Section 1.2, and are based on the concepts and technologies described in Section 1.3.

Both open source and commercial platforms are available. Open source solutions such as jBPM (*http://www.jboss.com/products/jbpm*) and ServiceMix (*http://servicemix.org*) concentrate mainly on individual subareas of integration; for example, business process modeling and execution. Commercial providers include world-leading software providers such as SAP (SAP NetWeaver Exchange Infrastructure), Microsoft (Microsoft BizTalk) and IBM (IBM WebSphere Business Integration), and providers that specialize in integration, such as TIBCO (TIBCO BusinessWorks) and Vitria Technology (BusinessWare).

Components of integration platforms

Typical components of integration platforms used in business-oriented integration processes that you will get to know as part of SAP XI are described as follows:

▶ **Mapper**
Mappers are used to transform data, thus tackling possible data and schema conflicts between the sender and recipient of a message.

▶ **Router**
Routers are used to set routing rules and thus to specify which intermediate points are used to send a message to the intended recipient. Routers are oriented around the metadata and content of a message, and as such are responsible for location transparency.

▶ **Repository**

Repositories contains reusable interface specifications and message mappings, and have information about the individual external systems to be integrated. SAP XI contains the *integration repository* (mappings and interfaces) and the *system landscape directory* (an overview of IT systems and software components).

▶ **Adapter**

Integration platforms provide various adapters for the interface technologies described in Section 1.3.3, and also provide general interfaces that extend the functionality of these adapters. Adapters are also available for the most common business applications (and their various versions).

▶ **Business process modeling**

Business process modeling makes it possible to model business processes (mainly graphically) and in many cases to translate the model into BPEL.

▶ **Runtime environment**

This is the runtime environment for mappers, routers, and adapters. As with SAP XI, the process engine is often another component of the runtime environment that makes it possible to execute the previously modeled business processes.

▶ **Configuration**

The configuration is used to administrate and configure real-world integration scenarios and business processes.

▶ **Monitoring**

The monitoring function provides tools for monitoring the runtime environment and makes it possible to analyze individual messages.

It almost always makes sense to use integration platforms[1] in complex integration projects. There are many reasons for this: it increases flexibility in terms of business process management and makes it possible to reuse interfaces, mappings, and sub-processes in a variety of integration scenarios. If business standard software is used, the integration platform takes care of version-based translations in the adapters and lightens the workload of the developers.

---

1 It depends on the respective requirements to decide which integration platform is appropriate for a project (e.g., scope of adapters, infrastructure requirements, expected message throughput). You can find a comprehensive checklist that supports this selection in *Enterprise Application Integration* (Keller 2002).

Also, despite the time it takes employees to get used to the individual characteristics of a product, the implementation period of integrating the project is reduced, as the main components already exist and therefore only have to be adapted or configured. This book helps you in the process of getting used to SAP XI.

1.5   Basics of Business Process Management

Business process modeling as a facilitator

In *business process management* (BPM), the focus is on a holistic view of business processes with the aim of improving them on an ongoing basis. The reasons for using BPM are as follows:

▶ Model-based planning and adaptation of innovative business processes

▶ Holistic view of business processes

▶ Standardization of business processes

Business process modeling is a central task in this context. It involves extracting and representing information required for the identification, optimization, and controlled execution of processes. Mainly informal and semi-formal graphical description languages with textual extensions are used for this purpose. These languages serve as a common basis of discussion for consultants, employees in the technical departments, and management, and facilitate communication between these parties.

Business process modeling consolidates processes

The main focus of process modeling is on business work processes. These range from manual processes that are executed without any technical support (such as storing goods in the inventory) to partially-automated processes (such as software system-supported order receipt) to fully automated processes (such as an automatic posting procedure or a database transaction). The task of business process modeling is to create a consolidated understanding of the business process from the technical and the business process viewpoint.

Figure 1.7 shows the content and context of the business process modeling tool ARIS and the BPM tools in the SAP NetWeaver stack. ARIS is used for process analysis and process design. As its basis, ARIS uses the SAP reference processes that are available with the ARIS toolset for SAP NetWeaver. The SAP Solution Manager as a component of SAP NetWeaver supports the technical implementation and monitoring business processes in the SAP system. To do this, it uses the XI component that allows processes to be modeled and executed within an application, but also across applications. The lower part of the figure shows how applications are connected.

It is clear how the integration of business process model, technical process configuration, and process execution should be planned. The integration of SAP XI with different applications using proprietary and standardized interfaces is very advanced and is already in production use. Integration of ARIS and SAP NetWeaver is available in an initial version, and its further development is currently a focal point of the cooperation between IDS Scheer AG and SAP.

Forced integration of ARIS and SAP NetWeaver

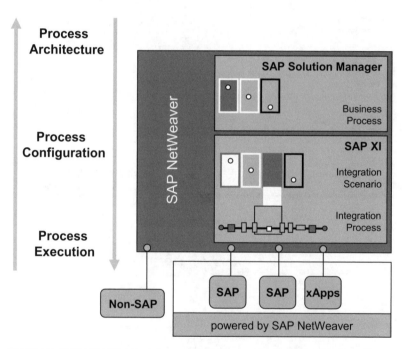

Figure 1.7 Connecting Business Process Modeling and Business Process Execution

Figure 1.8 shows how the four tools for mapping process flows (ARIS, SAP Guided Procedures, SAP XI [BPEL] and SAP Workflows) jointly specify the content of BPM runtime. Access can then be implemented independently of the selected technology using the portal (this is transparent to the user).

The vision—which has already been partly realized, as evidenced by the availability of initial services—is to use the ESA to bridge the gap between business modeling and technical implementation. The XI integration platform plays a central role as a link between processes and services.

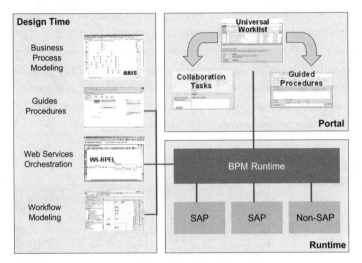

Figure 1.8 BPM Runtime Environment as a Process Integration Platform

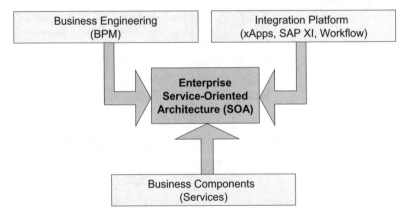

Figure 1.9 Enterprise SOA Brings Together Business Processes and Their Technical Implementation

In summary, albeit in simplified form, we can visualize the business components or services as components with standardized interfaces (as shown in Figure 1.9), which are integrated by means of the business process via an integration platform (such as SAP XI), in accordance with the business requirements.

This chapter describes how you can include SAP NetWeaver Exchange Infrastructure (XI) in an overall integration concept, as well as the functionality and interactions of SAP XI components.

2 SAP NetWeaver Exchange Infrastructure

2.1 SAP XI as Part of SAP NetWeaver

If you examine a company's processes today, you'll find that these processes are always business-related and that they run across different internal and external applications. They also involve the interaction of people (employees, customers, interested persons, suppliers, and so on) who must be integrated into the process. Along with these processes, a large amount of data (master data and transaction data) is created and stored either in databases or as unstructured documents, such as PDF or Word files.

Integration requirements in companies

Both data types must be made available to the user in a consolidated and aggregated form. After all, an employee does not want to look into several different lists to determine the aggregated revenues of his customers in a specific region or to identify the changes compared to the previous year. Instead, the employee wants to use a tool that provides all this information right away and presents it in an appealing manner; for instance, as a bar chart. Only this turns pure data into real information. And finally, the individual process steps carried out in different applications must be integrated via an integration platform to become consistent processes.

2.1.1 Challenges of Process Integration

In general, there are four main challenges regarding the integration process:

Processes are subject to change

▶ **System landscape**
Enterprises are divided into in separate business units with independent IT systems in heterogeneous system landscapes.

▶ **Integration of end users**
Role-based accesses to actions and interactions (collaborative processes) must be created for end-users.

▶ **Enterprise application integration**
Applications must interact with each other inside and outside the company to map end-to-end business processes.

▶ **B2B integration**
Interacting organizations, business partners (suppliers, customers, stakeholders) require the support of industry standards.

Figure 2.1 illustrates these four areas.

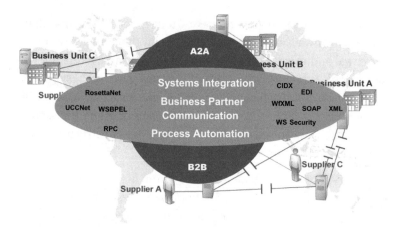

Figure 2.1 Challenges of Process Integration

Integrating People

Integration via front-end

In Section 1.2, the challenges of integrating business processes have already been described on the basis of the invoice verification process. If you recall, the invoice verification process checks whether the goods and services that have been ordered and delivered correspond to each other, and it determines whether or not the invoices have been paid yet. At the same time, it must be possible to audit the invoice verification process. This includes the following problems:

▸ Different schemas, formats, and goods receipt types must be processed. The different systems involved employ different interface technologies and communication types.

▸ The process is not automated. The auditor often manually interferes with the process, making the process inconsistent since the auditor has to use several different systems.

▸ The process is prone to errors since the auditor can simply forget an invoice that's included in the list of invoices to be verified.

▸ The process is time-consuming and cumbersome as it tends to reduce the user's productivity and motivation.

The reason for this time-consuming and error-prone process is that the human acts as the process integrator and not the software solution. To attain process efficiency, the procedure—and above all, the IT support of the invoice verification process—have changed significantly over time. Use of Internet technologies and new end-devices such as PDAs, mobile phones, etc., considerably optimizes the invoice verification process.

Man as a process integrator

For instance, you can use *optical character recognition* (OCR) software to scan invoices and display them in a portal along with the data from the purchasing application and the goods receipt system. This way, different user interfaces are merged into a uniform browser display. Thus, users no longer need to familiarize themselves with different application UIs and can work more efficiently.

Similarly, you can integrate office applications in the portal solution, for example, to create a document for the supplier stating that an invoice has been rejected. This means that a people integration layer is required to improve the invoice verification process.

Integrating Information

The integration of a search engine in the portal enables fast searches through structured and unstructured documents; for instance, to find additional invoices from the same supplier. In addition to providing extensive search options, the necessary components for integrating information must be able to merge different types of supplier master data, such as the supplier number maintained in different systems, into a cross-reference table. Moreover, the component should

Integration through a data warehouse

provide relevant information on the supplier in the way of analysis and reports.

Orders are often not completely fulfilled, or the delivery occurs after the agreed upon date. To analyze such deviations at an aggregate level (for example, deviations of a supplier in New England within the last few months), you need an appropriate application.

These are typically the functions provided by a business intelligence solution. The source systems, such as the warehouse, the ordering system, or the accounting system, provide separate documents such as purchase orders, goods receipt documents, and invoices that all pertain to the same purchase order. These documents are then imported into a data warehouse for instance, using an *Enterprise Application Infrastructure* (EAI) platform. The data warehouse allows you to consolidate the data and run certain analyses. Furthermore, it allows you to navigate into the details of purchase orders to identify the cause of the deviation. The latter is made possible by InfoCubes and so-called *operational data stores* (ODS).

If an integration layer exists that combines consolidated and aggregated information with the business process, you can enhance the invoice verification process with an analysis function. Otherwise, the information can be displayed along with the operational data as embedded analysis for the user.

Integrating Processes

Integrating the EAI platform and BPM

A third integration layer is necessary in the invoice verification process. In addition to integrating data from different systems, you'll need to determine when and under what circumstances individual systems and applications need to be integrated. As discussed in Chapter 1, this is the central task of the process integration layer.

Business process management

To continuously improve the process, you can use business process management (BPM) functions. For example, BPM functions allow you to combine the individual steps of the invoice verification process with each other to automate the process or to reduce the lead times of individual processes. BPM functionality is another element within a process integration layer and represents an essential part of modern integration platforms.

SAP NetWeaver
Exchange Infrastructure

SAP NetWeaver Portal

Office Integration

Quick Search

SAP NetWeaver
Business
Intelligence

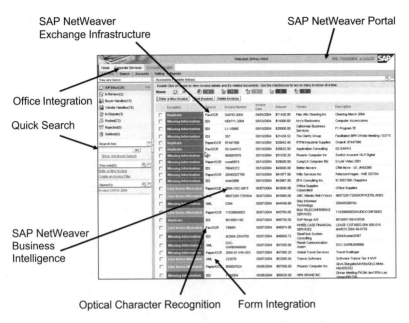

Optical Character Recognition   Form Integration

Figure 2.2 Using new Technologies in the Invoice Verification Process

SAP XI provides both functions—that of integration broker and the BPM function—into one integrated platform. Figure 2.2 shows how new technologies can be used to meet the specific integration requirements. As such, the relevant information (regardless of where it originates) is displayed in a standardized portal interface. Invoices have been digitalized upfront via OCR and distributed through an EAI layer. PDF forms are interactively integrated for further processing, information can be forwarded via email whenever necessary, and you can launch the appropriate analyses and reports for specific data.

Application Platform

Last but not least, different integration layers must run on one application platform. In this case, an application server is used. SAP NetWeaver Application Server combines two traits: In addition to an infrastructure for program development and execution, it also allows you to develop J2EE applications.

A common denominator: The application server

Lifecycle management plays an essential role for each of the components described here as it ensures that the components are kept in a valid, up-to-date, viable, and usable state. This is accomplished with implementation tools, change management processes, software logistics, upgrade options, and installation aides.

2.1.2   SAP NetWeaver

Overall integration platform

The example of an invoice verification process has shown that real business processes are carried out across several applications which require different kinds of integration. SAP NetWeaver contains all these integration layers, as shown in Figure 2.3.

As such, SAP NetWeaver represents the integration and application platform of SAP. In addition to SAP XI, you should also take into account all other SAP NetWeaver components when implementing integration projects.

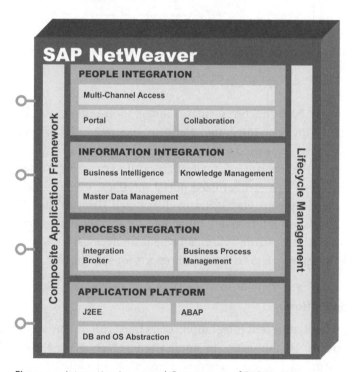

Figure 2.3 Integration Layers and Components of SAP NetWeaver

As you can also see in Figure 2.3 that SAP NetWeaver contains the *Composite Application Framework* (CAF), which provides design tools and methods as well as services and processes that allow you to implement and operate so-called *composite applications*. Composite applications are described in greater detail in Section 6.3.

The CAF uses all components of SAP NetWeaver and enables the integration of heterogeneous environments and *legacy applications*, particularly in strongly user-focused application environments.

SAP NetWeaver Exchange Infrastructure is used to enable a loose coupling of applications. The CAF plays a major role in conjunction with service-oriented architectures (SOA) and the enterprise SOA. Section 6.3 describes in great detail the role of SAP NetWeaver as a composite platform, how SAP NetWeaver evolves into the *business process platform* (BPP), and the central role of SAP XI.

2.1.3   IT Practices and IT Scenarios

Whereas the previous sections of this chapter described the components of SAP NetWeaver, the following sections introduce you to a new SAP concept, offering you a new perspective on SAP NetWeaver: IT practices and IT scenarios. The technical capabilities of the SAP NetWeaver components such as SAP XI are now (intentionally) moved into the background when talking about IT practices and scenarios. You have a better chance of convincing your IT manager of a certain technology in SAP NetWeaver when not talking about the technology itself (chances are, he's not understanding), but about what you can achieve with the technology (IT practices). Thus, the role of IT can change from a passive one that acts only upon request, to playing an active role in the decision-making process by suggesting easier, and often more efficient, processes.

New perspective

In the past, the SAP NetWeaver diagram shown in Figure 2.3 has often been referred to as the "refrigerator". One way to think of SAP NetWeaver is as a fridge, from which you take individual components from "compartments" to create an application. In essence, you "help yourself" by taking out of SAP NetWeaver what you need to "create your meal" (in this case, the application).

Link between the viewpoints of user department and IT department

However, this analogy isn't very useful if you want to create a link between the perspective of various user departments and the IT department to the application landscape and business processes. The user departments often don't have any insight into the technical architecture on which the applications are based. On the other hand, the IT department usually isn't familiar with the business processes. In other words, you may know what is in the fridge, but you may not know which meals you can prepare with the ingredients.

IT practices and IT scenarios allow companies to effectively combine the requirements of user departments with IT solutions. Therefore, IT practices provide specific solutions for implementing business requirements by means of IT.

For this reason, SAP has closed the "fridge" and cut it into slices that represent 10 essential IT practices. Figure 2.4 illustrates these 10 IT practices, with specific emphasis on end-to-end process integration in which the technical components of SAP XI are largely used.

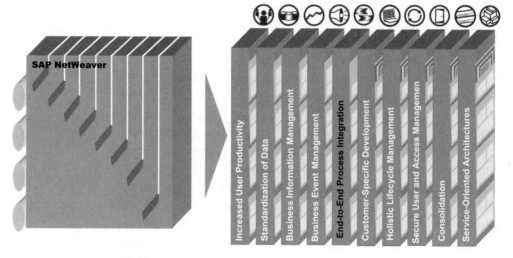

Abbildung 2.4 IT Practices

IT practices illustrate how IT can create business applications and processes. For example, a process containing data from the business warehouse can begin in the portal and send a message to SAP XI, eventually integrating suppliers in the business process. IT practices contain integrated and predefined IT scenarios based on SAP NetWeaver components and geared toward core enterprise business tasks. For example, IT practices allow a higher degree of information transparency (business information management) or solve problems inherent in implementations across different platforms (holistic lifecycle management).

Table 2.1 shows the essential options of SAP NetWeaver (Release SAP NetWeaver 2004s) with regard to IT practices and scenarios. You can find up-to-date IT practices and IT scenarios at *http://www.sap.com/solutions/businessmaps* (**Infrastructure and Services Maps** • **Technology** • **SAP NetWeaver**).

User Productivity Enablement	Running an Enterprise Portal	Enabling User Collaboration	Business Task Management	Mobilizing Business Processes	Enterprise Knowledge Management	Enterprise Search
Data Unification	Master data harmonization		Master data consolidation	Central master data management	Enterprise data warehousing	
Business Information Management	Enterprise reporting, query, and analysis	Business planning and analytical services	Enterprise data warehousing	Enterprise knowledge management	Enterprise search	
Business Event Management	Business activity monitoring			Business task management		
End-to-end Process Integration	Enabling application-to-application processes	Enabling business-to-business processes	Business process management	Enabling platform interoperability	Business task management	
Custom Development	Developing, configuring, and adapting applications			Enabling platform interoperability		
Unified Lifecycle Management	Software lifecycle management			SAP NetWeaver Operations		
Application Governance and Security Management	Authentication and single sign-on			Integrated user and access management		
Consolidation	Enabling platform interoperability	SAP NetWeaver Operations	Master data consolidation	Enterprise knowledge management	Enterprise data warehousing	
ESA Design and Deployment	Enabling enterprise services					

Table 2.1 IT Practices and IT Scenarios in SAP NetWeaver 2004s

Whereas the IT practice of end-to-end process integration and the underlying IT scenarios are closely related to the options of SAP XI, the IT scenario of business task management shows, for instance, that an IT practice (or an IT scenario) is not the same as an SAP NetWeaver component. The scenario is part of three IT practices at the same time. A business task can be a step within a workflow or a *guided procedure* that instructs a user step-by-step as to how to perform a particular task.

IT practices and SAP NetWeaver components

49

Guided procedures A common example is the process of purchasing goods or services from a Web site. A guided procedure would include the following steps:

1. Product selection

2. Shopping cart

3. Payment

As you can see, business task management involves activities typically carried out by a user, which is why this IT scenario is used both in end-to-end process integration and in the processing of business events as well as with user productivity.

Correspondingly, end-to-end process integration is not solely achieved by SAP XI. In an end-to-end process there might be also contained the processing of workflow steps, for instance with regard to exceptional situations in supplier integration, and thus calls for the availability of another technical component—the workflow engine. This shows that real processes are not just implemented by one single peace of technology but rather by several different technologies.

IT scenarios and business point of view In the next step, the IT scenarios lead to the point of view of the business departments. Table 2.2 shows the IT scenarios of the end-to-end process integration IT practice.

Within the IT scenarios, business departments address their requests to the IT department; for example, how industry standards such as RosettaNet or CIDX are mapped in a B2B scenario or how small partners or subsidiaries are integrated. Both examples are variants of the IT scenario, **Enabling Business-to-Business Processes**. A variant of an IT scenario consists of a set of IT processes that allow you to accomplish specific business goals.

For example, in a B2B integration (according to the RosettaNet standard), you must configure the system landscape, install the RosettaNet Business Package that contains the necessary RosettaNet processes (PIP), and you must configure and monitor the connection to the RosettaNet partner.

Enabling Application-to-Application Processes	Enabling Business-to-Business Processes	Business Process Management	Enabling Platform Interoperability	Business Task Management
► Application-to-application integration	► Integration of business partners via industry standards ► Integration of small business partners and subsidiaries	► Usage and customizing of pre-defined content ► Process automation ► Combination of local- and cross-business processes	► Enabling the coexistence of several portals ► Preserving application-to-application and business-to-business integration ► Providing web services interoperability ► Handling heterogeneous system landscapes ► Development of SAP NetWeaver-compliant applications	► Central access to tasks ► Support of offline processes

Table 2.2 IT Scenarios and Scenario Variants of End-to-End Process Integration

SAP customers can implement IT practices step-by-step with corre-   **Usage types**
sponding projects. In this context, you need to decide which SAP
NetWeaver components are needed for the implementation of a specific IT scenario (or IT scenario variant) since you won't always need
to install the entire SAP NetWeaver stack.

The next question is what is needed by the so-called *usage types*. A
usage type represents a logical view of the SAP NetWeaver platform.
This means that a usage type is not an installable unit; rather, it consists of the installation and configuration of different software components for a specific use.

Usage types represent the biggest link to the original SAP NetWeaver
components. However, because usage types are a configured collec-

tion of components, they comprise more than just the components of which they are made from. As shown in Table 2.3, the original components SAP XI and SAP Web Application Server have been merged into the usage type, Process Integration (PI), while the SAP BW and SAP Web Application Server components have become the usage type, BI Java Components (BI Java).

Original Component Name	SAP NetWeaver 2004s Usage Type	Usage Type Abbreviation	Required Server
SAP BW	Business Intelligence	BI	ABAP
SAP BW + SAP Web AS	BI Java Componets	BI Java	Java
SAP Web AS + certain Java Components	Development Infrastructure	DI	Java
SAP Web AS	Mobile Infrastructure	MI	ABAP + Java
SAP EP	Enterprise Portal	EP	ABAP + Java
SAP XI + SAP Web AS	Process Integration (XI)	PI	ABAP + Java
SAP Web AS	Application Server ABAP	AS ABAP	ABAP
SAP Web AS	Application Server Java	AS Java	Java

Table 2.3 Change of Component Names

A usage type can run together with other usage types in the same system, and they can also be installed in different systems. The relationships between IT scenarios and software components as well as between IT scenarios and usage types are referred to as *n-m relationships*. An n-m relationship is an IT scenario that's based on several usage types and can be installed on different systems.

To continue with the fridge analogy: The business department uses the SAP technology map with IT practices and IT scenarios like a menu and "orders" the relevant IT processes to reach a certain overall architecture (the meal). The ordered meal tells the IT department which components of SAP NetWeaver it has to use to prepare the meal—from IT practices to IT scenarios and scenario variants to the usage types.

To find out which usage types are necessary to implement a specific scenario variant, the IT department can use specific guides. For example, the SAP Online Help at *http://help.sap.com* contains different guides, such as the *Power User Guide*, *Developer Guide*, *Administrator Guide*, *Security Guide*, *Implementation Guide*, and so on, which are organized along the IT practices and IT scenarios.

Information organization along IT practices and IT scenarios

Figure 2.5 illustrates the relationship between IT scenarios, usage types, and the system on the basis of two IT scenarios.

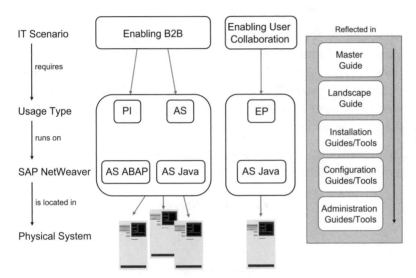

Figure 2.5 Relationship between IT Scenarios, Usage Types, and Software Components that is also reflected in all Guides

If you are familiar with the original component view, you may need some time to get used to the new one. If you look for the old view in the online help, you can find it on the home page of the SAP NetWeaver documentation in the SAP Help Portal (*http://help.sap. com*) by clicking on the **SAP NetWeaver** link, select **English** as language and then in SAP Library click at the bottom on **SAP NetWeaver by Key Capabilities**.

2.2 Functionality

The main purpose of SAP XI is to forward inbound messages to the appropriate receivers. At first glance, this task may not seem very

Tasks of SAP XI

demanding. For each inbound message, the appropriate receiver determines who receives the message.

However, if you consider that messages are often sent in different protocols, and that even within a specific protocol there are numerous different ways to map a message, the message distribution process becomes more complex. Therefore, to properly distribute messages, SAP XI must also act as a data converter. Messages must be converted from one protocol into another and from one type of presentation into another.

According to the *shared collaboration knowledge* principle, all the information handled in this process is supposed to be managed centrally. Thus, an inbound message does not contain any information on the target system. This information is instead derived with a complex set of rules consisting of the message format, the sender, and the message content.

Figure 2.6 illustrates the communication between two software components via an integration server.

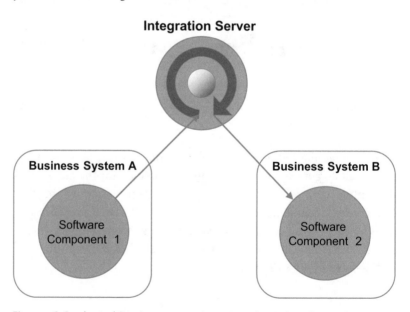

Figure 2.6 Sender and Receiver communicate via an Integration Server

The following sections trace the path of a message distribution process, as carried out by SAP XI.

2.2.1 Address Example

Let's suppose that a sending system distributes address data to differ- Initial example
ent receiving systems. For each Zip Code there is exactly one responsible receiving system. The sending system sends the address exclusively as SOAP documents. The receiving systems process different
formats each. The system that's responsible for zip code area *1xxxx* is
an internal SAP system that only communicates via IDocs.

From the point of view of the sender, an address consists of the following elements:

▸ **Name (contains the first and last name)**
▸ **Title (Mr./Ms.)**
▸ **Street**
▸ **City**
▸ **Zip code**

From the point of view of the receiver, an address consists of the following elements:

▸ **First name**
▸ **Last name**
▸ **Street**
▸ **Zip code**
▸ **City**

Before looking at the details of how the integration server handles
the addresses, we must introduce some essential terms and concepts
you'll encounter when using SAP XI.

2.2.2 Classification of Messages

Messages can be sent and received in different protocols: as email, as Adapter type
a file, as a SOAP document, as an IDoc, as a JMS or CORBA docu-
ment, and so on. As a data converter, an integration server must be
able to convert such formats into each other. For this, the SAP Integration Server first translates all inbound messages into an XI-inter-
nal format, which we'll refer to as *XI format* from now on. Only
when the document leaves the integration server will it be translated
into the format that's expected by the receiver. This procedure

ensures that all messages exist in a uniform format within the integration server (the XI format).

As such, adapters must be available for each supported format. The adapters are responsible for translating messages into the XI format (and vice versa). From the point of view of the integration server, the protocols differ only by the adapters used for the translation to the XI format. Instead of talking about different protocols, the *adapter types* of a message are discussed in the following sections.

Data type   In the XI format, each message has a concrete data type, which describes the elements and attributes of which the related messages consist. From a technical viewpoint, the data types are described as XSD documents.

The address example shown in Section 2.2.1 uses the data types displayed in Figures 2.7 and 2.8. These data types are described in greater detail in Section 2.4.2.

Structure	Category	Type	Occurrence	Details
▽ **Adress1**	Complex Type			
name	Element	xsd:string	1	length="50"
title	Element	xsd:integer	1	
street	Element	xsd:string	1	length="50"
city	Element	xsd:string	1	length="50"
zipcode	Element	xsd:integer	1	totalDigits="5"

Figure 2.7 Data Type of Address1 Presented by the Integration Repository

Structure	Category	Type	Occurrence	Details
▽ **Adresse2**	Complex Type			
firstname	Element	xsd:string	1	length="40"
lastname	Element	xsd:string	1	length="40"
street	Element	xsd:string	1	length="40"
zipcode	Element	xsd:string	1	length="5"
city	Element	xsd:string	1	length="40"

Figure 2.8 Data Type of Address2 Presented by the Integration Repository

Inbound/   To describe a concrete message in SAP XI, the data type's informa-
outbound   tion must indicate whether the message was inbound or outbound. This *communication category* is always described from the viewpoint of the connected system, not of the integration server. Messages sent to the integration server are referred to as *outbound messages*, while those sent by the integration server are referred to as *inbound messages*. From the SAP XI point of view, inbound messages are referred to as *inbound interfaces*, whereas outbound messages are called *outbound interfaces*.

Finally, the *communication mode* must contain information as to whether the message sender expects an immediate response (**synchronous communication mode**) or whether the sender keeps on working regardless of any response by the receiver (**asynchronous communication mode**).

Synchronous/
asynchronous

As you may have noticed, the address example uses asynchronous communication mode. Thus, addresses that arrive in the integration server as SOAP documents are asynchronous outbound messages of the **SOAP** adapter type and **Address1** data type. Messages sent by the integration server, on the other hand, are asynchronous inbound messages of the **IDoc** adapter type and **Address2** data type, as illustrated in Figure 2.9.

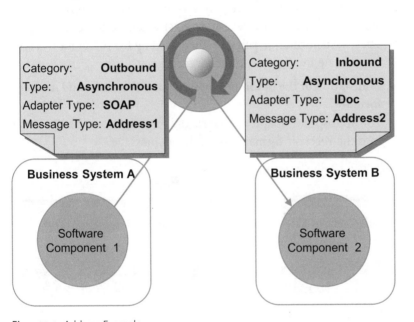

Figure 2.9 Address Example

The following subtasks must be carried out to distribute an inbound message:

Distributing a
message

1. **Translation of the inbound message to the internal XI format**
   Basically, two adapters are available for each format to be processed by SAP XI. These adapters are responsible for translating between the XI format and the external format. The adapters are integrated in SAP XI via an adapter framework that can also be

used to integrate project-specific adapters. The adapter sends the message in XI format to the integration server.

2. **Receiver determination/Interface determination**
   The integration server uses a complex set of rules to determine the receiver and the interface being used. The rules are based on the following elements:

   ▶ Sender details (if known)

   ▶ Message type

   ▶ Message content

3. **Transformation of the message in the derived data types**
   Similar to our address example, data types used by the sender and receiver match only in very few cases. For this reason you can store transformation rules (mappings) when defining data types. These transformation rules are then used by the integration server to translate messages into the target format.

4. **Translation of the outbound message into the outbound message format**
   The appropriate adapter converts the message from the XI format into the receiver format and sends the message.

Figure 2.10 illustrates this process.

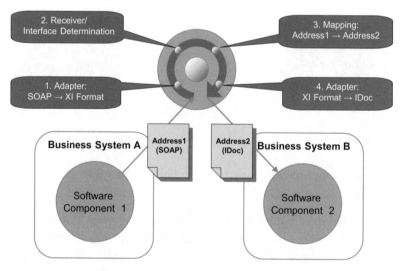

Figure 2.10 Message Distribution Process

2.2.3   Implementing a Message Flow

If you want to implement a new message path in SAP XI, it is useful to distinguish between the following tasks:

▶ **Technical configuration**
This task is responsible for structuring the XI system and integrating it with the existing SAP landscape. In particular, different technical RFC connections must be set up and assigned to each other in the XI system and connected SAP systems so the following processes can be mapped:

  ▶ Generation of proxies from the XI system in the connected SAP systems

  ▶ Exchange of RFC messages between the XI system and connected systems

  ▶ Central monitoring

All these settings must be made only once after you have installed the XI server.

▶ **Design**
In a second step, the required data and message types, as well as the mappings between those objects, must also be described. Entry of this information does not depend on any concrete implementation; in other words, it doesn't depend on the involved systems. The above objects can be developed in SAP XI or imported from external systems, and they are managed in the *integration repository*.

In the address example, the two address formats and the transformations between the formats are entered in this step.

▶ **Configuration**
To dispatch concrete messages, you must configure the abstract message flow for concrete systems. For this you'll need to enter the concrete integration partners and store the rules for the receiver. If necessary, you must complement adapter data (such as web services). All configuration data is stored in the integration directory.

In the address example, detailed information on the sending system and the receiving systems are stored in this step. Moreover, you must enter rules that enable the sending system to derive the appropriate receiver, the message type, and the communication channel from an address that has been received.

▶ **Runtime**

Message distribution

It is now possible to send messages to SAP XI; these messages are then forwarded to the appropriate receiver(s). A comprehensive monitoring concept is necessary to control these processes as you need to identify errors in the message flow. Inbound and outbound messages must be monitored for all involved components (adapters, integration server, and so on).

In the address example, it is important to analyze inbound SOAP documents, inbound and outbound internal XI documents, as well as the IDocs sent by the IDoc adapter.

2.3 Components

The SAP NetWeaver Exchange Infrastructure consists of several components, as described briefly in the following sections.

System Landscape Directory

The *System Landscape Directory* (SLD) maps the internal system landscape. This includes the involved systems and their interrelationships (for instance, which system acts as the integration server), as well as the software products installed in the system landscape.

Technical systems and business systems

When recording systems, you need to distinguish between technical systems and business systems. In the case of SAP systems, the SAP installation is mapped as a technical system, while the associated clients (logical systems) are mapped as business systems. In addition to SAP systems, you can also record any other system in the SLD.

The software products active in the system landscape are recorded regardless of the system on which they are installed. In this context, you can record different components for each software product and different versions for each software component. In a second step, software components installed on the system are assigned to each business system.

All business systems can later on be referenced as message senders or receivers while configuring message flows. If you think of the communication with external systems, it becomes evident that not every possible message receiver be recorded in the SLD.

Table 2.4 provides a brief overview of the properties of the SLD.

SLD Profile	
Tasks	Mapping of application systems and software products used in the company
Data	▶ Internal systems ▶ Software products ▶ Software components
Affected Processes	▶ Design phase: import of SAP objects ▶ Configuration: sender/receiver of messages ▶ Runtime
Required Maintenance	▶ During the installation of the XI system ▶ Future extensions of the system landscape ▶ Installation of new software products/releases

Table 2.4 System Landscape Directory

The *integration repository* stores formal descriptions of all messages that can be processed by SAP XI. These include, among others, the data types and the required transformations between data types. As such, the integration repository provides all metadata at design time and represents the central data basis for the integration server that exchanges messages at runtime.

Integration repository

Table 2.5 provides the corresponding profile of the integration repository.

IR Profile	
Tasks	Storage of message formats, data types, and associated transformations
Data	▶ Message formats (message interfaces) ▶ Data types ▶ Transformations (message mapping, interface mapping)
Affected Processes	▶ Integration server ▶ Adapter framework
Required Maintenance	During message design

Table 2.5 Integration Repository

Integration
directory The *integration directory* stores information on the systems that can act as message senders and receivers, and on the communication channels to be used to reach these systems. In addition, the integration directory provides the set of rules based on which the system can derive the appropriate receiver(s) and message formats for an inbound message.

Table 2.6 contains the profile of the integration directory.

ID Profile	
Tasks	▸ Storage of sender/receiver descriptions ▸ Storage of a set of rules to derive receivers and message formats from inbound messages
Data	▸ Derivation rules ▸ Sender and receiver descriptions
Affected Processes	▸ Integration server ▸ Adapter framework
Required Maintenance	During the configuration of message flows

Table 2.6 Integration Directory

Runtime
Workbench

The Runtime Workbench provides numerous tools that support the troubleshooting process:

- ▸ A component monitoring function allows you to check the connections to all systems involved.
- ▸ A message monitoring function provides you with access to all messages processed by SAP XI. It allows you to check the status of messages and to analyze errors that occur.
- ▸ The end-to-end monitoring function allows you to monitor the path of a concrete message through SAP XI.

2.4 Objects

Now that you've had a brief overview of the SAP XI components, let's look at the objects you'll use to map a message distribution process.

The organizational unit that groups all design objects is the *software component*. Software components are recorded in the SLD and contain a component name, a component version, and a reference to a software product that consists of a vendor, product name, and a product version.

Each software component must be assigned to the technical systems on which it is installed. Typical examples of software components include the components of an R/3 system; SAP delivers the components of its products with the corresponding definitions.

2.4.1 Software Products in the Integration Repository

In the address example, the first task is to create the software product **XI Book** and the software component **Address allocation**, both of which have version number 1. From a technical viewpoint, the software component corresponds to the development class of previous R/3 systems or to the packages in Java development. Software components can then be assigned to technical systems in the SLD and activated for the business systems on which the software is installed.

To define integration scenarios within a software component, you must first import the relevant software component into the integration repository. There you can assign one or more namespaces to it, which can contain the development objects described in the following sections. Apart from that, you can specify the SAP system from which you can import interfaces such as RFC modules or IDocs, if necessary.

Create the following namespace in the address example:

```
http://www.sap-press.com/XI/Adressallocation
```

Figure 2.11 displays the resulting software product. Because the practical part of this book details how the individual objects are created, this section just provides a quick overview of the process.

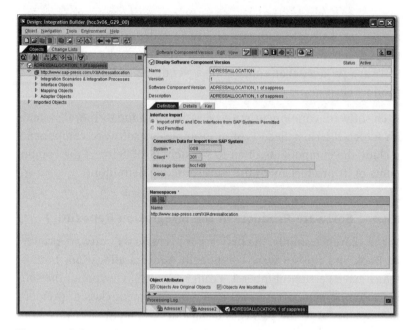

Figure 2.11 Software Components in the Integration Repository

2.4.2 Message Interfaces and Mapping Objects in the Integration Repository

Message interface This section describes the required interfaces. In the address example, a system sends an address in **Address1** format, which will be distributed in the **Address2** format. From the external systems point of view, there is an outbound interface in the **Address1** format and an inbound interface in the **Address2** format. These are created as *message interfaces* in SAP XI. A message interface consists of the following elements:

▶ A name

▶ A description

▶ A category (inbound/outbound/abstract)

▶ A mode (synchronous/asynchronous)

▶ A message type for inbound data

▶ A message type for outbound data

▶ A message type for technical messages

The category specifies whether messages are sent through the interface to (outbound) or from (inbound) SAP XI. If a format is used for both inbound and outbound messages, it must be recorded in the system twice. The mode indicates whether or not a response to a message is expected (synchronous or asynchronous mode).

Category and mode

Message types describe the exact data format of the interface. Depending on the communication type (inbound/outbound) and communication mode (synchronous/asynchronous), one or several of the following message types must be specified:

Message types

▶ **Input message type**
Data format of the message received by the SAP XI system (this information is required for outbound messages and all synchronous messages).

▶ **Output message type**
Data format of the message sent from the SAP XI system (this information is required for inbound messages and all synchronous messages).

▶ **Fault message type**
Data format in which processing information (for instance, in the case of erroneous processing) is sent from the SAP XI system (this information is possible for inbound messages and all synchronous messages).

For technical reasons, the message interface is not directly assigned the used data types. Instead, the message types simply contain a description and the data type. With the exception of data types used to define hierarchical data types, each data type is referenced by at least one message type.

The address example contains two different data types: The first address format (**Address1**) contains a name field that includes both the first and last name, whereas the second address format (**Address2**) contains separate fields for the first and the last name. Corresponding data types are internally stored as XSD documents; they can either be imported or recorded via a data type editor. For each field, you must enter the following information:

Data type

▶ A denominator
▶ A category (complex type or element)

▶ A type (XSD type or a previously defined data type)

▶ A cardinality (1 or n)

▶ If necessary, type-specific details such as the length of strings, for example

At design time, you must also enter the conversion rules to be applied with the interfaces. As shown in Figure 2.12, two different mapping objects exist:

▶ **Message mapping**
Message mapping specifies how to transform a message from one data type into another. Technically speaking, message mappings are XSLT documents that can either be imported or entered via the mapping editor contained in SAP XI.

▶ **Interface mapping**
Interface mapping defines the message mappings through which you can transform one message interface into another. Because a message interface can contain up to three different message types (input/output/fault), you must specify the associated mappings for each relevant message type. In other words, interface mapping is basically a collection of message mappings.

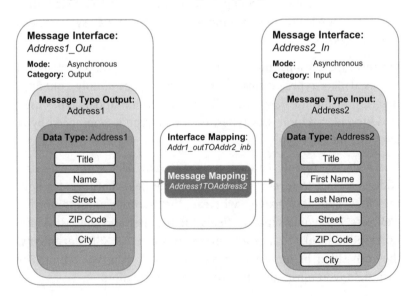

Figure 2.12 Design Objects

Figure 2.12 also illustrates that the following design objects are used in the address example:

- **Address1**, a data type for addresses with one name field
- **Address2**, a data type for addresses with separate first and last names
- A message type for the **Address1** data type
- A message type for the **Address2** data type
- An outbound interface for dispatching an asynchronous message in the **Address1** format
- An inbound interface for receiving an asynchronous message in the **Address2** format
- A message mapping from **Address1** to **Address2**
- An interface mapping from the outbound interface in the **Address1** format to the inbound interface in the **Address2** format

2.4.3 Configuration Objects in the Integration Directory

All objects described up to this point can be entered at design time, which means they are not related in any way to the actual senders and receivers of messages. In the following sections, you will configure the concrete message path: the sender sends a SOAP document to SAP XI which forwards an IDoc to the appropriate (internal) receiver. To do this, a wizard is available in the integration directory that generates all the required configuration objects on the basis of the actual sender and receiver descriptions.

Since knowledge of the wizard and configuration objects are an essential part of the address exercise in this chapter, this section provides you with a quick overview of the objects you'll use.

Unlike design time where all generated objects are assigned to a software component, this job is done at configuration time by the configuration scenario. For the address example, we'll create a configuration scenario called "Address allocation". | Configuration scenario

In the example, a SOAP document is received from an external system. Because external systems are not stored in the SLD, you must first create a *business service* that represents the sender of addresses. Here, the name of the sender and a communication channel is stored | Business service for the SOAP adapter type. The communication channel contains detailed information on how the sender's SOAP documents are transferred to SAP XI and how they will be processed by SAP XI. Because each sender can use different protocols to communicate with SAP XI, you can store numerous communication channels for each business service.

Now you can configure the following message path. Whenever SAP XI receives a SOAP document from the sender "Address allocator" that contains an "Address1 (outbound)" type message and whose address is located in Zip Code area 1, the message must be transformed into the "Address2 (inbound)" type and sent as an IDoc to SAP system "ZIP1".

The message path is configured using the configuration wizard, located in the integration directory. It basically needs the following information:

▸ The message's sender and format, and the adapter through which it was sent.

▸ To whom the message will be sent, the format to be received, and the adapter to be used.

▸ The mappings used to transform the involved formats.

The configuration wizard uses this information to generate the following objects:

▸ **Sender agreement**
The *sender agreement* defines how messages are sent into the SAP NetWeaver Exchange Infrastructure for a given sender and message interface. In the example, "Address1" (outbound) messages from the sender (the "Address allocator") are sent as SOAP documents to the SOAP adapter of SAP XI.

▸ **Receiver agreement**
The *receiver agreement* defines through which communication channel messages are distributed to a receiver. In the example, the receiver "ZIP1" receives messages as IDocs via the IDoc adapter.

▸ **Receiver determination**
The *receiver determination* defines to whom an inbound message must be distributed. Receiver selection can be determined by the message's content. Any number of receivers can be specified here.

In the example, we have stored one receiver for each Zip Code area, and the receiver is selected by using a corresponding rule.

▸ **Interface determination**
The *interface determination* defines the format in which the inbound message must be forwarded to the receiver, and which mappings must be used for the transformation. In this context, you can send several messages (with different message types) that refer to one inbound message. In the example, the message interface "Address2" (inbound) is assigned.

2.5 Advanced Concepts

This section describes additional details and functions of SAP XI. It discusses development models and adapter concepts and describes mappings, monitoring, and the special features of the different message senders and receivers.

2.5.1 Outside-In vs. Inside-Out

Numerous different methods are available for integrating applications with an SAP XI system. These methods are generally divided into two development models: the *inside-out model* and the *outside-in model*.

Interfaces allow applications to communicate with the SAP NetWeaver Exchange Infrastructure. The differences between the inside-out and outside-in models can be found in the development (the definition) and management (the way integration knowledge is saved).

With the outside-in model, the interface used by an application for communication is defined in a platform-independent format (such as XML) and is centrally stored. The integrated application imports the interface first before it is implemented. Outside-in

An example of the outside-in model in SAP XI is the integration via ABAP proxies. In SAP XI, the interface is mapped in the integration repository in the form of message interfaces, which are XML schemas. A connected R/3 system imports this interface information and uses it to generate an ABAP object that contains a method whose definition matches the definition of the message interface. Once the object has been generated, it can be used in the ABAP Workbench. Proxy generation is possible as of Release 6.40. Systems with Release 6.20 can be enhanced with the **APPINT 2.0** add-on, which allows them to generate proxies.

Inside-out

In the inside-out model, the interface used for communication purposes is developed within the connected application and imported during integration with SAP XI. In this context, it is essential further development of the interface occurs in the application and not in SAP XI. Every change to the interface requires a new import of the interface definition in SAP XI.

Examples of the inside-out model are integration via the RFC or IDoc adapters. In this case, an existing RFC-enabled function module or IDoc is imported in the integration repository and connected using the relevant mappings.

2.5.2 Generating ABAP Proxies

Using ABAP proxies

Generation of ABAP and Java proxies represents the outside-in model of SAP XI. In the case of ABAP proxies, ABAP proxy classes are generated on the basis of interfaces stored in the integration repository by means of the ABAP proxy generation (**Transaction SPROXY**). After that, the classes can be integrated into existing or new ABAP programs in the ABAP Workbench.

ABAP proxy generation includes the software components and the associated namespaces. The structure more or less corresponds to the structure used in the integration repository. According to the outside-in model, the namespaces include all object types that are mapped in ABAP in the context of the proxy generation. These include the message interfaces (with the exception of abstract interfaces), and the message and data types. Previously generated ABAP objects are displayed for each of these types.

To create an ABAP proxy, you must first create a package in the ABAP Workbench.[1] Once the package is created, you must call the ABAP proxy to generate ABAP objects from the required objects in the integration repository. The ABAP proxy generation also allows

---

[1] If you use SAP Web AS 6.40, you must additionally create a an **SAI_TOOLS** usage declaration for the package in order to generate ABAP proxies in this package.

you to change existing ABAP proxy objects; for instance, if you need to change the interface in the integration repository.

An EXECUTE method is created for each generated outbound proxy, which can be used to send a message via the proxy. Outbound proxies can only be integrated within the application that uses the proxy.

The generated inbound proxies process messages received from external sources. To accomplish this, a proxy interface and an implementing class are generated. After the proxy is created, the logic that processes the inbound message must be implemented in the implementing class. Inbound proxies are implemented in both the application and proxy objects.

2.5.3 RFC Adapter

The RFC adapter contained in the XI adapter framework represents one of the inside-out implementations of SAP XI. The RFC technology is widely used in the SAP R/3 environment to integrate applications in the SAP system. However, the RFC adapter in SAP XI can only be used with certain restrictions. For example, the context (session) in a called system is not kept if several RFC calls are made. Transactional contexts with several RFC calls also currently aren't possible, but is supposed to be available in the next major release.

Widely-used technology

The adapter engine uses the SAP Java Connector (JCo) in the background. If you are familiar with JCo, you shouldn't have any problem setting up and configuring the RFC adapter.

As with most other adapters, the RFC adapter basically consists of two components: the sender adapter and the receiver adapter. One sender and one receiver communication channel is needed for each connected system; however, it is possible to set up several communication channels for each system. For example, you might need to set up several communication channels for the receiver adapter if you are using different BAPI configurations.

When configuring the sender adapter, it is important to note that each activated communication channel virtually represents a separate RFC destination through the JCo. For each of these active sender channels, you must maintain a separate RFC destination in the connected R/3 system in **Transaction SM59**. At a minimum, the receiver adapter requires the logon data for the system to be integrated.

The implementation of the inside-out method for the RFC adapter can best be described as the integration of concrete function modules. The meta data of function modules, such as BAPI's, must be imported into the integration repository before they can be used in SAP XI. In contrast to the outside-in method, the function module (in this example, BAPI) is not maintained in the integration repository, but instead in the connected RFC system.

2.5.4 Other Adapters

Communicating with different platforms

This section describes some additional important adapters from the adapter framework including their functionality. Integration with different adapters represents an essential feature of SAP XI as it allows you to communicate with many different platforms.

- ▶ **File adapter**
  The *file adapter* allows SAP XI to exchange messages by means of a file transfer. The transport protocols supported by the file adapter are a local file system (NFS), FTP, and FTPS. You can use one of these protocols for each configured communication channel.

  The file adapter sends or receives the payload of an XI message through the adapter framework. There's a special characteristic regarding the sending of messages, which also occurs in other adapters: only the payload of a message is sent through the adapter. However, the payload does not suffice in order to use the logical routing from the integration directory. The additional information needed to do this—the sender and the message interface—are added in the adapter framework on the basis of the sender agreement assigned to the sender channel. Only messages of a specific message interface can be sent through a specific communication channel.

  On the other hand, a receiver adapter can be used to receive messages with different message interfaces. However, you cannot configure different file storage locations for a message interface. If you want to do that, you must create several communication channels.

- ▶ **SOAP adapter**
  The *SOAP adapter* allows you to send and receive XML messages that comply with the SOAP standard. The supported transport protocols are HTTP and HTTPS.

As is the case with the FTP adapter, the problem with the SOAP adapter is that a standard SOAP message does not contain any information on the sending service or the message interface that's used. If you use the SOAP adapter, the sending service can be derived from the parameters of the sender's URL, while the message interface must be directly specified in the communication channel.

▶ **JDBC adapter**

The *JDBC adapter* (see also Section 4.5.1) represents a special case in SAP XI in many respects. The central task here is to generate an SQL statement for a relational database from XI-XML messages, and to create an XML message from the result sets of a database operation. For this purpose, the JDBC adapter uses specific message formats, which must be defined as data types in the integration repository.

The JDBC adapter's receiver uses different message protocols to send an XI message to a database. The most simple way is the use of a native SQL string. If this message protocol is used, the system expects any SQL statement as the message content that can be processed by the connected database. The XML-SQL format represents another message protocol. This message type must meet the requirements of a specific, previously-defined format so the adapter can send it to the database. Possible formats are available for INSERT, UPDATE, DELETE, or stored procedures. The respective message format must be defined in the integration repository.

The sender of the JDBC adapter processes a SELECT and an UPDATE statement for each send operation. These statements must be specified in the adapter configuration. The result of a send operation is represented by the result set of the SELECT statement. This result set is transferred into an XML structure that must be defined in the integration repository, similar to the receiver adapter. You can, for example, use the UPDATE statement in the sender adapter to check a flag that marks the previously read result set as "transferred".

2.5.5 Mappings

A *mapping* converts data into different formats. In SAP XI, mappings can be used both in business processes and between a sender and receiver. They are stored in the integration repository.

Mappings always consist of an *interface mapping*. The interface mapping indicates which message interfaces are to be used as input and output mappings. Here you must specify one or several message interfaces for both input and output. The actual logic that defines how data is converted from one format into another is not located in the interface mapping itself, but in mapping programs stored in the interface mapping.

Mapping programs

Mapping programs can be mapped in different ways. The easiest way to create a mapping program is with the so-called *message mapping* that's created in the Integration Builder's graphical editor. This editor allows you to assign the individual components of the source and target messages to each other. If you cannot assign all messages to each other, you can also use predefined functions such as SUBSTRING, CONCAT, or SUBTRACT. You can also use conditions using the IF function, or you can use Java to build your own custom functions.

XSLT mapping

Another very powerful feature is the XSLT mappings. These mappings can be defined outside of SAP XI and be imported as archives with the Integration Builder. For example, the file adapter lets you create readable PDF or Excel files.

In addition, you can use mappings as ABAP classes or as a Java class on the J2EE engine. These allow you to program the respective mappings to suit your needs.

2.5.6   Monitoring Messages and Processes

SAP XI's monitoring function allows you to check and monitor the runtime of the XI system. It also allows you to view XI messages and logs on the flow of business processes. This way you can analyze the runtime behavior and error sources.

Messages of the integration engine

The most important element of message monitoring is **Transaction SXI_MONITOR** on the integration server. This transaction displays all messages that run through the integration engine. However, note that the standard configuration usually does not show any correctly processed synchronous messages. You can change this via the configuration of the integration engine in **Transaction SXMB_ADM**. All messages are assigned a status so you can directly see, for example, which messages contain errors as well as view the message content. A tree structure for the message content lets you view the message.

You can also call all messages on the integration server in the Runtime Workbench. Note, however, that the Runtime Workbench is much more difficult to handle than **Transaction SXMB_ADM**.

Messages received by the adapter engine and sent to the connected systems can be viewed in the message monitoring area of the Runtime Workbench on the adapter engine component. For example, if a system that uses the adapter isn't functioning properly, you can use the Runtime Workbench to access and analyze that system.

Messages of the adapter engine

Another monitoring feature provided by SAP XI is the business process engine monitoring function, which is called using **Transaction SXMB_MONI_BPE**. Developers already familiar with SAP Workflow won't have any problem using this transaction as the monitoring of the business process engine is very similar. For the purpose of evaluation you can use different variants of the Workflow log. For example, you can use the Workflow log that contains technical details that allow you to recreate the individual messages of a process.

2.5.7 Services and Partners

In SAP XI, services represent the senders and receivers of messages. SAP XI contains three different types of services: business systems, business services, and the integration process.

▶ **Business systems**
Business systems are services located within the system landscape. Typically, this is the system that you physically control. They are entered in the System Landscape Directory. Moreover, the systems are assigned products in the SLD, which allow you to determine which messages can be sent and received by a business system.

▶ **Business services**
In SAP XI, *business services* represent services of external providers. For example, a hotel reservation service that can be addressed via a SOAP interface. Business services are provided by systems that cannot be controlled by yourself. Because the business services are not entered in the SLD, you cannot determine via the SLD which messages can be send or received by a specific business service. For this reason, the senders and receivers of the message

interfaces from the integration repository are directly assigned to the business service in the integration directory.

▶ **Integration processes**
Integration processes in the integration directory represent configurable instances of integration processes in the integration repository. These are defined in the BPRL process designer in the integration repository. From a service's point of view, the configuration instance is treated like all other services; it can send and receive messages. It is not necessary to explicitly specify which messages of a service can send and receive, as this implicitly results from the design of the process in the integration repository.

Correspondingly, the major difference between the different partners in the XI configuration is represented by the location that stores information on the "capabilities" of the partner. In this context, the term "capability" describes the ability to send and receive messages.

PART II
Practices and Exercises

Before you can begin with the exercises and the case study,
you must carry out several steps to prepare your systems for
the examples. This chapter guides you through the necessary
steps to prepare for the exercises and the case study.

3 Basic System Configuration

The first order of business is to ensure your system meets the minimum requirements for the examples in this chapter. Once you've done that, you'll need to configure several settings necessary for working on the examples. For this, you'll need to have administrator privileges.

The following sections walk you through the necessary preparations for working on the individual exercises; they also pave the way for the case study. Some of these settings will need to be reconfigured later for some of the exercise chapters.

3.1 Prerequisites

To work on the exercises, you need an SAP XI system (Release 3.0), which should contain the highest available *support package* stack (SP), if possible. The exercises described here have been carried out on SAP XI 3.0 SP15, but you can also use lower releases.

Tested under
SAP XI 3.0 SP15

Apart from the XI system, you need two more systems or at least two different clients. In the following sections, we assume that you have successfully completed the installation and have customized the systems as described in the installation and configuration guides provided by SAP. Furthermore, it is assumed that the System Landscape Directory you use for the exercises is located in the XI system. You also need a user within the XI system for the preparatory steps. This user must have comprehensive rights. For instance, you can use the user **xisuper**, whose creation is recommended and described in the

SAP NetWeaver Exchange Infrastructure Installation Guide. It is also possible to use a copy of that user.

SAP GUI,
Java Web Start,
and SAP
NetWeaver Developer Studio for the
frontend
You will use many different applications in the frontend. For example, you will need the latest version of the SAP GUI (currently version 6.40), including the latest patches. You'll need the SAP GUI to access the XI functions in the ABAP part of the system. You can access the relevant Java components using Java applications, which are automatically downloaded via *Java Web Start* when used for the first time. For this, you need a Java SDK installation that contains Java Web Start, which is available for several platforms at *http://java.sun.com*. You should use the highest available version of the SDK under 1.5. Problems can occur on the SAP side of the system if you use older support packages.

Access to the XI system via the Java Web Start application occurs through port 5*XX*04, *XX* being the instance number of the SAP system. Most test systems use 00 as the instance number. You can determine the port number within the XI system via Transaction SMICM. To do that, navigate along the menu path, **Goto · http-Server · Display Data** and check the value of **J2EE HTTP port**. To implement the Java proxy example, you will also use SAP NetWeaver Developer Studio, which should also be installed in the frontend.

Source code of
the examples available online and in
the Appendix
You will use specific programs for different exercises. By importing ABAP code you can simplify your preparation for the exercises. These programs can be downloaded from the websites that accompany this book (*http://www.sap-press.com* and *http://www.sap-press.de/1383*), and you can also find the source code in Appendix A. You will be notified in the relevant exercises about which programs you should use.

3.2 Defining the Connected Systems in the System Landscape Directory

SAP systems that have not been previously included in an integration scenario require various settings so they can be used to send or receive messages. The following sections describe the necessary steps you need to integrate a business system with the XI system.

3.2.1 Creating the Systems—Technical Systems

A system definition in the *System Landscape Directory* (SLD) repre- sents the basis for later communications. When defining the sys- tems, you must specify how the new system can be accessed and which software products (including their versions) in the new sys- tem. These details are particularly useful for systems within the com- pany-internal IT landscape.

SLD as a central system directory

Open the SAP GUI and login as the superuser to your XI system in the client of the integration server. Start **Transaction SXMB_IFR** to navigate to the XI tools. Select the SLD and logon to it as the super- user. Later, you can also access the XI tools directly via the following URL: *http://<host>:<J2EE Port>/rep/start/index.jsp*. However, before you can do that, you must logon to the SAP GUI to change the super- user's default password.

Transaction SXMB_ IFR calls XI tools

Although SAP Web AS ABAP and SAP Web AS Java automatically login to the SLD as technical systems during the installation (provided the corresponding settings have been entered), you want to carry out this step once manually for the ECC 5.0 system[1] with system ID G50.

Technical landscape manages the host systems

For this purpose, you must click on the **Technical Landscape** link in the **Landscape** section (see Figure 3.1). You can select the different types of technical systems to view the systems that have already been registered.

To create an ABAP-based system, select **New Technical System**. The new system is based on an **SAP Web AS ABAP**. Select the correspond- ing option and navigate to the next step. The system now prompts you to specify details about the system to be integrated (see Figure 3.2). You must first enter the **Web AS ABAP Name** or the system ID (**SID**): You can find the three-digit alphanumeric ID in the relevant SAP system by selecting **System · Status** from the menu. In addition to the SID, you will also find the required database host name in the **Database data** section in the lower right-hand area. The installation number is displayed in the **SAP System data** section above the data- base host name. Once you have entered all values, click on the **Next** button to continue with the next step.

---

1 ECC stands for *Enterprise Central Component*. Among other things, this compo- nent contains the functions of R/3 systems and represents the center of mySAP ERP within an enterprise system landscape.

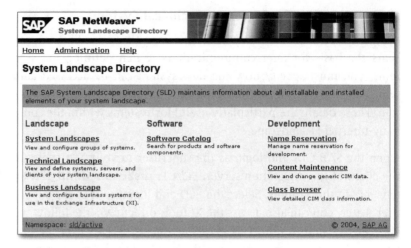

Figure 3.1 System Landscape Directory (SLD)

Technical System Wizard - System Details

Enter the required information about the technical system.

Details

Web AS ABAP Name (SID): `G50` ℹ️

Installation Number: `0123456789` ℹ️

Database Host Name: `g50db1` ℹ️

`<Back` `Next>` `Cancel`

Figure 3.2 Technical System Wizard—System Details

Technical System Wizard - Message Server and Central Application Server

Enter information about the message server and the central application server.

Message Server

Host Name: `host` ℹ️

Message Port (sapmsG50): `3650` ℹ️

Logon Groups: `PUBLIC` ℹ️

Central Application Server

Host Name: `host` ℹ️

Instance Number: `50` ℹ️

`<Back` `Next>` `Cancel`

Figure 3.3 Technical System Wizard—Message Server and Central Application Server

The next page of the wizard asks you for details about the central application server and the message server (see Figure 3.3). In most cases, these two servers are identical; however, you should verify this with the landscape administrator.

You can find the required data, for instance, in **Transaction SM51**. This transaction contains a list of all servers that belong to the system. Search for the **Enqueue** entry in the **Type** column: This is typically the central application server. The first column in this row contains an entry of the following type: **<host>_<SID>_<Instance number>**. In the example, the instance number is **50**. Copy the values into the relevant input fields of the wizard. The message port's number has the following structure: **36<Instance number>**. You can determine the available logon groups in your SAP system by using **Transaction SMLG**. Continue with the next step.

Transactions SM51 and SMLG contain important system data

In the next screen, you can specify additional application servers that belong to the SAP system in question. To do that, enter the relevant host name and add it to the lower list. If your SAP system only consists of the central application server, you can continue here without specifying anything.

ABAP-based SAP systems are divided into different clients. The following step shows you how to assign clients to your logical systems (see Figure 3.4).

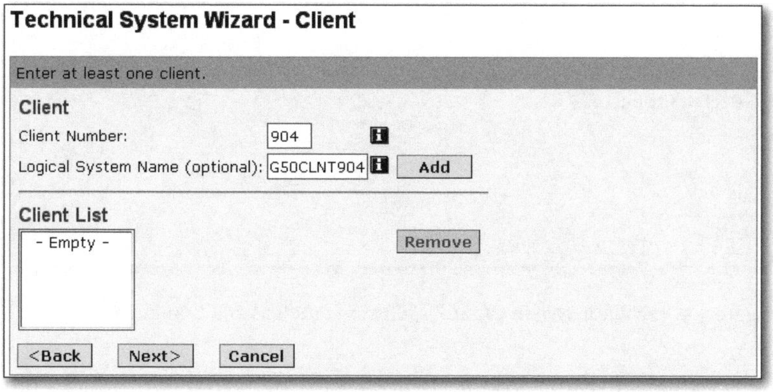

Each client is assigned a logical system

Technical System Wizard - Client

Enter at least one client.

Client

Client Number: 904

Logical System Name (optional): G50CLNT904 Add

Client List

- Empty - Remove

<Back Next> Cancel

Figure 3.4 Technical System Wizard—Client

You can view the clients and their logical systems in **Transaction SCC4**. If you discover that the clients you want to use haven't been assigned any logical systems yet, you can use **Transaction BD54** to create new logical systems and then assign those new systems using **Transaction SCC4**. Before you do that, however, you should consult with your landscape administrator as this step can be critical.

The names of logical systems usually have the following structure: **<SID>CLNT<Client>**. In our example, the name is **G50CLNT904**. The logical system is used for *application-link-enabling* scenarios (ALE); communication with IDocs, for example, represents such a scenario.

Installed software components can be viewed in the SAP system

Click on **Next** to obtain view a list of the installed software products. To specify the installed software products and components and their versions, you can select the SAP product or products installed in the new technical system. In this example, that's SAP ECC 5.0. If you enter **ECC** in the filter, the number of possible options can be restricted so the display is less complex (see Figure 3.5).

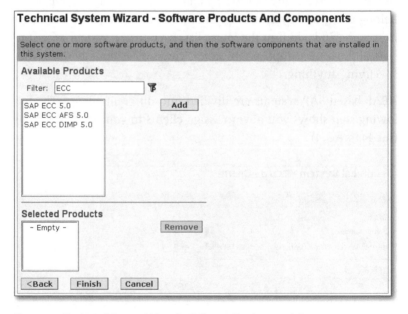

Figure 3.5 Technical System Wizard—Software Products and Components

Select your software product from the list of available products and click **Add** to add it to the list of selected products. This way you can also list the software components contained in the software product. You should deselect those components not installed in your system by unchecking the checkbox next to them. To see the list of components you can access in your SAP system, by select **System · Status** from the menu bar and click on the looking glass icon in the **SAP System data** section.

Once you have deselected non-installed components, exit the wizard by clicking the **Finish** button. The list of all **Web AS ABAP** systems now contains the newly created system (see Figure 3.6).

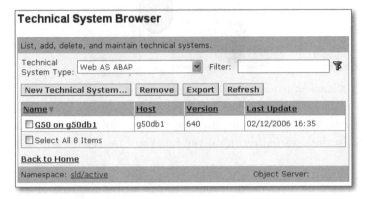

Figure 3.6 Technical System Browser

3.2.2 Creating the Systems in the SLD—Business Systems

Now that you have published the new technical system in the SLD, you must define which business systems can be accessed in the technical system. For this, you must once again go to the initial screen of the SLD and select **Business Landscape**. The system now displays a list of all existing business systems. Click on **New Business System** to call the appropriate wizard.

Business landscape for maintaining the business systems

First, you must enter the name of the new business system. The first system should have the name **SystemA**.[2] In the next dialog box, you must select the type of the technical system. Because you want to set up the new business system on the technical system you have just created, you must select **Web AS ABAP**. Continue to the next screen.

R/3 and ECC systems use SAP Web AS ABAP

You can now select your system from a list of all technical systems of the corresponding type. Once you have done that, the system dis-

---

2 The name of a business system cannot contain any special characters, which is why we do not use a blank space character at this point. In the following sections we'll use the names **SystemA**, **System A,** and **business system A** as synonyms. Of course, this applies to **SystemB**, accordingly.

plays all existing clients of this system (see Figure 3.7). Select the relevant client in this list and then click the **Next** button to continue.

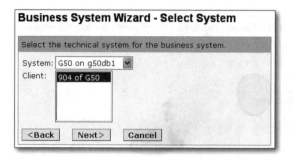

Figure 3.7 Business System Wizard—System Selection

Clients of the business systems are maintained as application systems

In the next step, the system displays a list of software products installed in the selected technical system. You can usually skip this step.[3]

The final step of the wizard prompts you to define the role of the business system (see Figure 3.8). Here you can choose between **Integration Server** and **Application System**.

Figure 3.8 Business System Wizard—Integration Server

Because we don't want the new business system to act as an information broker, you should select the **Application System** role. You must also select the integration server. The system displays a list of all business systems that have been created as integration servers. Select from the list the system you want to use for this course and exit the wizard by clicking the **Finish** button.

---

3   You do not need any additional software products for the practical exercises in this book. However, in other scenarios, you must use more than one software product. In such a case, you should check the products listed here.

The list of all business systems now contains the newly created business system, **SystemA** (see Figure 3.9). You must now repeat the steps to create a business system named **SystemB**. If necessary, you must also repeat the steps for defining another technical system.

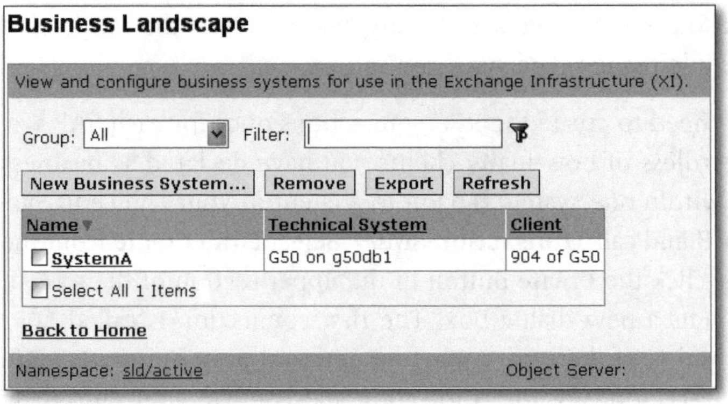

Both SystemA and SystemB must be configured

Business Landscape

View and configure business systems for use in the Exchange Infrastructure (XI).

Group: [All ▾]   Filter: [   ] 🜆

[New Business System...] [Remove] [Export] [Refresh]

Name ▾	Technical System	Client
☐ SystemA	G50 on g50db1	904 of G50
☐ Select All 1 Items		

Back to Home

Namespace: sld/active   Object Server:

Figure 3.9 Business System Landscape

3.3 Integrating the SAP Systems with the SLD

As a technical system in the SLD, the SAP systems you want to use are now familiar with different business systems. However, the job of the SLD is to provide up-to-date data about the connected systems at any time. For this reason, you must establish a connection between the SLD and the SAP systems to enable automatic updates of the available data. This can be made possible, for instance, by querying the clients or release statuses of the software components being used. Moreover, integration with the SLD is also necessary for later use of ABAP proxies.

SLD data must be updated regularly

> **Note**
>
> If you want to integrate an SAP system based on SAP Web AS 6.20, you must ensure that the **APPINT 2.0** Add-on is installed. This add-on contains the basic functions of SAP XI 2.0 that enable an SAP system to act as a local integration server.

APPINT 2.0 add-on for SAP Web AS 6.20

3.3.1 Creating the RFC Connections

First, you must create two RFC connections of the TCP/IP type. The **LCRSAPRFC** connection is used to import the exchange profile of

SAP XI. The exchange profile is an XML document that contains parameters used to define basic settings such as the host names and ports used by the XI components. The second connection, **SAPSLDAPI**, is used by the ABAP API for the connection to the SLD. In addition, you must maintain information on how and with which users the SLD can be accessed. Finally, you must test the connection and schedule regular data synchronisation.

LCRSAPRFC is a TCP/IP connection

You only need to create the RFC connections once for each SAP system, regardless of how many clients you have declared as business systems within one system. Logon to a client of your choice in System A or B and call **Transaction SM59**. Select **Edit · Create** from the menu, or click the **Create** button in the upper section of the screen, which opens a new dialog box. The first connection is called **LCR-SAPRFC** and is of the type **T-Start an external program via TCP/IP**. Enter a description for the connection and confirm your entries by pressing **Enter**.

This destination already exists in IDES systems

If you use an IDES system on an SAP Web AS 6.40, the system displays an error message saying that the connection already exists. In this case, you must exit the current transaction, search the relevant destination in the **TCP/IP Connections** category, and open it for editing.

ABAP and Java components find each other through a registered program ID

If the system does not return an error message, the layout of the lower part of the screen changes so you can enter additional parameters. For this, you must select the activation type, **Registered Server Program**. As the **Program ID**, enter a name with the structure **LCRSAPRFC_<XISID>**, where **<XISID>** represents the system ID of your XI system. You can determine the system ID by logging on to your XI system using the SAP GUI and selecting **System · Status**. Due to the registration you are carrying out with this step, a connection to the program of the same name can be established on the gateway server (in this case the XI system). This program should already have been registered on the Java side.

Although the program ID is not the cleanest of all solutions, it allows you to increase the speed of your work. By default, the program ID to be used is installed during the installation of SAP XI. However, depending on the type of SAP system you want to integrate, we recommend that you use program IDs of the structure **LCRSAPRFC_UNICODE** for Unicode systems or **LCRSAPRFC_NONUNICODE** for non-

Unicode systems. Note, if you do that, you must first register SAP XI on the Java side, which you can only do if you have the relevant administrator privileges. If you do, you can create separate entries for the **LCRSAPRFC** and **SAPSLDAPI** connections in compliance with the SAP installation guide.

The remaining values to be entered in this screen are the **Gateway-Options**. The **Gateway host** is the host name of your XI system, which you have seen in the URL of the SLD call in the previous section. The **Gateway service** is created according to the structure, **sapgw##**, with ## being the instance number of the XI system. You can import the instance number from the J2EE port when calling the SLD, as the port is structured according to the pattern **5##00**.

Connection data is stored in Transaction SMICM

Figure 3.10 displays the necessary settings in the TCP/IP connection, **LCRSAPRFC**.

Save your settings and run both the connection and the Unicode test via the corresponding buttons. Both tests should run successfully.

RFC Destination		LCRSAPRFC
Connection Type	T	TCP/IP Connection

Description

Description 1	LRC SAP RFC
Description 2	
Description 3	

Technical Settings   Logon/Security   Special Options

Activation Type

- ○ Start on Application Server   ● Registered Server Program
- ○ Start on Explicit Host
- ○ Start on Front End Work Station

Registered Server Program

| Program ID | LCRSAPRFC_<XISID> |

Gateway Options

| Gateway host | xihost | [Delete] |
| Gateway service | xigateway | |

Figure 3.10 Creating the RFC Destination LCRSAPRFC on the ABAP Side

SAPSLDAPI is created like LCRSAPRFC

Similar to the first RFC connection, you can now create **SAPSLDAPI**. The **Program ID** for this destination is **SAPSLDAPI_<XISID>** or—if you have already registered other programs on the Java side—**SAPSLDAPI_NONUNICODE** or **SAPSLDAPI_UNICODE**, respectively. Both the **Gateway host** and **Gateway service** remain unchanged. Once you have saved the settings, you must also run the connection and Unicode tests.

3.3.2 Configuring the SLD Integration

Maintaining the SLD access data in Transaction SLDAPICUST

Next, you'll need to configure the data exchange process with the SLD, based on those two connections. For this, call **Transaction SLDAPICUST** and click the **Display <-> Change** icon to go to the change mode. If there is an existing entry, you should consult with your landscape administrator to find out whether or not the entry is needed.

If so, you can create an additional row by clicking the **Insert Row** icon. Mark this row as **Primary** by clicking the corresponding checkbox and specify the host name of the XI system. When doing this, make sure that you don't enter the fully-qualified host name; just enter the host name up to the first point. Moreover, you must enter the J2EE port of your XI system in the corresponding column.

You must use the **XIAPPLUSER** user account for the integration; the default password is **xipass**. As your landscape administrator has probably changed this password, you should also contact him to obtain the correct password. You can enter the password in the column once you have clicked on the button.

Figure 3.11 shows an overview of the settings described so far. Save these settings and exit the transaction.

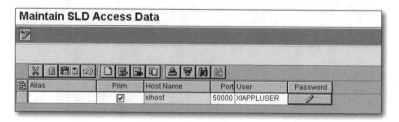

Figure 3.11 Maintaining the SLD Access Data

Due to the many configuration steps that need to be done, the process is prone to errors. For this reason, you can use a separate transaction to test the integration with the SLD. **Transaction SLDCHECK** checks all the settings made so far. If the check is successful, the transaction should call the SLD in a separate browser window and it should not display any error messages in red. If an error is displayed, you should double-check the settings you have made up to this point or refer to the decision tree provided by SAP, which you can find in SAP Note 768452 in the SAP Support Portal (*http://service.sap.com*).

Checking the SLD integration using Transaction SLD-CHECK

The final step in setting up the SLD integration consists of scheduling the automatic data transfer to the SLD. **Transaction RZ70** allows you to configure the data transfer.

Configuring the regular SLD update

You can keep almost all the default settings. On the left side of the screen, you can see that a batch job is scheduled which transfers data about the system to the SLD every 720 minutes (12 hours). Enter the host and gateway services of the XI system on the right in the **SLD Bridge: Gateway Information** section. These values correspond to those used in the RFC connections to the SLD.

Moreover, the lower part of the screen allows you to define the data collection programs to be used. At this point, it is helpful to have the system generate a proposal, which you can do by clicking the **Proposal** icon in the bottom-right of the screen. Next, click the **Start Data Collection** icon in the upper part of the screen to start the corresponding process. The system displays a detailed message telling you that all selected collection programs have been executed and that the data has been successfully transferred.

The first time the data collector is called, two new RFC connections of the TCP/IP type are automatically created within the SAP system. If an error message is displayed during the start of the data collector telling you that the new RFC destinations **SLD_UC** or **SLD_NUC** could not be called, you must make sure that the program IDs **SLD_UC** and **SLD_NUC** are registered in the SLD.[4]

SLD_UC and SLD_NUC may require additional program IDs

Figure 3.12 shows an overview of the settings. Now exit the results display and activate your configuration by clicking the **Match** icon in the top left-hand area of the screen.

---

4 You can find additional information on configuring the SLD integration in SAP Notes 700127 and 584654.

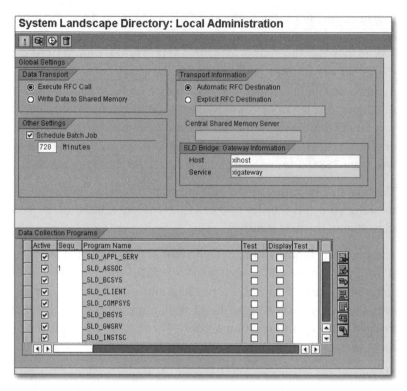

System Landscape Directory: Local Administration

Global Settings

Data Transport
- ◉ Execute RFC Call
- ○ Write Data to Shared Memory

Transport Information
- ◉ Automatic RFC Destination
- ○ Explicit RFC Destination

Other Settings
- ☑ Schedule Batch Job
  - 720 Minutes

Central Shared Memory Server

SLD Bridge: Gateway Information

| Host | xihost |
| Service | xigateway |

Data Collection Programs

Active	Sequ	Program Name	Test	Display Test	
☑		_SLD_APPL_SERV	☐	☐	
☑	1	_SLD_ASSOC	☐	☐	
☑		_SLD_BCSYS	☐	☐	
☑		_SLD_CLIENT	☐	☐	
☑		_SLD_COMPSYS	☐	☐	
☑		_SLD_DBSYS	☐	☐	
☑		_SLD_GWSRV	☐	☐	
☑		_SLD_INSTSC	☐	☐	

Figure 3.12 System Landscape Directory—Local Administration

3.4   Configuring the Local Integration Engine

Direct data exchange with SAP XI

Now that you have configured a regular data exchange between the SAP system and the SLD, you must configure the local integration engine of the SAP system. If you use an SAP system with an SAP Web AS 6.20 or higher, use the direct communication function between the central and the local integration engine. This connection is a prerequisite for the implementation of ABAP proxy scenarios. In the following sections, you will define the role of the local integration engine and establish the technical settings required for processing XML messages in the business systems. Additionally, you will establish a connection to the Integration Builder. Finally, you will set up a user that allows you to monitor the local integration engine from the Runtime Workbench.

3.4.1 Defining the Role of the Business System

Whereas the client of your SAP system that you want to use has already been assigned the role of a business system in the SLD, you must also make a corresponding local setting. In addition to defining the role, you must also specify the connection to SAP XI. Although connection data already exists in the SLD, local maintenance allows you to add authentication data as well. This logon data is needed later when you use ABAP proxies. You must specify the logon data in a separate RFC destination.

Defining the client role in Transaction SXMB_ADM

Open **Transaction SM59** in business system A to maintain the RFC destinations. Then select **Edit • Create** from the menu to create the new connection, **XI_INTEGRATIONSERVER**. In IDES systems, this connection may already exist. If so, you can customize the existing destination.

Select connection type **H–HTTP Connection to R/3 System** and enter a description of your choice. When you confirm your entries by pressing the **Enter** key, the lower part of the screen is adjusted accordingly. Go to the **Technical Settings** tab and enter the host name of your XI system as the target host. Select the service number of the ABAP port of SAP XI, which is usually structured according to the pattern, **80XX**. The path prefix is **/sap/xi/engine/?type=entry**. Figure 3.13 displays an overview of the data of the first tab.

Go to the **Logon/Security** tab and select the **SAP Standard** logon procedure. In the **Logon** section, enter the data of user **XIAPPLUSER** in the integration server client in the XI system. This data is used later for authentication with the XI service when SAP XI is called by the ABAP proxy. Figure 3.14 displays the settings of this tab.

Save the destination and run a connection test by clicking on the corresponding button. If necessary, you must confirm that you will accept all additional cookies. The results display should show status code **500**, which means that the XI service was called without data. If the system displays a different status code, you must check the logon data and, if necessary, whether the corresponding **sap/xi/engine** service has been released in **Transaction SICF** in SAP XI.[5]

---

5 Section 3.4.3 contains detailed instructions on how to proceed in **Transaction SICF**.

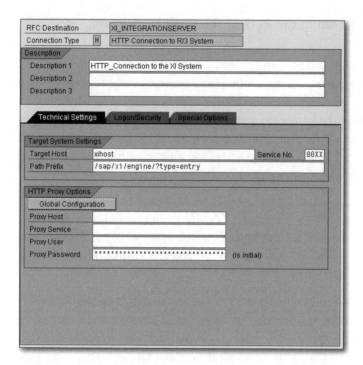

Figure 3.13 Technical Settings of RFC Connection XI_INTEGRATIONSERVER

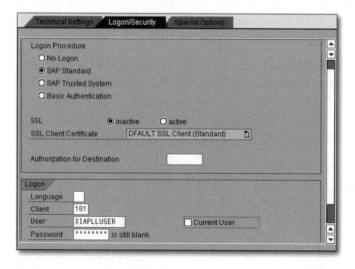

Figure 3.14 Logon Data of RFC Connection XI_INTEGRATIONSERVER

To define the role of the business system now and to integrate the stored destination, you must call **Transaction SXMB_ADM** in your business system. Select **Integration Engine · Configuration · Integration Engine Configuration** from the directory structure and execute this action by double-clicking or via the corresponding **Execute Function (F8)** icon. This takes you to the configuration data of the integration engine.

In this screen, select **Edit · Change Global Configuration Data** from the menu, which integrates the screen and causes some new icons to display. Next, select the **Application System** role for this business system and specify the **Integration Server** by entering **dest://XI_INTEGRATIONSERVER**. The keyword **dest://** ensures that the newly created RFC destination **XI_INTEGRATIONSERVER** will be used (see Figure 3.15).

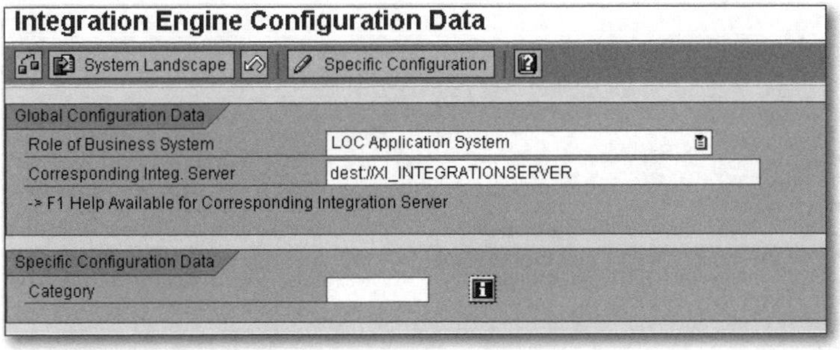

Integration Engine Configuration Data

System Landscape | Specific Configuration

Global Configuration Data
Role of Business System   LOC Application System
Corresponding Integ. Server   dest://XI_INTEGRATIONSERVER
-> F1 Help Available for Corresponding Integration Server

Specific Configuration Data
Category

Figure 3.15 Configuration Data of the Integration Engine

Save the settings and go one step back until you reach the tree structure of **Transaction SXMB_ADM**.

3.4.2 Defining and Activating Message Queues

Asynchronous messages are processed in such a way that all messages are first arranged in *queues* which ensures the dispatch or reception of individual messages in correct sequence based on the type of delivery. Because local integration engines can also receive such messages, the queues must be defined and activated.

Defining and activating queues to process asynchronous messages

Select the path **Integration Engine · Administration · Manage Queues** from the directory structure and execute this step by double-clicking the path entry. The system then displays a list of queues that must be created. The queues are distinguished by the type of processing (inbound vs. outbound), by the delivery options **Exactly**

Once (EO) and **Exactly Once In Order** (EOIO), and by the priority of the message.

Furthermore, a queue for particularly large messages must be created. Make sure that all queues are marked and that the **Register Queues** action has been selected. Select **Queues • Execute Action** from the menu or the corresponding icon to register the queues. Once you have completed this step successfully, a confirmation message is displayed in the status bar. Select the **Activate Queues** option in the **Action** area and run the activation process by clicking on the **Execute Action** button (see Figure 3.16).

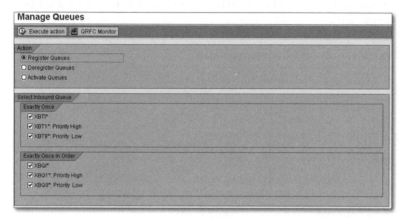

Figure 3.16 Managing Queues

If the activation process was successful, exit the transaction.

3.4.3 Activating the XI Service

You must activate the XI service on each integration engine

As already described during the configuration of the SLD integration, the integration engines communicate with each other through a service provided using the Internet Communication Framework (ICF). This service must be released in each system that contains a separate integration engine.

Call Transaction SICF in your business system to access the directory structure of the existing services. Within the directory structure, navigate along the path **default_host • sap • xi** and consider the services located in this directory (see Figure 3.17). Check to see whether the **engine** service has already been activated (i.e., if it is displayed in black color). If it hasn't been activated, select this service and click on **Service/VirtualHost • Activate** in the menu bar. Confirm the security question that displays with the first **Yes**. The second **Yes** option activates all subdirectories and services for a directory, which is not necessary at this point. Exit the transaction as soon as the activation is complete.

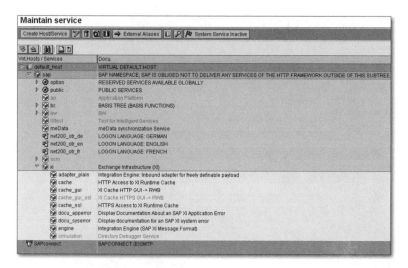

Figure 3.17 Maintaining the Services

3.4.4 Establishing the Connection to the Integration Builder and the Runtime Workbench

The last step in the configuration of the integration engine involves creating a connection to the contents of the Integration Builder. Like the central integration engine, local integration servers also require information on the objects that have been created in the Integration Builder. This is a particularly important prerequisite for the configuration of ABAP proxy scenarios. The connection is established by using an RFC connection with the fixed name **INTEGRATION_ DIRECTORY_HMI**, where HMI stands for *HTTP Method Invocation*.

Start **Transaction SM59** to create a new connection. The destination should be assigned the name **INTEGRATION_DIRECTORY_HMI** and be a **Type H—HTTP Connection to R/3 System** connection. In addition, enter a description of your choice and confirm your entries by pressing the **Enter** key.

Creating the RFC connection INTEGRATION_ DIRECTORY_HMI

If a security message displays, you can skip it. The lower part of the screen now changes and you can specify the **Target Host** by entering the XI system's host name. The service number describes the XI server's J2EE port and is structured according to the 5XX00 schema. The **Path Prefix** to the target host is firmly defined: **/dir/hmi_cache_refresh_service/ext** (see Figure 3.18).

Figure 3.18 RFC Destination INTEGRATION_DIRECTORY_HMI—Technical Settings

Connection uses the user XIISUSER

Now go to the **Logon/Security** tab and make sure that the **Basic Authentication** logon procedure is selected. Moreover, you must check whether the SSL setting corresponds to your landscape. To log on, you must use the user **XIISUSER** in the client of the central integration server within your XI system.

In addition, you must set the appropriate language. Depending on the language settings of the XI system, English can be used in most cases. The initial password of this user is **xipass**. However, you should check with your landscape administrator to see if the password has been changed. You may need to scroll down within the input screen to access the password field.

The **Special Options** tab requires the configuration of various settings (see Figure 3.19). The **Timeout** in terms of milliseconds should be set to 900. In the **HTTP Setting** section, make sure that the compression option is set to **inactive** and that no compressed response is expected. Regarding **HTTP Cookies**, all cookies should be accepted.

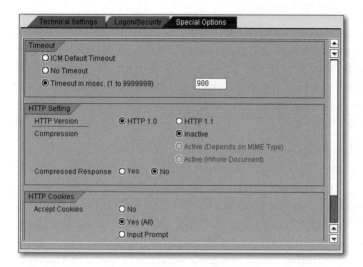

Figure 3.19 RFC Destination INTEGRATION_DIRECTORY_HMI—Special Options

Save the connection and select **Test • Connection** from the menu or click on the **Test connection** icon. Select the **Accept All Further Cookies** option in the security prompt that displays and click on **Yes**. If instead of the security prompt an input field pops up in which you must enter the user name and password, either the logon data was incorrect or it wasn't entered correctly.

Return code 200 in case of successful connection test

The subsequent screen displays the result of the connection test. If the test was successful, the first row below the title displays the entry **HTTP/1.1 200 OK**; this is further explained in the subsequent rows. Exit the test and **Transaction SM59**.

To monitor the configuration of the local integration engine, the Runtime Workbench later tries to log on with a specific user, which we now have to create. You must create the user **XIRWBUSER** in every client of the SAP system that has been set up as a local integration engine.

User XIRWBUSER to log on to the business system

To do this, call **Transaction SU01** and enter the name of the new user. Select **Users • Create** from the menu or click on the corresponding icon. The system now displays the **Address** tab in which you only need to maintain the last name of the user. Enter the password in the **Logon data** tab and repeat this entry. Make sure that the type of the user is **Service**. Go to the **Roles** tab, select the **SAP_XI_RWB_SERV_USER** role, and save the user.

Mass generation of the roles SAP_XI* and SAP_SLD*

Sometimes the XI authorization roles and the associated profiles have not yet been used in the business systems and therefore haven't been generated yet. If that's the case, you must call **Transaction PFCG** in the business systems. Then select **Utilities • Mass generation** from the menu and enter **SAP_XI*** to specify all roles whose names begin with "SAP_XI".

If you select **Program • Execute** from the menu or click on the corresponding icon, the system displays a list of profiles it has found, including their generation statuses. Next, select **Roles • Generate profile** from the menu and generate the profiles. Repeat these steps for the **SAP_SLD*** profiles. If users exist that already use these roles, you must also carry out a mass comparison according to the same schema by selecting **Utilities • Mass comparison** from the menu in **Transaction PFCG**.

3.5 Adapter-Specific System Settings

General configuration of different adapter types

Although you will have to configure more settings in the following exercises, you will primarily deal with content-related aspects. The settings made in this section, however, involve the system administration level and are therefore described separately.

3.5.1 Checking the ABAP-Proxy Integration

Testing the ABAP-proxy integration via Transaction SPROXY

The local integration engine, which requires the same information on existing repository objects as the central integration engine, is used by ABAP proxies to integrate the SAP system. To verify this on your system, start **Transaction SPROXY**.

The system displays the **ABAP Proxy Generation** screen, which shows all existing elements of the integration repository. You will generate proxy classes on the basis of repository information in the corresponding exercise.

3.5.2 Settings for the Use of the RFC Adapter

Use of the RFC adapter on the sender's side requires an RFC connection that—similar to the destinations already created—bridges the gap between the ABAP world of the SAP system and the Java world of the adapter framework in SAP XI. Depending on whether you carry out the exercise scenario on your own or in a team, you must perform this step once or several times with the relevant variation.

Sending RFC adapters are connected to an RFC destination

To create a new RFC destination in your system, call **Transaction SM59**. Create a new TCP/IP type connection whose name should be structured according to the schema **SystemA_Sender-<Participant number>**.

Assigning the RFC connection and communication channel with the program ID

This differentiation of participants is necessary to allow each group participant to create a separate communication channel. If you want to use the same communication channel for all participants in the RFC exercises, you do not need to add the participant number. The name of the connection for the trainer is **SystemA_Sender-00**.

> **Note**
>
> The participant number is preceded by a hyphen (-). If you use an underscore here, the system returns an error message.

Next, you'll need to enter a description for the destination. Go to the **Technical Settings** tab and select the activation type **Registered Server Program**. Enter a **Program ID** that corresponds to the name of the RFC connection. Technically speaking, the differentiation of multiple instances of an RFC communication channel occurs at this point; however, it is useful to use a meaningful name for the RFC connection here for reasons of clarity.

As you did before with other RFC destinations, you must enter the host name and the gateway service of the XI system in the **Gateway Options** section. Save the settings without testing the connection. At this stage, a test would fail because the corresponding communication channel hasn't been registered.

Figure 3.20 shows an overview of the settings described here.

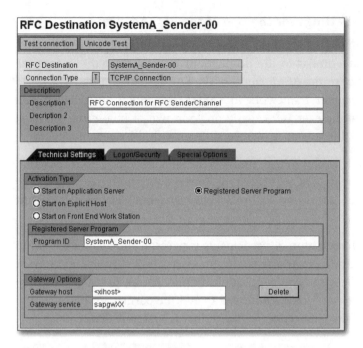

RFC Destination SystemA_Sender-00

Test connection	Unicode Test

RFC Destination	SystemA_Sender-00
Connection Type	T	TCP/IP Connection

Description

Description 1	RFC Connection for RFC SenderChannel
Decription 2	
Description 3	

Technical Settings	Logon/Security	Special Options

Activation Type

○ Start on Application Server   ◉ Registered Server Program
○ Start on Explicit Host
○ Start on Front End Work Station

Registered Server Program

Program ID	SystemA_Sender-00

Gateway Options

Gateway host	<xihost>		Delete
Gateway service	sapgwXX		

Figure 3.20 RFC Adapter SenderChannel

3.5.3 Settings for the Use of the IDoc Adapter

Settings required in all involved systems

Message delivery with the IDoc adapter requires you to configure many elements both on the side of the business system and of the XI system. RFC connections are used to deliver the messages to the receiving system. This holds true for the delivery of the IDoc to the SAP NetWeaver Exchange Infrastructure and for the delivery from SAP XI to the business system. However, the XI system requires the metadata of the defined IDocs, which is queried through an RFC destination. This second RFC connection is defined as a *port*. Because the system that stores the metadata in the IDoc exercise is also the receiving system, you don't need to maintain the second RFC connection in the XI system. Instead, you'll make the necessary settings for automatic processing of inbound IDocs in the corresponding exercise, and in the case study later in this book.

RFC-KOMM allows logon via RFC

You must first create a new user, **RFC-KOMM**, in your systems A and B, as well as in the XI system via **Transaction SU01**. The user should have the same last name. Define a password in the **Logon data** tab and enter it a second time. In addition, you must make sure that the user type **Communications** is selected.

Go to the **Profiles** tab and select authorizations that are as comprehensive as possible. Save your entries. The newly created user enables the connection between the XI system and the business systems for IDoc communication via the RFC destination.

Start **Transaction BD54** in SystemA to make the logical name of the client of SystemB known to SystemA. Confirm the warning that the table of logical systems is a client-independent object.

Each business system must know the logical name of the sending business system

Select **Edit • New Entries** from the menu or click the **New Entries** button. Enter the logical system of the client of SystemB and a description. You can find the logical system by calling **Transaction SCC4** in SystemB. In most cases, the name has the structure **<SID>CLNT<Client>**. Save your entries.

SystemA now knows the name of the logical system of SystemB. Repeat this step in SystemB to make SystemA known so it can be used later in the case study.

Delivery of IDocs occurs via RFC connections between SAP systems. This holds true for the delivery from business systems to SAP XI and vice versa. This means that, in each business system, you must create a destination to SAP XI as well as a connection from SAP XI to each business system.

Sending IDocs via RFC connections

Go to the XI system and call **Transaction SM59** to maintain the RFC connections. Create a new RFC connection of the type, **3—R/3 Connection**, and call it **SystemA_IDoc**. Repeat these steps for SystemB.

> **Note**
>
> The name of the RFC connection does not contain any participant number because the system only recognizes the logical system of the sender so multiple creations wouldn't make any sense in this case.

Enter the host name of SystemA in the **Target Host** field and add the **System Number** in the field to the right (see Figure 3.21). Go to the **Logon/Security** tab and maintain the data of the **RFC-KOMM** user you have previously created in the SAP systems and carry out a connection test, which should now be successful.

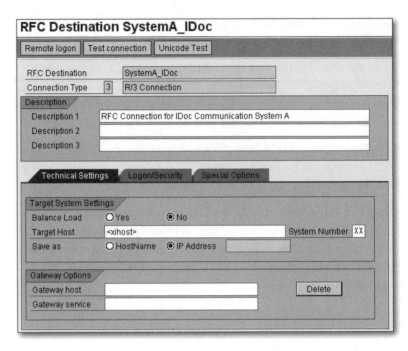

Figure 3.21 RFC Connection for the IDoc Adapter—Technical Settings

The test of the remote login will fail, however, because the **RFC-KOMM** user has only been created as a communication user and therefore cannot be used to log on. Save the RFC connection and create an RFC destination called **XI_System** in the two business systems. This destination uses the **RFC-KOMM** user to connect to the integration server client of the XI system.

Accessing IDoc metadata of the business systems

For the port that establishes the connection to the IDoc metadata, you must "pack" the newly created RFC connection in a different way. To do this, call **Transaction IDX1** in your XI system and create a new port by clicking on the icon that represents a blank sheet. Assign a name with the structure **SAP<SID>** to the port; in our case, the port for SystemA is called **SAPG50**. Perform this step also for SystemB.

Add a meaningful description and select the newly created RFC destination **SystemA_IDoc** or **SystemB_IDoc** respectively. Save the settings and take a look at the saved entry in the directory structure on the left. Figure 3.22 shows that the client has been attached to the name of the port. However, later in this book, the name of the port is **SAP<SID>** or **SAPG50**, respectively.

The automatic dispatch of IDocs in the case study requires the definition of transactional ports that can be used for transferring data via transactional RFCs. A transactional RFC corresponds to the quality-of-service EOIO.

Case study
uses transactional
ports

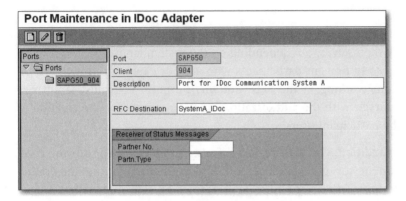

Figure 3.22 Port Mainnance in IDoc Adapter

Because you will only send IDocs from business system A in the case study, you only need to perform the following steps in SystemA. Start **Transaction WE21** and highlight the **Transactional RFC** item in the tree structure on the left. Select **Port • Create** from the menu or click the **Create** icon. Enter the port name **XI_SYSTEM** in the screen that displays and confirm your entry. Select the RFC destination **XI_System** you have just created and save the port.

Figure 3.23 displays the settings for the port of the transactional RFC call.

Port	XI_SYSTEM
Description	Transactional Port to the XI-System

Version
- ○ IDoc rec.types SAP Release 3.0/3.1
- ◉ IDoc record types SAP Release 4.x

RFC destination	XI_System

Figure 3.23 Creating a Transactional Port

3.6 Course-Specific Preparations

Exercises that are carried out in a course require various preparations

The basic system settings made thus far are primarily used to integrate SAP systems with SAP XI. If you want to work through the exercises in this book in a training course, you must set up the configuration described up to this point only once. However, the following steps may be necessary for each course that is to carry out the exercises.

In principle, you can also have the students carry out these settings by themselves, but depending on the system landscape, it can make sense to prevent participants who are not experienced with SAP XI from working in the SLD. For this purpose, you must familiarize yourself with the authorization objects required for the creation of the participant users.

In addition, you will create a software product with a software component for each student and import them into the Integration Builder. These steps must be performed so each student gets a separate software product so they can work independently. Thus, the following steps will increase the level of clarity and are intended to prevent individual students from interrupting each other when processing various objects.

Creating users in all involved clients

Depending on the experience of your students with regard to using enterprise software, you should define the authorizations to be assigned to the system users of the participants. You can use **Transaction SU01** to create a new user in the XI system by entering the name of the new user and selecting **Users · Create** from the menu or by clicking the corresponding icon. In the **Address** tab, you must at least enter a last name for the user. If necessary, users can complete the remaining details later on. In the **Logon data** tab, it is mandatory to enter the initial password. Finally, the **Profiles** tab contains a list of user profiles that have been assigned. Assign names to the users in the client of SystemA according to the schema, **SYS_A-##**, and in SystemB according to the structure, **SYS_B-##**, so you can tell which system you are currently working with. You should use the schema, **XI-##**, for the users in the XI system.

Table 3.1 lists the most important profiles for the exercises in this book. Each student should at least be assigned the first three profiles to be able to implement an entire integration scenario. There are some inherent risks in authorizing access to the SLD. Therefore, you should only assign it to experienced users. The authorization is primarily important for creating software products and software components. The last profile for the administration of the XI system should only be assigned to the instructor.

Depending on how you implement the exercises, the users need different roles

User profile	Description
SAP_XI_DEVELOPER	Design and development of integration processes
SAP_XI_CONFIGURATOR	Configuration of business integration content
SAP_XI_MONITOR	Monitoring of XI components and messages
SAP_XI_CONTENT_ORGANIZER	Maintenance of content in the SLD
SAP_XI_ADMINISTRATOR	Technical configuration and administration

Table 3.1 Important User Profiles in the XI System

Once you have assigned the relevant profiles, you must save the user; you can use it as a template for creating other users. Depending on the type of SAP system you want to integrate with the XI system, you should consult with your landscape administrator regarding the profiles to be used. If you use an IDES system, you can also use the profiles **IDES_USER** and **IDES_DEVELOP**. In addition, you may need to assign privileges for the use of RFC connections, depending on how you implement certain exercises.

3.6.1 Creating and Assigning the Software Product

Start **Transaction SXMB_IFR** to access the XI tools and log on to the System Landscape Directory. In the SLD overview, you can find the **Software Catalog** item in the **Software** menu.

Software products must be created in the SLD

In the software catalog, click on the **New Product** button and create a new software product called **SP_Training_XI_##**. **SP** is used to mark the software product and **##** represents the participant number. You can enter any name as a **Vendor**, but you should use a URL here to ensure that the name is unique. Make sure the vendor name does not contain more than 20 characters. Although you can use any version number, you should first enter version **1** (see Figure 3.24).

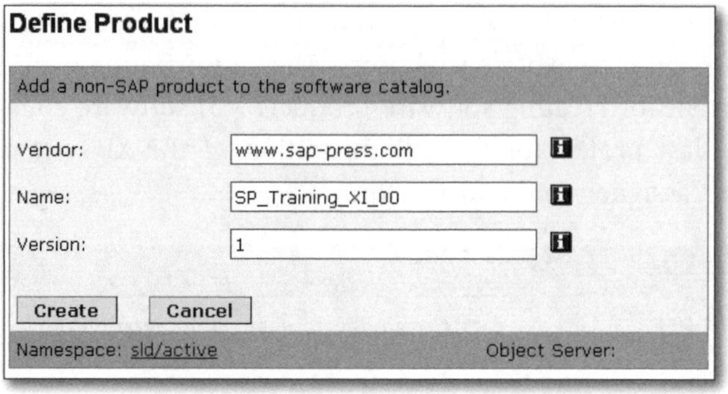

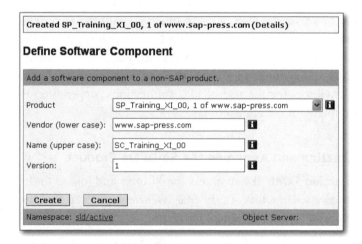

Figure 3.24 Defining a Software Product

Software products require a software component and a version number

Click the **Create** button to create the software product. The system now displays a message about the successful creation followed by an input screen for a software component within the new product. Because the product doesn't need more than one component in the exercise scenarios, the software component is assigned the name **SC_Training_XI_##**, and is set to version 1 (see Figure 3.25).

Figure 3.25 Defining a Software Component

If you want to use your own software component for the case study, you can create it in the manner described here.

Because a software product usually consists of more than one component, you can create additional components once you have saved the first one. In our case, however, that's not necessary.

Return to the initial screen of the SLD and select **Technical Landscape** to note that you will run your software product on the machines that also run the SAP systems. Select the system you have previously created from the list of technical systems. This takes you to the datasheet of the technical system which displays the installed software products in its lower section.

Assigning the software product to a technical system

In this section, you can use the **Add** link to add additional software products. The system now displays a search screen that allows you to search your software product. Enter **SP** in the filter field and confirm your entry by pressing the **Enter** key. The list below the filter field then displays your software product, which you can now select. If you click on the product, the software components contained therein are displayed in the field below, allowing you to select your component(s) (see Figure 3.26).

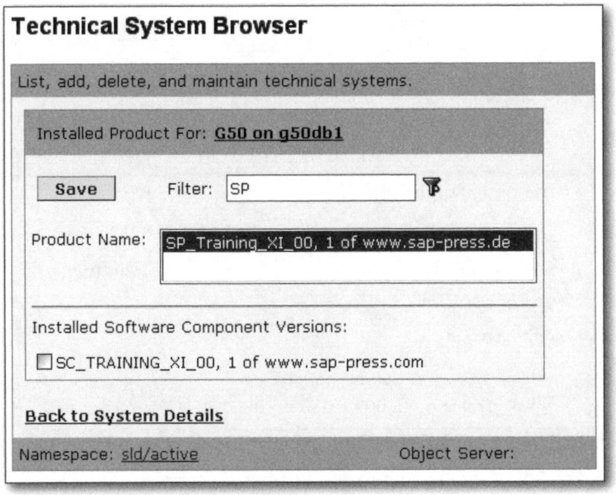

Technical System Browser

List, add, delete, and maintain technical systems.

Installed Product For: **G50 on g50db1**

| Save | Filter: SP |

Product Name: SP_Training_XI_00, 1 of www.sap-press.de

Installed Software Component Versions:
☐ SC_TRAINING_XI_00, 1 of www.sap-press.com

Back to System Details

Namespace: sld/active   Object Server:

Figure 3.26 Adding a Software Product

Save your selection. This returns you to the datasheet of the technical system, which displays your product in the installed software products section.

Assigning the soft-
ware product to a
business system

Once again, return to the initial screen of the SLD and click on the **Business Landscape** link to define that your business system uses this software product. To do this, click on **SystemA** in the list of business systems. This takes you to the datasheet of the business system that also contains a section for installed software products. You will see that your software product is displayed there because it is available as the Technical System. However, it is not used (or *marked*) by this business system.

You can change that by selecting the checkbox next to your product and saving this change (see Figure 3.27).

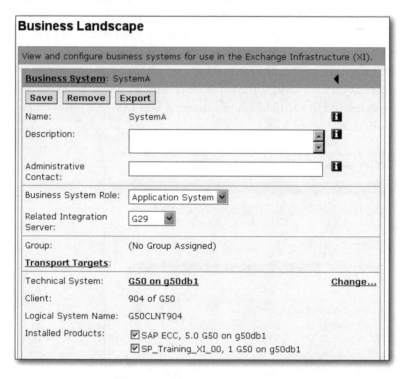

Figure 3.27 Assigning the Software Product to the Business System

Depending on the SAP XI support package being used, this is where you might notice inconsistencies between several participants. This is because there is a locking mechanism hasn't been used and each participant saves the selections he or she sees on the screen. As such, previously selected products can be deselected again. For this reason, you should make sure that the products of other participants are selected when selecting your own product.

3.6.2 Importing the Software Product in the Integration Repository and Setting it Up

In addition to displaying the installed applications and components of a business system, the newly created software product is also used to organize the development of integration scenarios in the Integration Builder. Before doing so, however, you must import the information on the new product and the software components into the integration repository.

Software products are needed to organize the development

First, return to the XI tools web site and select the **Integration Repository** in the **Integration Builder: Design** section. This starts the associated Java Web Start application. Logon using your user info from the integration server client of the XI system. However, prior to logging in, you must change the initial password of that user.

Select **Tools · Transfer from System Landscape Directory · Import Software Component Versions** from the menu. This command compiles a list of all available software components, including their versions. Select your software component **SP_Training_XI_##** in version **1** and import it (see Figure 3.28).

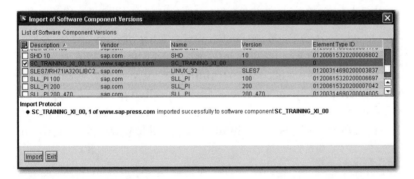

Figure 3.28 Importing Software Component Versions into the Integration Builder

> **Note**
>
> Sometimes it is possible that the new software component is not included in the list. In this case, you can select **Environment · Clear SLD Data Cache** from the menu to invalidate the SLD cache and repeat the import process.
>
> Depending on the quantity of software components, both the compilation of the list and the import can take several minutes.

Setting up the software component in the integration repository

Once you have imported the software component, the tree structure on the left side of the Integration Builder contains a new item with the name of your software component. Expand this branch so you can also see the versions of this software component. Double-click on the software component version to open the corresponding datasheet and select **Software Component Version · Display/Edit** from the menu bar within the datasheet. The color of some fields now changes from gray to white.

You must now enter two changes within the datasheet. On the one hand you will maintain the data for a connection to an SAP system so that you can later import RFC and IDoc interface information, and on the other hand you will create a namespace for each participant in which you can create all additional objects within the Integration Builder.

Permitting the import of SAP objects

In the **Interface Import** section, select the option, **Import of RFC and IDoc Interfaces from SAP Systems Permitted**. Once you have done that, the fields below this option are made available for input. Enter the data of an SAP system; for example, **SystemA**. As you can see, you still need to specify the user and password to trigger an import based on this data. Critical logon data is not required until the import starts.

Creating namespaces for the course participants

The lower part of the datasheet contains a list of namespaces that is still empty. Enter a new namespace according to the structure, **http://www.sap-press.com/xi/training/##**, where ## again represents your participant number. When specifying the namespace, it isn't important whether the URL actually exists. Your company's Internet domain is used to eliminate a possible namespace collision.

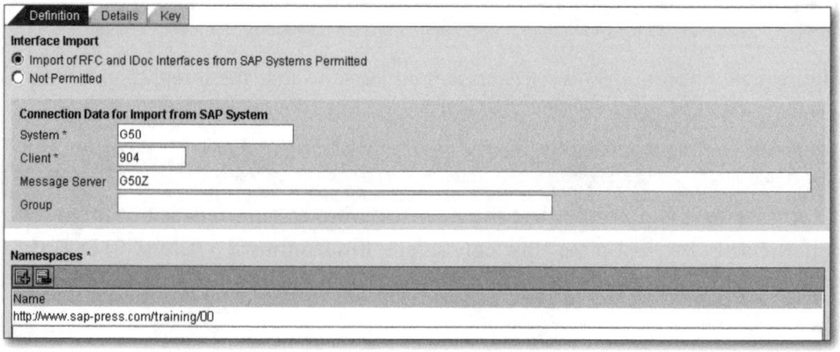

Figure 3.29 Editing the Software Component Version

Figure 3.29 displays the settings of the software component version with the first namespace.

Save your settings. The color of the object in the lower tab now changes from red to white. Moreover, the tree structure gets additional branches below the software component version. The two data types **ExchangeFaultData** and **ExchangeLogData** are automatically created in the **Data Types** branch.

You must now activate the changed object so the changes you saved can take effect and be transferred to the connected adapters and integration engines. To do this, go to the **Change Lists** tab above the tree structure on the left. You'll see the change list of your user in the tree structure. Expand the tree structure to the lowest level. In addition to the software component you have changed, you can see two data types that were automatically been created when you created the namespace.

Right-click on the **Standard Change List** branch to open the context menu, and then select **Activate**. You can now select specific objects that you want to activate. Select all objects (if that hasn't been done yet) and activate them.

You have now successfully prepared your systems for the exercises that follow in the remaining chapters. Depending on whether you perform the exercises on your own or in a group, you can carry out the corresponding steps for additional participants.

To ensure that all the preparatory steps have been done correctly, use the checklist provided in Table 3.2. If you encounter any errors or problems during the course of the exercises that you cannot solve with the help of this book, you can also refer to the *Troubleshooting Guide—SAP XI 3.0/2.0*. You can find the Troubleshooting Guide in the SAP Support Portal (*http://service.sap.com*) by selecting the quick link **instguides** from the menu path, **SAP NetWeaver · Release 04 · Operations · SAP XI**.

Change lists

Checklist and SAP XI Troubleshooting Guide

Area	Configuration	OK
Prerequisites	Systems A and B run on SAP Web AS 6.20+	
	SAP GUI version 6.20+ is installed in the frontend	
	Java Web Start < 1.5 is installed in the frontend	
	Port 5XX00 of the J2EE Engine is released in the XI system	
	Port 80XX is released in all business systems and the XI system	
Define the connected SAP systems in the SLD	Create the technical systems of Systems A and B in the SLD	
	Create business systems A and B in the SLD	
Integrate the SAP systems with the SLD	Create RFC connection LCRSAPRFC in business systems A and B	
	Create RFC connection SAPSLDAPI in business systems A and B	
	Settings in Transaction SLDAPICUST in Systems A and B	
	Execute Transaction SLDCHECK in Systems A and B successful	
	Configure the data exchange in Transaction RZ70 in Systems A and B	
Configure the local integration engine	Create the RFC destination XI_INTEGRATIONSERVER and definition of the role of the business system in Transaction SXMB_ADM in Systems A and B	
	Define and activate message queues in Systems A and B	
	Activate the XI service in Systems A and B	
	Create the RFC connection INTEGRATION_DIRECTORY_HMI in Systems A and B	
	Create user XIRWBUSER in Systems A and B (if necessary, mass generation and mass comparison)	
Adapter-specific system settings	Start of Transaction SPROXY in both business systems	
	Create RFC connections SystemA_Sender-<Participant number> in business system A	
	Create RFC-KOMM users in both business systems and the XI system	

Table 3.2 Checklist for Basic System Settings

Area	Configuration	OK
	Mutual publishing of the logical systems in Systems A and B	
	Create RFC connections SystemA_IDoc and SystemB_IDoc in the XI system	
	Create RFC connections XI_System in both business systems A and B	
	Create ports for business systems A and B in the XI system	
	Create the transactional port XI_System in business system A	
Course-specific preparations	Create system users in the business systems and in SAP XI	
	Create and assign of software products in the SLD	
	Import and setup of the software product in the integration repository	

Table 3.2 Checklist for Basic System Settings (cont.)

The exercises in this chapter show how to use SAP NetWeaver Exchange Infrastructure (XI) components by presenting scenarios that are linked in content but technically independent to prepare you for the case studies in Chapters 5 and 6.

4 Technical Exercises

Use of the available concepts and adapters of the SAP NetWeaver Exchange Infrastructure (XI) is the basis for implementing complex integration scenarios. This chapter shows you how to configure adapters, create mappings, and monitor the course of scenarios. The individual exercises build on each other and get more complex so you gain the knowledge necessary to implement the case studies presented in Chapters 5 and 6. Although the individual exercises depend on each other, you can use the lists of every exercise to track which objects are reused so you can start with a more advanced lesson. Predefined objects aren't used in the exercises, so you can reproduce all of the steps for completing the integration scenario at any time.

All exercises are designed in such a way that they can be performed by a group of participants at the same time. Still, some steps can only be carried out once. For steps that must be performed by the instructor, you will be notified either prior to or during the course. **Appropriate for several participants**

Although the exercises are appropriate for workgroups, you can also complete them on your own. In this case, perform the steps to be implemented by the instructor as well. Even if you are going to complete the exercises alone, we recommend you to use a user number as this simplifies the comparison of your work with the described procedure. In this case, you should use the instructor's number of 00.

Most exercises are completed as a development consultant, and particularly in the beginning of the exercise block, you will assume the role of the system administrator or the lead developer. In some places, you will have the opportunity to develop your own small applications in ABAP or Java. You hardly need any prerequisites **Possibility of your own developments** because the sample listings can be found in the Appendix of this book as well as in digital form on the web site for this book under *http://www.sap-press.com* and *http://www.sap-press.de/1383*.

Exercises as a
preparation for the
case study

The exercises deal with selected adapters and aspects of the XI environment. Various elements played a role when selecting the integration scenarios. When an adapter can be reused in a later exercise, its necessary aspects are discussed in that section. In hands-on exercises that are independent of each other, you will get to know the elements of SAP XI.

Even though the individual exercises do not have to be completed in the given order, there is a reason why we chose this order. In this chapter, you will implement integration scenarios that can be regarded as a preparation for the case study in the next chapter. Using XI messages, you will create a material in another system and verify its success. In a final step, the creation of material master data is reported to the person responsible for all material. A business process ensures that these reports are delivered in bundles per agent.

Procedures of the
exercises

At first, you will use an ABAP program in System A, which records the data of a material to be created and transfer this data to the XI system using the RFC adapter (see Section 4.1). There, the material master record is converted to a file in XI format via the file adapter. In the next exercise, this file is read via the file adapter and converted into an IDoc which is transferred to and directly processed on System B (see Section 4.2). In the third example, you will check to ensure that the material has been created successfully. Based on an ABAP proxy, you will send a call to the XI system. This request is converted to a web service call provided by System B. The response of this control is returned synchronously to the calling System A (see Section 4.3). The agent uses an ABAP program to report the successful creation of the material master records using a business process (see Section 4.4).

Even though the contents of the individual exercises are based on one another, you can start with any of the exercises by using the appropriate templates.

4.1 Exercise 1: RFC-to-File

In the first exercise you will use your own ABAP program to call a remote-enabled function module that transfers the entered material master data via the RFC adapter to the XI system. Once there, data is converted to the XI XML format and stored as a file. To keep things simple, the file is created directly on the file system of the XI server. Later, you will see what changes are necessary to store the file per FTP on another machine.

Course of the first exercise

Although the file technically remains on the XI system, from a logical viewpoint you will configure the receiving file adapter for System B. The communication in this integration scenario is asynchronous because no business response is returned after sending the material data. The roles of System A and B, as well as the adapters used in this exercise, are schematically illustrated in Figure 4.1.

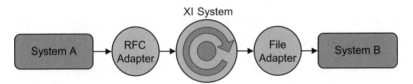

Figure 4.1 Scheme of Exercise 1: RFC-to-File

4.1.1 Basic Principles

Because this book does not focus on development of ABAP programs and remote-enabled function modules, we will only give you a basic explanation of the used program and the function module. You can get an appropriate transport with the function module and the program for 20 participants and 1 instructor from the book's web page and implement it in your System A. For implementing the transport, consult your landscape administrator, if necessary.

New ABAP compo-nents

If you want to create the program and the function module yourself, you will find the corresponding sample source code in Appendix A of this book.

First, log on to the client of System A as the user **SYS_A-##**, where ## is your participant number. There, you can view the remote-enabled function module using the Function Builder in **Transaction SE37**. Select the function module **Z_RFM_MATERIALINPUT**.

Structure of the function module

You will see that from the function module's point of view the parameters are only imported and no value is returned. This is one of the two prerequisites for asynchronous communication from a sending RFC adapter.

Except for the interface definition, the function module does not contain any ABAP code. This means that the function module is used as a kind of dummy that forwards the transferred data to SAP XI and serves as the definition of an interface. The information about where the data transferred to the function module is to be forwarded is contained in the calling program.

Function of the ABAP program

The program `Z_PROG_MATERIALINPUT_##`, which you can find together with the function module in the same transport request and that you can view in **Transaction SE38**, has two functions:

▸ First, it accepts the basic material master data that will be used to create a new material in System B.

▸ Second, it calls the function module (described earlier) with the parameters listed in Table 4.1.

The calling of these parameters is explained in the second exercise, in Section 4.2.

Transferred Data	Description
MATNR	Material number
MAKTX	Material description
ERSDA	Creation Date (will be added automatically)
ERNAM	User name of creator (will be added automatically)
MTART	Material type
MBRSH	Industry sector
MATKL	Material group
MEINS	Quantity unit
BRGEW	Gross weight
GEWEI	Weight unit
MTPOS_MARA	General item category group

Table 4.1 Data Transferred to the Function Module Z_RFM_MATERIALINPUT_##

In this call, two things need to be mentioned, in particular:

▸ The remote-enabled function module is called in a specific destination (i.e., in the system behind this RFC connection). In the case of the destination **SystemA_Sender-##**, this is the XI system, so the values transferred to the function module are forwarded to the XI system.

▸ The second aspect is the call in the background that causes the communication to be asynchronous.

4.1.2 Design

At first, you need to create the various data and message types as well as the message interfaces with the required mappings in the Integration Repository. In a later phase of the configuration, these elements will be linked to the connected business systems (System A and System B).

Creating the design objects in the Integration Repository

First, call **Transaction SXMB_IFR** from one of the connected systems or the XI system itself. This opens the menu of the XI tools in your web browser which will look familiar to you if you already carried out the preparation of the exercises (see Chapter 3). At the top-left, select the entry to the **Integration Repository**.

First steps in the Integration Repository

After the Java Web Start application has been updated and you have logged into the XI system as the appropriate user, the user interface to the Integration Repository is displayed. Ensure that you do not logon using the initial password; instead, change it during the logon to the SAP GUI.

On the left side, you will find the software components that have already been declared. This also includes the software component SC_ Training_XI_## with the namespace http://www.sap-press.com/xi/ training/##, which is where you will store your elements in the Integration Repository.

If you take a look at the individual categories within the namespace, you will notice that there are only two data types that have been generated during the namespace creation. For a better overview, restrict the view to your software component. In the tree structure, click on your software component, and above the tree select the icon **Only display selected subtree**.

The Integration Repository should then be presented as shown in Figure 4.2.

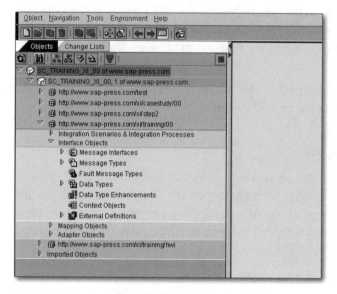

Figure 4.2 Entry to the Integration Repository

An overview of the elements required for this exercise is given in Table 4.2. The roles of individual elements and their connections have already been explained in Chapter 2.

Object Type	Sender Side	Receiver Side
Message interface	Z_RFM_MATERIALINPUT_##	MI_Material_Asnyc_In
Message type		MT_Material
Data type		DT_Material
Interface mapping	IM_Z_RFM_MATERIALINPUT_##_to_MI_Material_Async_Out	
Message mapping	MM_Z_RFM_MATERIALINPUT_##_to_MT_Material	

Table 4.2 Elements in the Integration Repository for the First Exercise

Solutions to interrupted connections

Note

If the connection to the Integration Repository is interrupted while an object is being edited, you can click on the **Administration** option in the XI tools on the right side and release the locked object for editing in the **Lock Overview** area.

Creating Elements for the Sending System

Due to the use of an RFC adapter, this scenario has a particular aspect: all elements on the sender side are replaced with the interface definition of the RFC module. Instead, the interface is imported from System A (and not created in the Integration Repository) to accelerate work and reduce the error rate.

Design objects on the sender side

To import the RFC interface, expand the bottom directory **Imported Objects** and right-click to open the context menu to find the **Import of SAP Objects** function. In the following window, select the option **According to Software Component Version** in the **Connection Data** area because the system data has already been stored (see Figure 4.3). If this option is not available, enter the host name and the system number of System A. Next, enter your user **SYS_A-##** and the appropriate password before continuing.

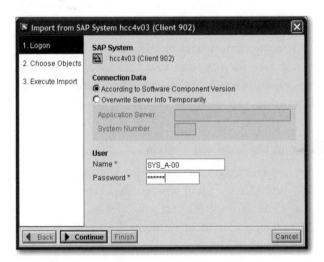

Figure 4.3 Import of RFC Interfaces—Login

The next step lets you choose between RFC and IDoc interfaces. Expand the RFC option. All remote-enabled function modules in System A are determined and displayed. Because this data collection can take a while, it is possible to import all interfaces before starting the exercise when you perform these steps in a group. From the list, select your function module **Z_RFM_MATERIALINPUT_##** (see Figure 4.4) and continue with the import.

Import the RFC interface

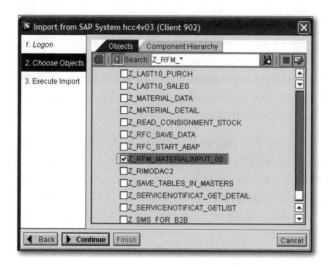

Figure 4.4 Import of RFC Interfaces—Selection

In the final step of the import process, check your selection and finish the import. After the import has completed, you can see your newly imported interface for your software component version in the directory **Imported Objects • RFC**. It is marked with a separate icon that indicates that this element has not yet been activated.

Creating Elements for the Receiving System

Design objects on the receiver side
While all elements are created on the side of the sending system by importing the RFC interface, you will create a data type, a message type, and a message interface for the receiving system. It is recommended to begin with the individual elements (i.e., with those on the lowest hierarchy level), which in this case is the data type.

Creating a data type
Within your namespace, expand the **Data Types** directory and open the creation dialog via the **New** entry of the context menu. In this window, you have the option to enter the name of the new object along with a description (see Figure 4.5).

The namespace and the software component version are automatically completed because you called the dialog in the appropriate context. Also, it is important to note the left area of this screen, which lists the elements that can be created within the Integration Repository. You can change the kind of element you want to create at any time. You will see a similar structure later when working in the Integration Directory.

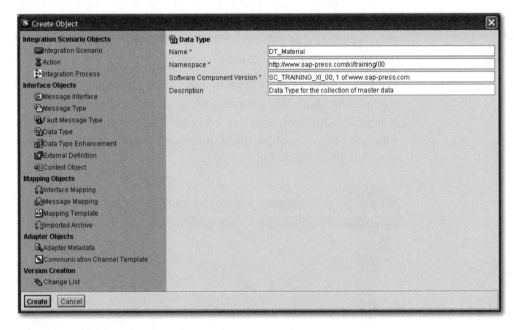

Figure 4.5 Dialog for Creating an Object in the Integration Repository

Name the new data type **DT_Material** and click on **Create**. The details window of a new data type is displayed on the right side. Because the structure of this window is typical of all detail views in the Integration Builder, it is used to explain some functions.

Next to the menu line of the Integration Repository is a separate details menu, the most important functions of which are also displayed as icons to its right. In addition to the icons for switching between the display and changing mode, and for creating a copy, you will also find an icon for the where-used list of this element, for example. The icon group to the right allows you to control the view. For example, you can hide header data or detach the details window as an independent element.

In the case of your data type, the lower area of the details window contains a list of all data type elements. Using the relevant icons you can add new rows to the top of the table and enter the elements from Table 4.1. Please note that this is the type **xsd:string**. Only the

Structure of the data type DT_Material

BRGEW element has the type **xsd:decimal**; you will later perform a calculation using this value (see Figure 4.6). Additionally, add the missing element NTGEW of the type **xsd:decimal**. You will use this element to calculate the net weight of the material (based on the gross weight) in the message mapping. Save the data type after all of the elements have been inserted.

Creating a message type

Since data types in the XI environment are exclusively used for the modularization of data formats, and cannot appear in a mapping or interface themselves, they are embedded in message types. While data types can only be assigned to message types in a 1:1 ratio, data types can be combined in any ratio.

Structure	Category	Type	Occurrence	Details	Default	Description
DT_Material	Complex Type					
MATNR	Element	xsd:string	1			
MAKTX	Element	xsd:string	1			
ERSDA	Element	xsd:string	1			
ERNAM	Element	xsd:string	1			
MTART	Element	xsd:string	1			
MBRSH	Element	xsd:string	1			
MATKL	Element	xsd:string	1			
MEINS	Element	xsd:string	1			
BRGEW	Element	xsd:decimal	1			
NTGEW	Element	xsd:decimal	1			
GEWEI	Element	xsd:string	1			
MTPOS_MARA	Element	xsd:string	1			

Figure 4.6 Editing a Data Type

To create a message type, open the appropriate context menu by right-clicking on the directory **Message Types**. Select the **New** option. The familiar creation dialog box is displayed, this time for a message type. Name the new object **MT_Material** and enter a description. Continue with the detail view by clicking **Create**. Pay attention to the **Data Type Used** area in the middle; this is where you should insert the data type you just created. You have three different possibilities of doing so:

Methods for selecting the data type

▶ The most obvious method is typing the name and the namespace, which, however, involves the risk of mistyping.

▶ The second option is to select the object in an ABAP-based SAP system, such as in the input help. For this, click on the hand and question mark icon to the right of the namespace field. A window opens, containing all of the data types created in your software component version for selection. The two fields **Name** and **Namespace** are then populated.

▶ The third option is to Drag and Drop the selection. This is particularly suitable if your software component version contains a lot of data types, but there are only few in your namespace. You can also pick the data type from the directory structure to the left and drop it on the hand next to the namespace field. Only by dropping it over the hand you can ensure a correct data transfer.

As you can see, all three possibilities work, even without activating the data type.

After selecting the appropriate data type, the lower area of the details window shows the structure of the used data type (see Figure 4.7). Check the structure and save the message type.

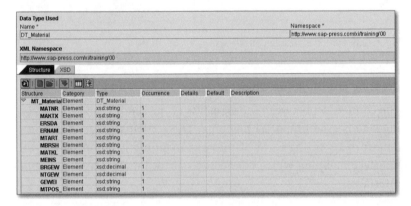

Figure 4.7 Editing a Message Type

The last object on the receiver side is the message interface, which determines if a message can be received or sent and whether the message is sent synchronously or asynchronously.

Creating a message interface

To create this message interface, open the context menu of the corresponding directory. Enter the name **MI_Material_Async_In** and an appropriate description, and then click **Create** to get to the details window. You can choose between the options **Inbound**, **Outbound**, and **Abstract** for the interface category; the individual categories have been discussed in Chapter 2. Because we are dealing with the interface on the receiver side, select **Inbound**. The communication mode determines whether a response regarding the contents is expected or not. Because this is a one-way scenario, select the **Asynchronous** mode.

You have probably noticed that the input options for message types change with every time the attributes are modified. You should now see the fields for the **Input Message** and the **Fault Message Type**. You will, however, only use the former (see Figure 4.8). Using one of the three methods discussed earlier, select the message type **MT_Material** as the input message, and then save your message interface.

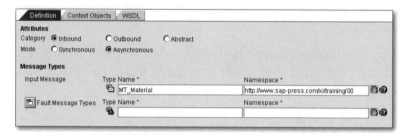

Figure 4.8 Editing a Message Interface

Creating the Mapping Objects

The connection between the elements of the sending and the receiving side is established via mapping. The contents conversion of the data formats in the form of message mapping is embedded in the interface mapping which connects a pair of inbound and outbound interfaces.

Creating the message mapping

At first, the independent message mapping should be created. In your namespace, open the context menu of the directory **Mapping-Objects • Message-Mappings**. In the creation dialog, enter the name **MM_Z_RFM_MATERIALINPUT_##_to_MT_Material**, where ## represents your participant number. Choose a description and create the object.

Selecting the outbound and the target message

The center area of the details window is divided into two parts, allowing you to select the sending message type on the left side and the receiving message type on the right side. First, start with the message type on the sending side: You have the option to either use the input help or to drag the appropriate message type to the label, **Enter a source message**. In this exercise, there is no explicit message type on the sender side, so use the RFC interface.

Regardless of the used selection method, you must choose which RFC message of the interface you would like to use. This is because a synchronous communication is expected for an RFC interface. Therefore, you can choose between the two messages **Z_RFM_ MATERIALINPUT_##** and **Z_RFM_MATERIALINPUT_##.Response**. Select the former because no response is expected.

The left part of the center area now lists the elements of the RFC interface. For the receiving part, select your **MT_Material** message type.

If you look at the elements on the right side, you'll find a red mark next to every entry. This indicates an incomplete mapping for the respective target element. Since we didn't change anything in the **Occurrences** column when creating a data type, the default value of **1..1** is applied. This means that this element is mandatory. If one of the target fields does not receive a value from the mapping, an error occurs. The connection between the elements of the two message types can again be established via three different methods:

Methods for mapping elements

▸ The most obvious possibility is the connection via drag and drop, where it isn't important which side is dragged to the other. The two elements are displayed in the lower screen area and connected automatically.

▸ The second option is to double-click on the source and on the target element to move them to the lower screen area where they are displayed as rectangles. There you can connect the two rectangles by dragging the white area of the sending element to the corresponding area of the receiving element. In particular, this method should be used if the mapping is to be extended by predefined functions.

▸ The third method is suitable for connecting a large number of elements of the same name. For this, parent elements must be selected on both sides. In this mapping, these are **Z_RFM_ MATERIALINPUT_##** on the sender side, and **MT_Material** on the receiver side. Then, above the sending message type, select the icon **Map selected Fields and Substructures if Names are Identical**. An alert dialog box appears, asking you to confirm the action. After dismissing the dialog, all of the elements on the sender side are connected to those on the receiver side. It's important to note that mapping of element names is case-sensitive.

Perform a mapping using the third method and have the result displayed in the overview by clicking on the **Dependencies** icon. The two message types then move apart and give way to the display of connection lines. You will also notice that the marks next to the receiver elements have now turned green. Only the **NTGEW** element is still red because it was not automatically provided with a value.

For demonstrating the integrated mapping functions, we assume that the net weight of the material is 90 percent of the gross weight. To map this, first select the **NTGEW** element on the receiver side and then the **BRGEW** element on the sender side by double-clicking on these items so both are displayed in the bottom area. To make this calculation, you first need a multiplication function that calculates the net weight from the gross weight with a constant of 0.9.

In the toolbar at the bottom of the screen, select the functions for **Constants** and click on the **Constant** function to the right, which is then displayed as a rectangle in the work area of the mapping. The cog wheel means that you can maintain parameters within this function. Double-click on the constant rectangle and change its value to **0.9** for the 90 percent of the net weight.

Now change to the **Arithmetic** area in the toolbar to insert the **mul** (short for *multiply*) function in the work area. Connect the **BRGEW** and **Constant 0.9** elements to the **mul** function by dragging the white subareas. In fact, these functions would be sufficient for calculating the correct net weight. However, the three decimal places permitted for the **xsd:decimal** type might be exceeded. If this message mapping were tested, it would result in an error.

Before the result of the calculation can be mapped to the **NTGEW** element, it must be formatted using the **FormatNum** function from the **Arithmetic** functional area. Configure the internal parameter **Number Format** of the function so the result matches the scheme **000.000**. Insert the **FormatNum** function between the **mul** function and the target element **NTGEW** (see Figure 4.9). All rectangles and the mark next to the **NTGEW** target element should now be displayed green. Save the message mapping.

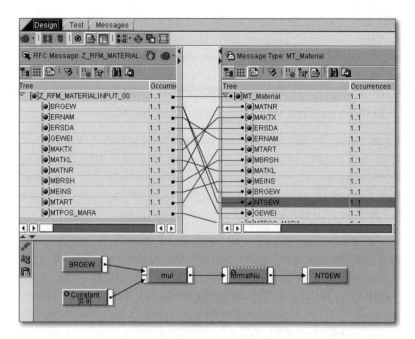

Figure 4.9 Message Mapping of the RFC-to-File Exercise

To ensure that the new mapping works, a test function is added to the Integration Repository, which you can select via the **Test** tab in the top area of the details window. On the left side of the test area, there is the structure of the sending message type whose elements are populated with test values. Be sure to use a decimal point as the decimal character for the **BRGEW** element.

Testing the mapping

The test itself is started with the **Start Transformation** icon (indicated by a vise) at the bottom-left of the test area. If the test program does not find any errors, the structure of the receiving message type with its respective values is displayed on the right. In particular, you should verify whether the **NTGEW** element has been populated correctly.

The last object of the integration scenario you are creating in the Integration Repository is the interface mapping. Start the creation dialog by opening the context menu of the directory **Mapping-Objects • Interface Mappings** in your namespace. Name the interface mapping **IM_Z_RFM_MATERIALINPUT_##_to_MI_Material_Async_In**, and then enter a description for the object and create it by clicking the **Create** button.

Creating the interface mapping

This object's detailed view is divided into the upper interface area and the lower mapping area. In the interface area, first select the sender interface; that is the RFC interface **Z_RFM_MATERIALINPUT_ ##**. Note that the RFC interface is not stored in your namespace; instead, you will find it in the directory **Imported Objects • RFC**. Perform the same steps for the target interface, **MI_Material_Async_In**.

By selecting the two interfaces, you have now specified which interfaces will communicate with each other as well as which message types are used. However, you still need to determine how the two data formats are converted to each other, since there might be different message mappings for the same message pair.

In the lower mapping area, click the **Read Interfaces** button to display the message types of the used interfaces (see Figure 4.10). After the **Source** and **Target Message** fields have been filled, click in the **Name** field located in the **Mapping Program** section area (located between the the source and target message fields) and select the input help that appears. A list is displayed, which contains all message mappings existing between the interfaces in this scenario of sender and receiver; you should only see mappings of the scheme **MM_Z_RFM_MATERIALINPUT_##_to_MT_Material**. Select the mapping with your participant number.

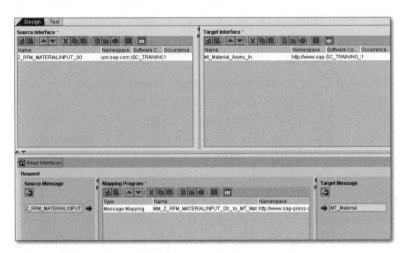

Abbildung 4.10 Interface Mapping of the RFC-to-File Exercise

If you have a closer look at the **Mapping Program** area (see Figure 4.10), you will notice that the tabular structure allows you to select several mappings. All selected message mappings are processed sequentially according to their order in the table. When creating the message mapping, for example, you can use the **Test** tab to perform a test which, in addition to the message mapping, also checks interface compatibility. Save your interface mapping after it has been successfully tested.

As you can see, all newly created objects were usable throughout the entire Integration Repository although they were not activated. However, you will not be able to access all of these objects in the Integration Directory in this state, so the next step is to activate your change.

Activating the new design objects

For this, go to the directory structure on the left and select the **Change Lists** tab. The tree structure is hidden and your software component version is displayed, which you should fully expand. Beneath that list, you will find a **Standard Change List** containing all newly created objects. Verify that all elements presented in Table 4.2 are included in the change list, and then select the **Activate** option from the change list's context menu. A window containing all objects of the list is displayed. You have the option to exclude specific objects from the activation. Activate the entire list and return to the **Objects** tab. Notice that the icons indicating that the new objects are not yet activated have disappeared.

4.1.3   Configuration

Based on the objects created in the Integration Repository, you can now set up the communication between systems A and B in the Integration Directory. The Integration Directory can be called either via **Transaction SXMB_IFR** (via the direct link in the web browser), or by selecting **Environment · Integration Builder (Configuration)** in the Integration Repository menu.

First steps in the Integration Directory

As with the Integration Repository, the interface is divided into two parts; however, the objects are no longer arranged according to software component versions. Instead, they are arranged according to scenarios and object types. Above the directory structure you'll see three tabs: Change Lists, Objects, and Scenarios. The **Change Lists** tab serves the same function as in the Repository. The **Objects** tab lists all objects of the Directory by their type. Because the number of these objects will significantly increase over time you have the option to arrange them in configuration scenarios on the **Scenarios** tab. Except for the scenario, you will create for all of your objects in the Integration Directory; this exercise uses all elements listed in Table 4.3.

Object Type	Sender Side: System A	Receiver Side: System B
Communication channel 1	RFC_SenderChannel_##	File_ReceiverChannel_##
Sender agreement	| SystemA | Z_RFM_ MATERIALINPUT_## | |	
Receiver agreement		| SystemA | | SystemB | MI_ Material_Async_In
Receiver determination	| SystemA | Z_RFM_MATERIALINPUT_##	
Interface determination	| SystemA | Z_RFM_MATERIALINPUT_## | | SystemB	

Table 4.3 Elements in the Integration Directory for the RFC-to-File Exercise

Setting Up the Business Systems and Their Communication Channels

Creating a Configuration Scenario

To create the **XI_Training_##** scenario, use the context menu of an existing scenario or click the **Create Object** icon to the bottom left of the menu bar. Save the object so the scenario is displayed in the listing on the left side, select the new scenario, and then restrict the view by clicking on the icon **Only Display Selected Subtree** above the list.

Change to the **Objects** tab and open the directory **Service Without Party • Business System**. Below the branch you will see at least the two business systems **SystemA** and **SystemB** which were declared in the System Landscape Directory when you prepared in Chapter 3 for the exercises. Click the **Add to Scenario...** option in the context menu of **SystemA** and select the scenario you just created.

Due to this mapping, this business system and its communication channels are displayed in your scenario as well. Repeat this step for the business system **SystemB** and return to the **Scenarios** tab.

The adapters available for the appropriate business systems are mapped in the Repository as communication channels (see Figure 4.11). Therefore, you need to configure a sending RFC adapter for System A and a receiving file adapter for System B.

Using the context menu from the path **Service Without Party · Busi-ness System · SystemA · Communication Channel**, open the creation dialog and enter the name **RFC_SenderChannel_##** along with an appropriate description. In the details window, use the input help to set the adapter type to **RFC**. Select the direction **Sender** for this adapter. For the fields **Transport Protocol**, **Message Protocol**, and **Adapter Engine** in the upper area, just use the default values.

Creating an RFC sender channel

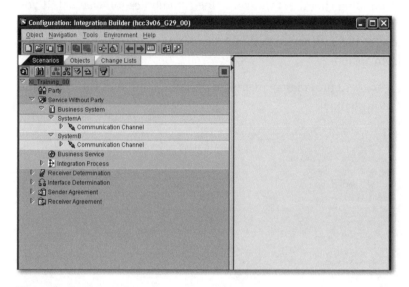

Figure 4.11 Integration Directory

The **RFC Server Parameter** area establishes a TCP/IP connection to the RFC destination on the side of System A. During the preparation of the exercises (in Section 3.5.2), you created an RFC connection named **SystemA_Sender-##**. This RFC connection is registered on the gateway server of the XI system and waits for a corresponding counterpart.

Connection to the existing RFC connection

In the **Application Server** field, enter the host name of the XI system, and in the **Application Server Service** field, enter the gateway service of the XI system according to the scheme **sapgwXX**, where *XX* represents the instance number. The **Program ID** follows the scheme **SystemA_Sender-##** and, like the two values mentioned earlier, exactly matches with the values entered in the corresponding RFC connection in System A. The **SNC** option specifies whether communication over RFC connection takes place via Secure Network Connection. The **Unicode** checkbox must be enabled if System A is a Unicode system.

The **RFC Metadata Repository Parameter** section is used to identify and log onto the system, and provides metadata about the used RFC interfaces. This integration is required because the metadata are checked by the XI system when calling the sending RFC adapter. In this example, the RFC interface is imported from System A during the design phase. Enter the host name and the instance number of System A, as well as your user **SYS_A-##**, your password, and the corresponding client, before saving the communication channel. If you enabled the communication channel at a later stage, the connection test for the destination **SystemA_Sender-##** is carried out successfully from System A.

Figure 4.12 provides an overview of all the settings of this communication channel.

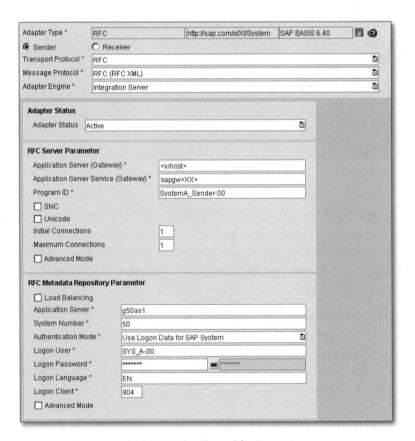

Figure 4.12 Setting up the RFC Sender Channel for System A

The receiving communication channel for System B is created with the context menu from the path **Service Without Party · Business System · SystemB · Communication Channel**. The name of the new channel should be **File_ReceiverChannel_##**. In the details window, select the **File** adapter type using the input help and specify the direction **Receiver**. Set the parameter **Transport Protocol** to **File System (NFS)**, which means that the XI system can use its own local file system to access the directory in which the file is to be created.

An alternative to the *Network File System* (NFS) is the *File Transfer Protocol* (FTP), which allows access to file systems of remote computers. If you select FTP, you can specify the server and user data to log on to a remote FTP server. The **Message Protocol** field should be set to the **File** value which causes the written file to be stored in the XI format. The **File Content Conversion** characteristic, however, allows you to write the file as a list containing several entries.

The **File Access Parameters** determine the directory to which the file is written, and the scheme according to which its name is structured. After consulting your landscape administrator, it is recommended to use */tmp* for Unix installations or *C:\temp* for Windows.

The **File Name Scheme** can be freely chosen. However, you should select the name *xi_output_##.dat* for this exercise, where ## represents your participant number. During the course of this scenario, we will refer to this file so you need to take this into account in Section 4.1.4 if you select a different name.

The **Processing Parameters** specify how to create the file, that is if the name scheme specified earlier is used as-is or if, for example, a time stamp, a counter value, or the message ID is to be included in the file name. Select the **Add Time Stamp** option as well as the write mode **Directly** and the file type **Binary** (see Figure 4.13).

The write mode, **Directly**, causes data to be written out when no temporary file is used. The selected file type, **Binary**, makes it so not only text can be output.

In addition to the basic settings, you also have the option of specifying the path of the file storage dynamically using variable replacement or to trigger an operating system command before or after the message processing. Save the receiver channel.

Creating a file receiver channel

Setting the source file

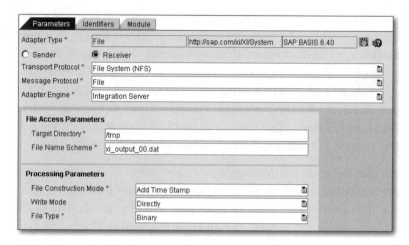

Figure 4.13 Setting up the File Receiver Channel for System B

Creating the Connection Elements

Connection
elements between
the sender and
the receiver side

Based on the basics we just created, and the objects in the Integration Repository, the integration scenario can be completed using some connection elements. The first two missing elements you need to create are the sender and the receiver agreement. This determines how a message is converted from or to the interface of a specific business system so the XI system or the receiving system can further process the message. In the case of the incoming RFC communication channel, for example, the message must be converted from the RFC adapter format to the XI XML format.

Creating a sender
agreement

Let's start with the sender agreement, which you can create using the context menu of the **Sender Agreement** directory: In the creation dialog, select business system A as a service. The sending interface is the RFC interface **Z_RFM_MATERIALINPUT_##**, which you imported to the Integration Repository. In the details window of the new object, you can specify the communication channel of the sender by opening the input help and selecting the sender channel **RFC_SenderChannel_##**. Save the sender agreement.

Creating a receiver
agreement

As you did for the sender agreement, create a receiver agreement for business system B and the receiving interface **MI_Material_Async_In**. Note that you also need to specify the sending business system A. In the details window, select the channel **File_ReceiverChannel_##** as the communication channel of the receiver and save the agreement.

For logically routing, messages in the XI system first need a receiver determination, which specifies available receiver services for a pair of business system and interface. Create a new receiver determination with the corresponding context menu for the sending business system A and the interface **Z_RFM_MATERIALINPUT_##**.

Creating a receiver determination

In the details window, the **Configured Receivers** area allows you to specify various possible receivers. If the review result of the relevant condition is true, the message is delivered to this system. This means that the message is delivered to several systems. For example, the condition can check elements of a message for a specific content.

If none of the configured systems is specified as the receiver, you can specify a default receiver below the receiver table. In the **Service** column of the existing row, select business system B as a potential receiver. Since the message in this exercise should be delivered to this receiver, you don't have to set a condition.

Save the receiver determination and then look at the lower area **Configuration Overview for Receiver Determination**, which now includes the **SystemB** entry. Expand the entry: As you can see in the entries, no matching interface determination and no appropriate interface mapping could be determined. Above this listing, click on the **New** icon to create a new interface determination.

Creating the interface determination

By calling the creation dialog from this context, all mandatory fields can be populated so you only need to enter a description. In the details window of the **Configured Inbound Interfaces** area, use the input help to select your message interface **MI_Material_Async_In** from the namespace. To the right of it, specify the only interface mapping available for the combination of the sending and receiving interfaces (see Figure 4.14). Save and close the interface determination and return to the receiver determination.

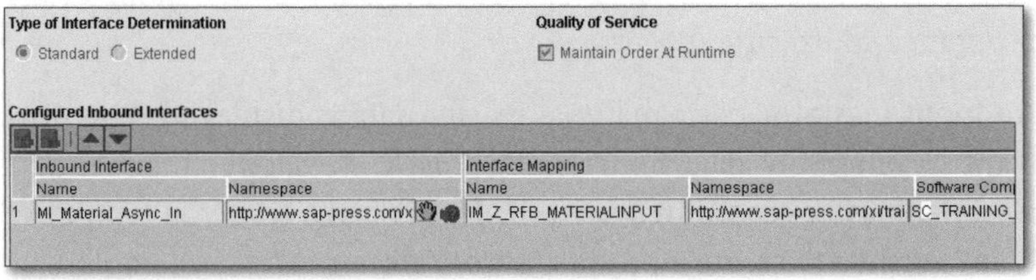

Figure 4.14 Editing the Interface Determination for the RFC-to-File Exercise

In the lower area, click the **Refresh** icon so the receiver agreement for the receiving System B is also displayed with the target interface and the matching interface mapping (see Figure 4.15).

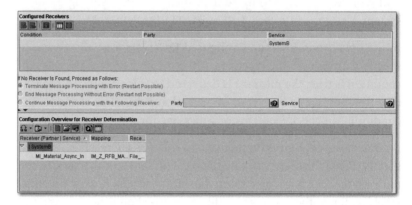

Figure 4.15 Editing the Receiver Determination for the RFC-to-File Exercise

Save the receiver determination and activate all newly created objects using the **Standard Change List** in the **Change Lists** tab. You have now created and activated all objects for this integration scenario.

4.1.4 Process and Monitoring

Now that you have created all design and configuration objects, you've completed the task of preparing the integration scenario for the course. Next, you will monitor the process and examine any possible errors.

Course of the Scenario

The configured integration scenario is started by calling the program Z_PROG_MATERIALINPUT_##. Log in to the client of System A using your user **SYS_A-##** and call **Transaction SA38**; type the name of the program and execute it.

An input mask for basic material master data is displayed. You now want to enter the data for creating this XI developer manual as a material master record in System B. This is just a test; you won't use it any further to create a production or sales order, for example.

The used data correspond to the mandatory fields of the two views Basic Data 1 and 2 from the materials management in SAP R/3 or SAP

ECC, respectively. Because this data is used in the second exercise to actually create a material using an IDoc, we recommend you use the data from Table 4.4.

Field	Recommended Value
Material	XI_BOOK-##
Material description	arbitrary (for example, SAP XI developer book ##)
Material type	FERT (Finished product)
Industry sector	1 (Retail)
Material group	030 (Documentation)
Quantity unit	ST (Piece)
Gross weight	arbitrary (for example, 1.2)
Weight unit	KGM (kilogram)
General item category group	NORM (Normal item)

Table 4.4 Recommended Values for Creating a Test Material

This data works in an IDES R/3 or ECC system without further adaptation. For the second exercise (see Section 4.2), you can later use the appropriate template files.

Entering the recommended values

Enter the data in the individual fields and note that the input help displayed for some fields only returns values of the sending system that might not exist in the receiving system (see Figure 4.16).

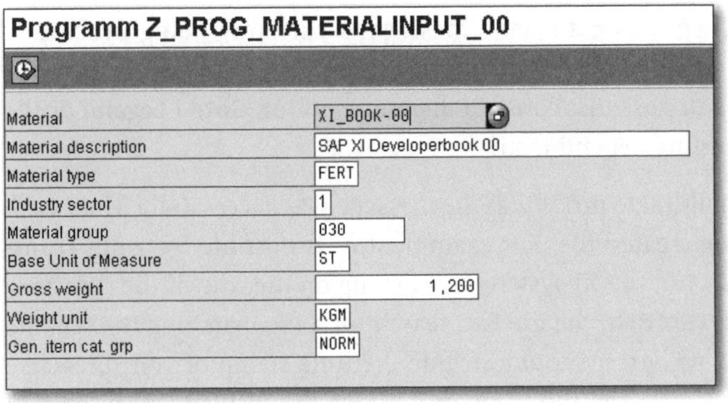

Figure 4.16 Calling the Program Z_PROG_MATERIALINPUT_##

After you have clicked on the menu option **Program • Execute** or the corresponding **Execute** icon you will receive a success message. This message only notifies you that the function module belonging to the program has been called successfully. However, it does not confirm that the message has been successfully delivered.

Monitoring the process Correct delivery and processing of the message can be verified in the XI system, for example. Log on to the appropriate client and call **Transaction SXMB_MONI**. Double-click on the path entry **Integration Engine • Monitoring • Monitor for Processed XML Messages**. This opens a selection mask that allows you to select all processed messages.

If the XI system is used only for training or testing purposes a restriction is hardly necessary. Otherwise, you could restrict the selection to messages with the sending server **SystemA**, for example.

Execute the message query via the **Program • Execute** menu option or the corresponding **Execute** icon. If your message has been successfully delivered and processed you should see an entry showing a black-and-white checkered flag in the status column (see Figure 4.17).

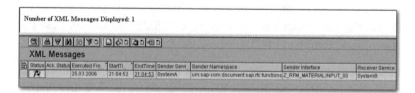

Figure 4.17 Display of the First Message in Transaction SXMB_MONI

A green flag means that the message is currently being processed. Most other icons represent an error in our case. You can display the legend of all possible icons via the menu option **Goto • Legend** or the corresponding **Legend** icon.

Viewing the created file To get an ultimate proof that the message was successfully processed, look at the created file. For example, this is possible by using **Transaction AL11** in the XI system, by clicking on the row of the directory alias **DIR_TEMP**. In the file list, search for a file matching the scheme *xi_output_##.dat*; it should include the time stamp of your message. Double-click on the file to open it. Since the display is limited to a specific width and the lines are not wrapped automatically, we recommend you use the file tools to import the transport request from the web page of this book to locally view the file.

Troubleshooting in Monitoring

To find the cause of an error in the message display of **Transaction SXMB_MONI**, double-click in any field of the corresponding row. This brings you to the **Display XML Message Versions** view. In the case of an asynchronous message, you will see the different statuses of the message on its way through the central integration engine. In the directory structure to the left, navigate to the place that has an error icon. In the windows on the right side, look for an error message indicating the cause. In most cases, the error was caused by a mapping or an object that was inadvertently selected from the input help.

Process analysis

In some cases, however, the error was caused by incorrectly configured communication channels or adapters. To check this, start **Transaction SXMB_IFR** which is used for calling the XI tools. On the bottom right, select the **Runtime Workbench** and logon using your user **XI-##**.

Checking the adapters

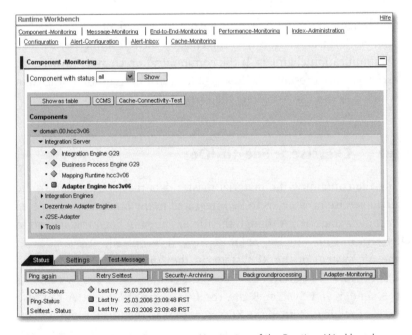

Figure 4.18 Entry Point to Component Monitoring of the Runtime Workbench

You will see the options for the Runtime Workbench, most of which you will become familiar with while working on the following exercises and the case study. Even though you already know a different way to display a message overview using **Transaction SXMB_MONI**, you can use the **Message Monitoring** menu option to view the message status in the XI system. First select **Component Monitoring**, and display the components with every possible status. In the directory structure of the components, select the path **domain.XX.<XIhost-name> • Integration Server • Adapter Engine**. A status view opens beneath the directory structure providing you with information about the general status of the adapter engine. On the top-right, click the **Adapter-Monitoring** button (see Figure 4.18).

Selecting the adapter type

After expanding the namespace http://sap.com/xi/XI/System, a new browser window opens and displays the selection of all available adapters. A gray diamond next to an adapter type indicates that a communication channel for this type hasn't been created. A green square indicates that all communication channels of this type have been correctly configured and that no error has occurred during processing. A red circle, however, indicates that at least one communication channel of this type is faulty.

You'll need to see if an error occurred for the adapter types **RFC** or **File**. For a closer analysis, you can click on the relevant type to list all communication channels. If the communication channel displays an error, you are presented with a detailed error description to the right which you can use to correct the error.

4.2 Exercise 2: File-to-IDoc

Course of the second exercise

The file containing the material master data that you created in the first exercise now needs to be integrated in the business system B to become a material. Although the file has already been transferred to System B from a logical point of view, it technically still resides on the file system of the XI system, in the */tmp* or *C:\temp* directory, respectively. This allows us to keep the arrangement that System A is the sender and System B the receiver because System A can also access the file system of the XI system to read the file. System A reads the file using the file adapter and transfers it to the XI system from where the record will be sent as an IDoc to System B.

A diagram of the used adapters and their use are shown in Figure 4.19.

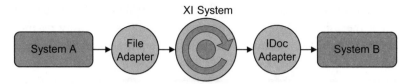

Figure 4.19 Scheme of the Second Exercise: File-to-IDoc

If you didn't work through the first exercise, you can obtain the templates for the file at *http://www.sap-press.com* and *http://www.sap-press.de/1383*. In this exercise, you will reuse several design elements of the receiving side from the first exercise.

Jumping in at Exercise 2

4.2.1 Basics

After you are familiar with the receiver side of the file adapter, it's time to get to know the sender side. File mapping to an IDoc presents a certain challenge in this exercise because IDocs contain very sophisticated and complex data structures. Despite the age of this format, they still play an important role in the SAP environment, which has something to do with their option of automatic processing.

Overview of the new objects

In this scenario, you will create a partner agreement in System B. This agreement ensures that the incoming material master data is automatically processed in the form of the IDoc (i.e., that the corresponding material is created automatically).

The partner agreement you will create is not a new element for SAP XI, but an element of the traditional ALE communication. The partner agreement can only be created once for a sending system (i.e., System A) because the differentiation is made according to the logical system of the sending application. The client of the sending System A, however, can only be assigned a single logical system.[1]

Function of the partner agreement

Log on to System B and call **Transaction BD54** to verify that the name of the logical system (System A) is known. Every system must know the names of the logical systems of the IDoc partners. The name of the logical system is usually structured according to the scheme **<SID>CLNT<client>**; in the training course, the logical system of System A is called **G50CLNT904**.

Creating the partner agreement

---

1 If you perform this exercise with several participants, it is recommended that the instructor be present for the following steps.

Leave **Transaction BD54** and call **Transaction WE20**. The left part of the screen shows the existing partner agreements sorted by partner types. The right side contains detailed information about the selected agreement.

From the menu bar, select **Partners • Create**, or click the **Create** icon to create a new partner agreement. Enter the name of the logical system of System A (the one you just checked) as the partner number. Note that the partner type **LS** (logical system) is selected in the details window. Ensure that the partner status value in the **Classification** tab is set to **A** for active.

Configuring the inbound parameters

Next, you need to specify that incoming IDocs of the **MATMAS** (Master Material) type are automatically processed according to a specific pattern. For this purpose, save the partner agreement and in the lower area **Inbound parmtrs** and click the **Create inbound parameter** icon. In the new screen template, select the message type **MATMAS** (see Figure 4.20).

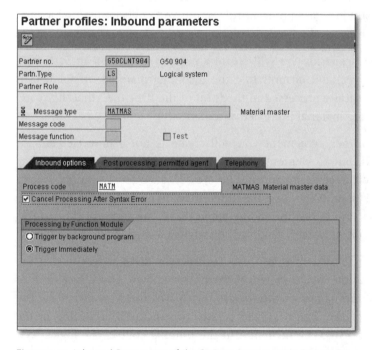

Figure 4.20 Inbound Parameters of the Partner Agreement in System B

Below the **Inbound options** tab, select the predefined process code **MATM**. If a syntax error occurs, don't terminate the process as this helps you easily identify potential errors later on. However, if you successfully tested your integration scenario in the previous example, you can enable the **Cancel Processing After Syntax Error** option by selecting its corresponding checkbox. The **Processing by Function Module** options are to be performed immediately. Save these settings to complete this Transaction.

4.2.2 Design

Object creation in the Integration Repository is much easier after working through the first exercise. If you have already gone through all the processes, you can reuse some design objects from the first exercise. Reused objects are indicated with an asterisk (*) in Table 4.5.

Overview of the new design objects

Object Type	Sender Side	Receiver Side
Message interface	**MI_Material_Async_Out**	**MATMAS.MATMAS02**
Message type	**MT_Material** *	
Data type	**DT_Material** *	
Interface mapping	**IM_MI_Material_Async_Out_to_MATMAS_MATMAS02**	
Message mapping	**MM_MT_Material_to_MATMAS_MATMAS02**	

Table 4.5 Elements in the Integration Repository for the File-to-IDoc Exercise

The sender side, which corresponds to the receiver side from Exercise 1, is already complete except for the outbound message interface. Open the creation dialog in the path **Interface Objects**, and create the message interface **MI_Material_Async_Out**. It is taken from the **Outbound** category and is used in the **Asynchronous** mode. The output message corresponds to the **MT_Material** message type already created in the last exercise (see Figure 4.21). Save the completed interface.

Creating the outbound message interface

Figure 4.21 Editing the Outbound Message Interface for the File-to-IDoc Exercise

On the receiver side, you first need to import the metadata of the **MATMAS.MATMAS02** IDoc. You can import the metadata the same way as you imported the RFC interface in Exercise 1. In the Integration Repository, navigate to your software component version and open the import dialog via the context menu of the **Imported Objects** directory. If systems A and B run different SAP systems so that the required IDoc type is unknown in System A, you can log on to the business system B. Otherwise you can import from System A.

In the next step, expand the **IDocs** area, mark the **MATMAS.MATMAS02** type and import it. Like the interface definition of RFC interfaces, the interface definition of IDocs can be used both as a message type and as a message interface so more objects are not required on the receiver side.

Create a new message mapping named **MM_MT_Material_to_MATMAS_MATMAS02**, assign the **MT_Material** message type on the sender's side, and the **MATMAS.MATMAS02** IDoc type on the receiver's side. When using IDocs, message mapping is a challenge because the data structure is very complex and can contain several hundred entries. To keep track, Table 4.6 presents the relevant fields of this example.

Data Element of MT_Material/Constants	Data Element of MAT-MAS. MATMAS02	Segment of MAT-MAS. MATMAS02
Constant: 1	BEGIN	None (IDOC)
MT_Material	E1MARAM	None (IDOC)
MT_Material	SEGMENT	E1MARAM
Constant: 005	MSGFN	E1MARAM
MATNR	E1MARAM	
Constant: KBG	PSTAT	E1MARAM
Constant: KBG	VPSTA	E1MARAM
Constant: 000	BLANZ	E1MARAM
ERSDA	E1MARAM	
ERNAM	E1MARAM	
MTART	E1MARAM	

Table 4.6 Assignment of Data Elements in the Message Mapping of the File-to-IDoc Exercise

Data Element of MT_Material/Constants	Data Element of MAT-MAS. MATMAS02	Segment of MAT-MAS. MATMAS02
MBRSH	E1MARAM	
MATKL	E1MARAM	
MEINS	E1MARAM	
BRGEW	E1MARAM	
NTGEW	E1MARAM	
GEWEI	E1MARAM	
MTPOS_MARA	E1MARAM	
MT_Material	E1MAKTM	E1MARAM
MT_Material	SEGMENT	E1MARAM/E1MAKTM
Constant: 005	MSGFN	E1MARAM/E1MAKTM
MAKTX	E1MARAM/E1MAKTM	
Constant: D	SPRAS	E1MARAM/E1MAKTM
Constant: DE	SPRAS_ISO	E1MARAM/E1MAKTM

Table 4.6 Assignment of Data Elements in the Message Mapping of the File-to-IDoc Exercise (cont.)

As you'll notice, element names in the **DT_Material** data type were not chosen by chance. Some fields of the IDoc structure are populated with constants that were not queried in the material input mask.

Structure of the IDoc type

In particular, pay attention to the fields **BEGIN** and **SEGMENT** as well as to the segments themselves which control the creation of the IDoc or its segments, respectively. While **BEGIN** must be assigned a specific value, you can assign any field to the **SEGMENT** fields (and the segments themselves) because this only determines the number of segments in the IDoc. You will work with this more later in this section.

Additionally, it's worth mentioning the **MSGFN** fields found in every segment. These fields specify the function to be used by the data in the receiving system. The **005** constant stands for changing or creating.

If you closely examine the structure of the IDoc, you will notice that most segments allow for multiple integration. Most IDocs are appropriate for mass processes. This IDoc can be used for creating several material master data sets; however, the IDoc in this example is only used to create a single material master record. Documentation of this and all other IDoc types can be found in **Transaction WE60**.

Deactivating fields If you examine the table containing the element assignment, you will see that only two of the segments are provided with data. The unused segments can be disabled to prevent them from generating fields. For such a segment, open the context menu and select the **Disable Field** function. The icon next to the segment is then crossed out and the segment is no longer checked for data. Disable all segments except **E1MARAM** and its child segment **E1MAKTM**.

Next, create the message mapping (see Figure 4.22) using Table 4.6 and test it. If it runs smoothly, save it. The work area shows how the constant is assigned to the **BEGIN** element.

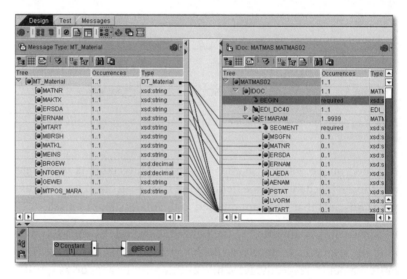

Figure 4.22 Message Mapping of the File-to-IDoc Exercise

Creating the inter-
face mapping Next, create the interface mapping **IM_MI_Material_Async_Out_to_
MATMAS_MATMAS02** based on this message mapping **MM_MT_
Material_to_MATMAS_MATMAS02** via the context menu in the appropriate path. Use the two message interfaces **MI_Material_
Async_Out** and **MATMAS.MATMAS02**, import the interfaces into the lower area of the details window, and assign the message mapping you just created (see Figure 4.23). In the **Test** tab, test the interface mapping and save the object.

Since this was the last new design object for this exercise, you should now apply all changes in the **Change Lists** tab before any changes are made to the Integration Directory.

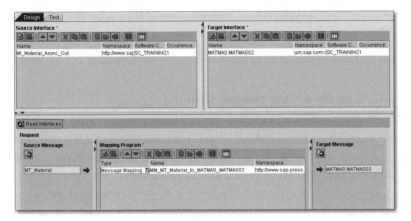

Figure 4.23 Interface Mapping for the File-to-IDoc Exercise

4.2.3 Configuration

Now use the XI tools menu or the direct URL to make changes to the Integration Directory. In the previous exercise, you already created the basic elements for the configuration. Since there are hardly any overlaps with the first exercise at the configuration level, you will create all required objects — even the communication channels — and use the Configuration Wizard to create the connection elements. This Wizard saves you from several steps and contributes to a smooth implementation. An overview of all configuration objects in this exercise is shown in Table 4.7.

Overview of configuration objects

Object Type	Sender Side: System A	Receiver Side: System B
Communication channel	File_SenderChannel_##	IDoc_ReceiverChannel
Sender agreement	| SystemA | MI_Material_Async_Out | |	
Receiver agreement		| SystemA | | SystemB | MATMAS.MATMAS02

Table 4.7 Elements in the Integration Directory for the File-to-IDoc Exercise

Object Type	Sender Side: System A	Receiver Side: System B
Receiver determination	| SystemA | MI_Material_Async_Out	
Interface determination	| SystemA | MI_Material_Async_Out | | SystemB	

Table 4.7 Elements in the Integration Directory for the File-to-IDoc Exercise (cont.)

Setting up the Communication Channels

Creating the file sender channel

Open the **Scenarios** tab in the **XI_TRAINING_##** scenario. To create the sending communication channel for the file adapter, open the creation dialog using the menu path, **Service Without Party · Business System · SystemA · Communication Channel**. The new communication channel should be named **File_SenderChannel_##**. First enter a description and create the new object.

In the details window (see Figure 4.24), select the **File** adapter type and ensure that **Sender** is selected. Set the **Transport Protocol** to **File System (NFS)**, since a local directory is accessed. With the **Message Protocol**, the **File** setting ensures that the file is read without being converted. The **Adapter Engine** is the Integration Server.

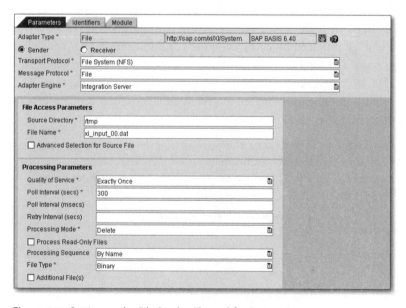

Figure 4.24 Setting up the File Sender Channel for System A

In the **Source Directory** field, select the setting you used for the receiver channel in the RFC-to-File exercise (see Section 4.1.3). If you followed the recommendations, this is */tmp* for Unix, or *C:\temp* for Windows. The file name should be *xi_input_##.dat*, where ## represents the participant number. Note that this file scheme differs in two ways from the scheme of the receiving communication channel in the first RFC-to-File exercise: the file was written to the directory as *xi_output_##.dat*, and a time stamp was added. Therefore, it is necessary to rename the file from the first exercise.

In the **Processing Parameters** area, you can keep the **Quality of Service** as **Exactly Once**. Set the **Poll Interval (Sec)** to a value between 3 and 10 minutes, otherwise the load on the Integration Server will be too high. The **Retry Interval** field specifies the number of seconds the adapter should wait before retrying after a failed read. (This value is not relevant to this exercise.) The **Processing Mode** of the communication channel can take various characteristics depending on your permissions at the operating system level.

One option is the **Archive**, which causes the file to be moved to another folder. Alternatively, the file can be deleted or left unchanged in the test operation, which causes the data record to be sent continuously. Use the archiving with a time stamp if an appropriate folder is available. The file cannot be archived in the source directory. If you do not have an appropriate folder, you could just delete the file. The processing order can be freely chosen, however, you should set the **File Type** to **Binary**.

All other fields of the communication channel can be left empty. Just make sure that the **Adapter** is set to **Active**. Save the communication channel.

The receiving communication channel for IDocs is created only once (as described in the basics of this exercise) because there is no possibility of distinguishing between several participants.[2]

Creating the IDoc receiver channel

Navigate to the directory path **Service Without Party • Business System • SystemA • Communication Channel** within your scenario. Using the menu, create the communication channel **IDoc_Receiver-Channel** and enter the description. Set the Adapter Type to **IDoc**, and

---

2 The IDoc communication channel can only be created once by the instructor.

set the direction to **Receiver**. The three following fields (Transport Protocol, Message Protocol, and Adapter Engine) normally don't offer options, so just ignore them (see Figure 4.25).

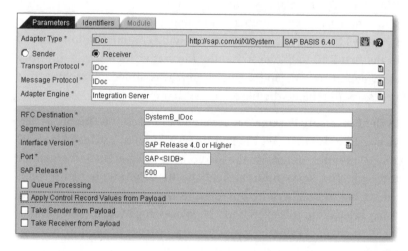

Figure 4.25 Setting up the IDoc Receiver Channel for System B

For the **RFC Destination**, select the **SystemB_IDoc** connection, which you created while preparing for the exercises. The **Segment Version** is used for integrating with legacy SAP systems, and can only be used for sending those segments that already existed in a specific R/3 release. The **Interface Version** field (which is mandatory) serves the same purpose but refers to the entire interface definition. For this field, select the **SAP Release 4.0 or Higher** option. Enter the port for System B, which was created according to the **SAP<SIDB>** scheme during the preparation (SIDB is the system ID for System B). In the **SAP Release** field, enter the release of the receiving SAP system. In the case of SAP ECC 5.00, the entry is **500**. Save the object and activate the two new communication channels.

Since not all communication channels of a business system are automatically displayed in all scenarios using these business systems, the two new objects must be added to the scenarios of every participant. In the **Objects** tab, change to the path of the two business systems, **SystemA** and **SystemB**. Using the menu for the new communication channels, you can use the **Add to Scenario** option. Add the two new objects to your scenario and check the display in the **Scenarios** tab.

To ensure that the file communication channel has been configured correctly, you can view the adapter in the Component Monitoring. Open the Runtime Workbench and display all components by clicking on the entry on **Component Monitoring**. In the list, click on the **Adapter Engine**. A new area appears below the list (on the right side) which contains the **Adapter Monitoring** button. Select the **File** adapter type and check its status.

Controlling the file adapter

If no errors occurred, the status should be green. If an error has occurred, you will find a detailed description of the error status. Some errors only occur during data processing, so you should return to the adapter monitoring if you encounter problems at a later stage.

Creating the Connection Elements

In this exercise, the connection between the two communication channels or between the sender and the receiver interface is created using the Configuration Wizard. The Wizard is started with the menu path **Tools · Configuration Wizard**, or by clicking the corresponding icon in the Integration Directory's toolbar. The Wizard collects data for the configuration and creates the appropriate objects. In the progress bar on the left side of the wizard, you can use the orange mark to identify your current position in the configuration process.

Calling the Configuration Wizard

In the first step, you can select whether to configure an internal or partner communication. Internal communication takes place entirely within the enterprise landscape, while partner communication either entirely or partially involves external business partners. For our scenario, select the **Internal Communication** option.

Determining the communication type

In the next screen (see Figure 4.26) you can specify the values for the sending side. Before you specify other values, however, you should select the sending **Adapter Type**; in this exercise, this is the file adapter. Next, select **Business System** as the **Service Type**, and **SystemA** as the **Service**. In the **Interface** field, specify the interface as **MI_Material_Async_Out**. When selecting the values using the input help, you may need to delete the search criteria and search once more to find a specific interface. If you used the input help for entering the interface, the namespace is populated automatically. Otherwise specify your namespace as http://www.sap-press.com/xi/training/##.

Setting the sender parameters

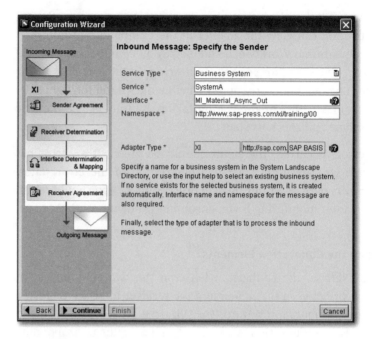

Figure 4.26 Configuration Wizard—Information about the Sender in the File-to-IDoc Exercise

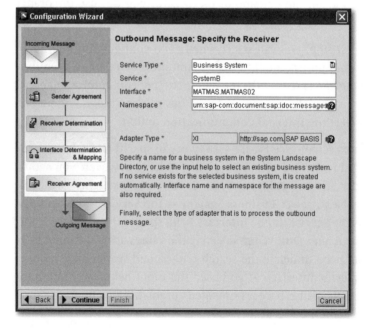

Figure 4.27 Configuration Wizard—Information about the Receiver in the File-to-IDoc Exercise

When you continue to the next step, you are presented with the same input mask for the receiver side (see Figure 4.27). As before, first select the **Adapter Type (IDoc)**. Specify the **Service Type** as **Business System**, set the service to **SystemB** and set the **Interface** to **MATMAS.MATMAS02**. By selecting the IDoc adapter type, the namespace is already defined.

Setting the receiver parameters

In the next input mask, the communication channel on the sending side is queried to be able to automatically create the sender agreement | **SystemA** | **MI_Material_Async_Out** | |. Specify your sending file communication channel **File_SenderChannel_##** of System A.

Determining the sender channel

The following step is for creating the receiver determination | **SystemA** | **MI_Material_Async_Out**. At first, it checks to see if a receiver determination for the sending interface already exists for the relevant system. If the object does exist, it is extended. Otherwise, a new object is created which does not require any input. Since this training scenario shouldn't contain an appropriate receiver determination yet, this step is only for your information.

Creating the receiver determination

The next step for creating the interface determination | **SystemA** | **MI_Material_Async_Out** | | **SystemB** can either be used for information or for checking as well (see Figure 4.28). Ensure that the **MATMAS.MATMAS02** interface has been selected and that the interface mapping **IM_MI_Material_Async_Out_to_MATMAS_MATMAS02** is displayed. If the mapping isn't displayed, this usually indicates that it has not been created (or at least not activated).

Creating the interface determination

The last object checked for this scenario is the receiver agreement | **SystemA** | | **SystemB** | **MATMAS.MATMAS02**. To create this object, you only need the receiving communication channel **IDoc_Receiver-Channel**, which should have been entered already. Continue to the last step.

Creating the receiver agreement

After you have made the necessary changes, you can directly assign the new objects to a specific scenario. Select your scenario (**XI_Training_##**) and click the **Finish** button. The required objects are now created, and reused objects are modified. After the objects have been generated successfully, you receive a detailed log on the updated and created objects. Finally, the changes must be activated in the **Change Lists** tab.

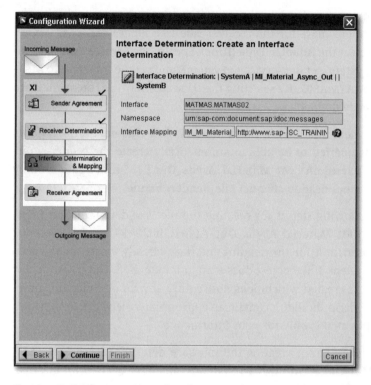

Figure 4.28 Configuration Wizard—Information about the Interface Determination of the File-to-IDoc Exercise

4.2.4 Process and Monitoring

Controlling the process

The process of the integration scenario in this exercise is triggered by creating the file *xi_input_##.dat* in the directory of the sending file adapter. When creating and placing the file, you can either use the template or and download the file from the web page for this book. (You can also rename the file from the first exercise.) Additionally, you may need to remove the write protection of this file when working on a Unix system. For this, use the *chmod* command.

Depending on the poll interval that has been set in the communication channel, the file is archived or deleted after several minutes. If the process is successful, you can look at your new material **XI_BOOK-##** in **Transaction MM03** of business system A shortly after the file disappears. In the first screen, select your material and confirm your input by pressing the **Enter** key. Select the two views Basic Data 1 and 2, and check the details. To keep the used IDoc structure small, only these two basic views have been created (see Figure 4.29).

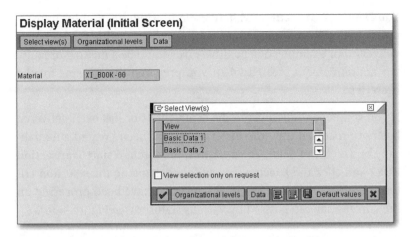

Figure 4.29 Entry Point for Displaying the Material XI_BOOK-##

Using two utilities, however, you have the option of adding more views; **Transaction WE60** stores the documentation of the entire IDoc type with all its field names. If you are already familiar with material management in the SAP system and now want to know which field of the input mask corresponds to a field in the IDoc, you can get this information by pressing **F1** for help. For example, open any material using **Transaction MM03** and highlight a field. Press the **F1** key and in the help, click the **Technical Information** icon. In most cases, the **Field Data** area contains the exact field name matching that of the IDoc.

Possibilities of extending the sent data

If the material hasn't been created in System B (even after you have waited for a while) you will need to troubleshoot the problem. The first possible source of an error is the file adapter since it doesn't read and archive the file, for example. In the **Component Monitoring** of the Runtime Workbench, re-check the status of the corresponding adapter. Some errors are only obvious while a message is being processed.

Checking the file processing

The next item to troubleshoot would be the message monitoring on the XI system. You can open it via **Transaction SXMB_MONI** or the message monitoring in the Runtime Workbench. There you can see if the message has reached the XI system and analyze if a content error has occurred for an Integration Builder object. However, if the message shows a green flag, it has been successfully forwarded to System B.

You can use **Transaction SM58** (the monitoring function for transactional RFC calls) to see if there were problems with the technical delivery. For example, one possible error could be a missing or faulty partner agreement created when you prepared the systems for the exercises.

Checking the incoming of the IDoc

If you still haven't discovered the error, the IDoc has been delivered but not processed (i.e., the material has not been created automatically on receipt of data). To check this, in System B start **Transaction BD87** and click the **Execute** icon without changing the selection criteria. You will receive a list of all IDocs that have been processed on the current day categorized by various statuses (see Figure 4.30).

Status Monitor for ALE Messages

IDocs	IDoc status	Number
▽ 🍃 IDoc selection		
📄 Changed on is in the range 02.04.2006 to 02.04.2006		
▽ 🔧 G51CLNT902		13
▷ 🗃 IDocs in outbound processing		5
▽ 🗃 IDoc in inbound processing		8
▽ ⦿ IDoc with errors added	56	4
▽ 🗂 MATMAS		4
🔲 EDI: Partner profile not available		4
▽ △ IDoc ready to be transferred to application	64	1
▽ 🗂 MATMAS		1
ℹ️ & &, &, &.		1
▽ 🗀 Application document posted	53	3
▽ 🗂 MATMAS		3
ℹ️ Messages have been issued: number &		3

Figure 4.30 Status Monitor for ALE Messages

Navigation in the Status Monitor for ALE Messages

To determine the exact source of error when processing a message, click on the appropriate category (e.g., **Application document posted**). The selection is restricted to the messages in this category. Because System B only differentiates processing of IDocs by the names of the logical systems, delivered messages cannot be distinguished by participants.

If you double-click on one of the messages in the list, the corresponding details are displayed. On the left side, expand the **Status records** directory and the numbers underneath. Every number represents a specific message. In this exercise, you will find messages, even for messages that have been successfully processed.

If you double-click on one of these numbers, the status record is displayed. To see a descriptive error message, go to the menu bar and select **Goto · Application Log** or click on the appropriate button. You will see warnings and error messages that have occurred while the message has been processed, and you can see if you have overlooked a field or filled it with the wrong data (see Figure 4.31). IDoc fields are checked, as well as the input in the relevant transactions.

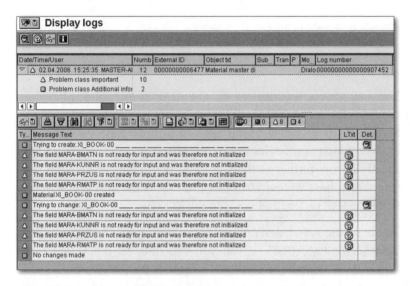

Figure 4.31 Application Log of an IDoc Message

4.3 Exercise 3: ABAP-Proxy-to-SOAP

In the second exercise, you imported the data you created as a file in the first exercise into the business system B using an IDoc. Additionally, you could also verify that the material master record has been properly created. However, in real life, it isn't always possible that you can access both the sending and the receiving system. *Course of the exercise*

Therefore, we will implement an integration scenario in this third exercise that allows you to control the successful material creation from System A. You will create an ABAP proxy in System A and call it synchronously. The request is forwarded to a web service on System B and a response is returned shortly afterwards. The XI system serves as the mediator between the different adapter and data formats.

The scheme of this exercise for synchronous communication is illustrated in Figure 4.32.

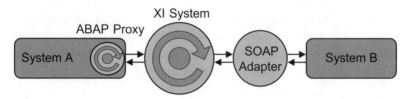

Figure 4.32 Scheme of Exercise 3: ABAP-Proxy-to-SOAP

4.3.1 Basics

Origin of the web service

The web service is addressed via the SOAP adapter and is based on the BAPI **BAPI_MATERIAL_EXISTENCECHECK**, which is provided by System B. As of the technical basis of SAP Web AS 6.20, remote-enabled function modules can be addressed as web services without specifying any further settings. As with the import of RFC and IDoc interfaces, these web services can also export the WSDL description from the SAP system and use it in the XI system.

Web Service Repository

To obtain the WSDL description for the appropriate BAPI, use a Business Server Page (BSP), which you can find via the URL scheme *http://<Host SystemB>:<Port 80XX>/sap/bc/bsp/sap/webservicebrowser/ search.html?sap-client=<client>*. The *XX* in the port number represents the instance number of the respective server. The specifications about host and port can be obtained from the **Transaction SMICM** by choosing **Goto • Services**.

Open the appropriate URL in the web browser and log on as user **SYS_B-00**. In the search field, enter the name of the BAPI (**BAPI_ MATERIAL_EXISTENCECHECK**), and confirm your selection by pressing **Enter**. The search result shows the BAPI with two links on the right side (see Figure 4.33).

The question mark (**?**) opens the function module's documentation, if there is any. The **wsdl** label opens the WSDL description of this function module in a separate window. Because Microsoft Internet Explorer, for example, automatically adds functions for collapsing and expanding individual sections to WSDL descriptions, it is necessary to save the source text of the display. This can be done by choosing **View • Sourcecode**. Save the document as *BAPI_MATERIAL_*

EXISTENCECHECK_SystemB.wsdl on your local machine. You will import this file into the XI system during the design phase.

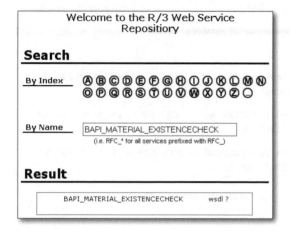

Figure 4.33 Web Service Repository

The calling ABAP proxy class is created based on a message interface existing in the Integration Repository. Because inbound and outbound data formats match those of the web service, you will use the imported WSDL definition as the data and message type of the outbound message interface as well.

4.3.2 Design

In contrast to the previous exercises, you are now facing your first synchronous scenario. This means you not only have to create the design objects for access to the web service, but also for the way back. In this respect, this example is easy because you are using the existing WSDL interface so you don't have to create any data or message types. In other cases, a synchronous scenario can involve creating up to four different data types and the corresponding message types. While the message mapping is created separately for every direction, the same interface mapping is used for both directions. The new objects to be created for this exercise are listed in Table 4.8.

Overview of the design objects

Object Type	Sender Side	Receiver Side
Message interface	MI_ABAP_PROXY_MAT_EXIST_ ##__Sync_Out	MI_ws_bapi_material_ existencecheck_Sync_In
Message type	ws_bapi_material_existencecheck	
Data type		
Interface mapping	IM_ABAP_PROXY_MAT_EXIST_##_to_ws_bapi_material_ existencecheck	
Message mapping (request)	MM_ABAP_PROXY_MAT_EXIST_##_to_ws_bapi_material_ existencecheck	
Message mapping (response)	MM_ws_bapi_material_existencecheck_to_ABAP_PROXY_ MAT_EXIST_##	

Table 4.8 Elements in the Integration Repository for the ABAP-Proxy-to-SOAP Exercise

Creating the Interface Objects

Importing the WSDL description

First, use the menu path **Interface Objects • External Definitions** to change your namespace. Create the external definition **ws_bapi_material_existencecheck**, which contains the WSDL description of the web service on System B. In the details window, ensure that the **wsdl** category is selected, and next to the File field click the **Import external definitions** icon. Select the **BAPI_MATERIAL_EXISTENCECHECK_System B.wsdl** file on your local machine, which you just transferred from the Web Service Repository (see Figure 4.34).

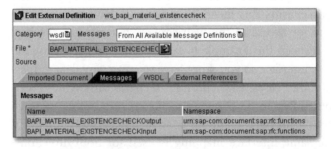

Figure 4.34 Importing the External Definition for the ABAP-Proxy-to-SOAP Exercise

After the import, you can see the contents of the file in the **Imported Document** tab. Select the **Messages** tab to see both of the message types created by the import. Based on the corresponding function module, the web service contains the definition for the inbound and the outbound message. Additionally, you can use the message names to determine the connection to the corresponding BAPI.

The import of the external definition is only handled as a message type with integrated data types. As a result, the message interface must be created manually on the receiving side. Open the creation dialog by choosing **Interface Objects • Message Interfaces** and create the **MI_ws_bapi_material_existencecheck_Sync_In** message interface.

Creating the synchronous inbound interface

Although the web service processes both inbound and outbound messages due to its synchronous character, it is primarily used as an inbound interface in this scenario. Accordingly, set the **Inbound** category and the **Synchronous** mode. This combination gives you the option of specifying both an input and an output message. When selecting a message type from a web service, you cannot use the drag and drop method. Therefore, the easiest option is to use the input help. Below the newly created external definition, select the message type **BAPI_MATERIAL_EXISTENCECHECKInput** for the input message and the corresponding counterpart for the output message (see Figure 4.35). Save the message interface.

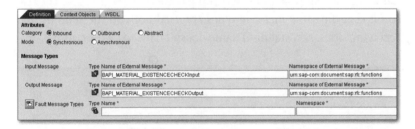

Figure 4.35 Creating the Message Interface for the Web Service of the ABAP-Proxy-to-SOAP Exercise

Now that the receiver's interface objects have been created, a message interface is still needed for the sender side. The data and the message type are based on the imported WSDL description. Open the creation dialog for message interfaces and create the interface **MI_ABAP_PROXY_MAT_EXIST_##_Sync_Out**. The included participant number is not necessary in the Integration Builder, however, the ABAP classes created later must be distinguishable.

Creating the message interface for the ABAP proxy

The new interface belongs to the **Outbound** category and the **Synchronous** mode. For the Output Message, select the **BAPI_MATERIAL_EXISTENCECHECKInput** message type from the external definition, **ws_bapi_material_existencecheck**. The Input Message is of the **BAPI_MATERIAL_EXISTENCECHECKOutput** type from the same external definition (see Figure 4.36). It may be a little confusing to select a type labeled Input for the Output message, but the messages are named from the point of view of the web service. Save the interface and activate all interface objects.

Figure 4.36 Creation of the Message Interface for the ABAP Proxy of the ABAP-Proxy-to-SOAP Exercise

Creating the Mapping Objects

Creating the message mapping for the way to the web service Despite previously naming the mapping objects, we won't strictly name the message mappings according to their message types. The reason is that the same message types are used both on the sending and receiving sides, so a standard name doesn't have to be descriptive.

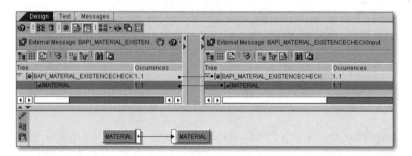

Figure 4.37 Creating the Message Mapping for the Way to the Web Service in the ABAP-Proxy-to-SOAP Exercise

As such, create the message mapping **MM_ABAP_PROXY_MAT_EXIST_##_to_ws_bapi_material_existencecheck** in the directory **Mapping Objects • Message Mappings**. This serves as the mapping for the way from the ABAP proxy to the web service. As an outbound message, select the **BAPI_MATERIAL_EXISTENCECHECKInput** type from the external definition **ws_bapi_material_existencecheck**, which can be found in the directory **External Definitions**. The target message is of the same type. The mapping of the way to the web service is fairly easy because only the two **MATERIAL** fields need to be connected (see Figure 4.37). Test and save the message mapping.

The message mapping **MM_ws_bapi_material_existencecheck_to_ ABAP_PROXY_MAT_EXIST_##** for the way back is created according to the same pattern. However, both the outbound and inbound messages are **BAPI_MATERIAL_EXISTENCECHECKOutput**. The mapping can quickly be implemented by clicking the icon **Map Selected Fields and Substructures if Names Are Identical**.

Creating the message mapping for the way back

This simple mapping is used to take the first steps in the area of user-defined mapping programs. For this, you will create a user-defined function within the graphical mapping. The function's goal is to fill an element with a specific content depending on the contents of another element. Therefore, the function is an IF construction that could basically be implemented using one of the predefined functions as well. If the web service detects that the tested material is available, it provides a return code without a descriptive message. If an error occurs, however, a detailed error description is returned. The adaptation of the success and failure responses is to be achieved using the new function.

Extending the message mapping by a user-defined function

One of the affected elements is **MESSAGE**, which should include a description. The controlling element is **NUMBER**, which contains a value of **000** in the case of a successful connection.

To create a user-defined function, first double-click on the **MESSAGE** target element and add the outbound field **NUMBER** to the work area. In the bottom-left of the work area, click the **Create New Function** icon to create a user-defined Java function. Name the function **Successmessage** and enter a description (see Figure 4.38).

Creating a user-defined function

Because it is a simple function it is sufficient to only load the values (**Value**) in the cache. In the list of arguments, use the appropriate icon to create another argument **b** that, just like argument **a**, is of the **String** type. The arguments are the transfer parameters to the function.

If you work in SAP XI 3.0 with Support Packages lower than SP15, you must create an advanced user-defined function with two arguments for this exercise. When the function is called, argument **a** is populated with the **NUMBER** element and argument **b** with the **MESSAGE** element. If **NUMBER** is not **000**, a success message must be forwarded. Click **Create Function** to continue.

Figure 4.38 Creating the User-Defined Function for the ABAP-Proxy-to-SOAP Exercise

Structure the source code You now have the option of creating a Java function that is only valid within this mapping. This procedure may not be confused with the deployment of Java classes, which is referred to as *Java mapping*.

You are still working within the graphical mapping of SAP XI. In the lower part of the work area, the selection of functions has switched to the **User-Defined** area, and you can see your new function as a selection option. The newly displayed window represents a small Java editor that already contains a few settings. Insert the source code from Listing 4.1 in the implementation part of the function (see Figure 4.39). You do not have to import any additional classes because the most important classes are imported automatically.

```
if (a.equals ("000"))
  return "The material is available";
else return b;
```

Listing 4.1 Source Code of the User-Defined Function of the Message Mapping

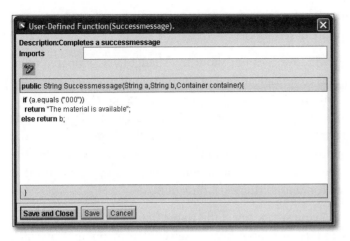

Figure 4.39 User-Defined Function for the ABAP-Proxy-to-SOAP Exercise

Save the new function and insert it between the existing **NUMBER** and **MESSAGE** (source) and **MESSAGE** (target) rectangles by clicking on the function name. Drag the connections between the three objects so **NUMBER** is connected to the upper white field of the function on the left side. The upper input field of the function is automatically assigned to argument **a**. Connect **MESSAGE** (source) to the second white field on the left side and assign the function result to the target field (see Figure 4.40).

Integrating the user-defined function

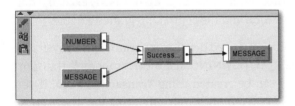

Figure 4.40 Integration of the User-Defined Function for the ABAP-Proxy-to-SOAP Exercise

Save and test the entire mapping. Use the value **000** for **NUMBER** and another value including any message input for testing. In case **NUMBER** equals **000** the message stored in the function should appear in the **MESSAGE** field.

The two message mappings for both directions of the exchange must now be embedded in the interface mapping **IM_ABAP_PROXY_MAT_EXIST_##_to_ws_bapi_material_existencecheck**. Open the cre-

Creating the synchronous interface mapping

ation dialog for the new interface mapping and enter the name and an appropriate description.

The details window does not show any changes yet compared to an asynchronous communication. For the outbound interface, select the interface **MI_ABAP_PROXY_MAT_EXIST_##_Sync_Out** using the input help. The target interface is the message interface, **MI_ws_ bapi_material_existencecheck_Sync_In**. In the lower area of the details window click on the **Read Interfaces** button and examine the **Request** label underneath. The simple label turns into two tabs that can be used for configuring each direction.

First, in the **Request** tab, select the **Name** field in the list of mapping programs and use the input help to select your mapping. Now click on the **Response** tab and repeat this step. In both cases, the input help should display only one entry. Save the interface mapping and activate all mapping objects of this exercise.

Generating the ABAP Proxy

Providing an ABAP package

The **MI_ABAP_PROXY_MAT_EXIST_##_Sync_Out** message interface created in the Integration Repository is the basis of proxy generation. An ABAP class is automatically created to allow communication with this interface from an ABAP program. In contrast to remote-enabled function modules, however, no adapter is used. Data is exchanged in XI format between the local and the central Integration Engine.

For the remaining steps, you need developer permissions in System A as well as a package **Z_XI_TRAINING** and a corresponding transport request. The package can be created using **Transaction SE80**. If you already developed the RFC modules yourself during the first exercise (see Section 4.1) or downloaded the appropriate transport from the web site for this book, you can use the corresponding objects.

Generating a proxy class

Log in to System A via the user **SYS_A-##** and call **Transaction SPROXY**. The structure of this screen is similar to the Integration Repository: The created software component versions are displayed on the left, with the namespaces listed beneath them. Within the namespaces, however, only the objects of the **Interface Objects** branch are displayed.

In your namespace, expand the branch **Message Interface (outbound)** and double-click the message interface **MI_ABAP_PROXY_ MAT_EXIST_##_Sync_Out**. You will be asked if a proxy should be created for this interface; answer with **Yes**. You are then asked for specific settings for the proxy class. Enter the package **Z_XI_TRAINING** and the prefix **Z**.

After confirming this information, a warning dialog pops up during the generation process, informing you that there have been name collisions or name shortenings. The reason for this is because the names of the generated ABAP objects may contain a maximum of 30 characters while the Integration Builder accepts longer names.

The details window of the newly generated proxy class contains four tabs. The **Properties** tab informs you about the classification of the object as well as the name **ZCO_MI_ABAP_PROXY_MAT_EXIST_##**. The **Name Problems** tab lists all elements that caused problems during the generation process. The name of the class has been shortened but is still descriptive and distinguishes the individual participants.

Properties of the proxy class

In the right column of this list, you can see which object in the Integration Repository corresponds to the rows and their contents. The second row displays the structure of the message type **BAPI_ MATERIAL_EXISTENCECHECKOutput**. Change the last two letters to **OU** so the structure is named **ZMI_ABAP_PROXY_MAT_EXIST_##_ OU** (see Figure 4.41). The counterpart to the message type **BAPI_ MATERIAL_EXISTENCECHECKInput** should also be renamed to **ZMI_ ABAP_PROXY_MAT_EXIST_##_IN** for consistency. The last structure, which corresponds to **BAPIRETURN1**, should be renamed to **ZMI_ ABAP_PROXY_MAT_EXIST_00_RE**.

Message Interface (Outbound)	MI_ABAP_PROXY_MAT_EXIST_00_Sy_	New (revised)		
Properties	Name Problems	Generation	Structure	Preconfiguration

Object	Name	Problem	Name in Integration Builder
Class	ZCO_MI_ABAP_PROXY_MAT_EXIST_00	Name shortened to 30 characters	MI_ABAP_PROXY_MAT_EXIST_00_Sync_Out_
Structure	ZMI_ABAP_PROXY_MAT_EXIST_00_OU	Name name already exists (number attach...	BAPI_MATERIAL_EXISTENCECHECKOutput
Structure	ZMI_ABAP_PROXY_MAT_EXIST_00_IN	Name name already exists (number attach...	BAPI_MATERIAL_EXISTENCECHECKInput
Structure	ZMI_ABAP_PROXY_MAT_EXIST_00_RE	Name shortened to 30 characters	BAPIRETURN1

Figure 4.41 Naming Problems when Generating the ABAP Proxy for the ABAP-Proxy-to-SOAP Exercise

The **Generation** tab displays a list of all created objects, regardless of any naming problems. The **Structure** tab displays a hierarchical

Activation of the proxy class

arrangement of all objects. For example, you can see that the new class **ZCO_MI_ABAP_PROXY_MAT_EXIST_##** contains a method called **EXECUTE_SYNCHRONOUS**. Below this method you can view the parameters from the point of view of an ABAP program.

Save the proxy class and specify the corresponding transport request. Check the objects by choosing **Proxy · Check**, or by clicking the **Check** icon. The list of checking messages should contain four yellow warnings but no red error messages. Confirm the list and activate the objects using the menu option **Proxy · Activate** or by clicking the **Activate** icon. After you've activated the objects, the activation log can contain warning messages; however, you can ignore the log in this case since there shouldn't be any errors.

For checking, you can call the Class Builder using **Transaction SE24** and display the class **ZCO_MI_ABAP_PROXY_MAT_EXIST_##**. Within the **Methods** tab, you can see that the method **EXECUTE_SYNCHRONOUS** has been created in addition to the constructor. Additionally, the **GET_PROTOCOL** and **GET_TRANSPORT_BINDING** methods are displayed, which have been created but not yet implemented. These two optional methods are not required for this exercise.

4.3.3   Configuration

Overview of configuration objects

Change to the Integration Directory and log in, if necessary. Before you use the Configuration Wizard to configure the objects, you first need to create a communication channel for the receiver side. On the side of the sending system, no communication channel is used because communication with a proxy does not require an adapter.

The configuration objects you will create for this exercise are listed in Table 4.9.

Object Type	Sender Side: System A	Receiver Side: System B
Communication channel		SOAP_Receiverchannel_##
Receiver agreement		| SystemA | | SystemB | MI_ws_bapi_material_existencecheck_Sync_In

Table 4.9 Elements in the Integration Directory for the ABAP-Proxy-to-SOAP Exercise

Object Type	Sender Side: System A	Receiver Side: System B
Receiver determination	**SystemA | MI_ABAP_PROXY_MAT_EXIST_##_Sync_Out**	
Interface determination	**| SystemA | MI_ABAP_PROXY_MAT_EXIST_##_Sync_Out | | SystemB**	

Table 4.9 Elements in the Integration Directory for the ABAP-Proxy-to-SOAP Exercise (cont.)

Open the context menu in your scenario **XI_Training_##** in the path **Service Without Party · Business System · SystemB · Communication Channel** and create a new communication channel. Name it **SOAP_Receiverchannel_##** and enter a description. Continue with **Create** and in the details window, select the **SOAP** adapter type. The communication channel is created as a **Receiver**. Ensure that the **Transport Protocol** is set to **HTTP**. The other parameters in the header can be left unchanged.

Creating the SOAP communication channel

In the **Connection Parameters** area, enter the URL of the target system according to the following scheme: *http://<host SystemB>:<ABAP-Port>/sap/bc/soap/rfc/sap/BAPI_MATERIAL_EXISTENCECHECK?sap-client=<client>*. The client of System B is required to determine against which client to perform user authentication. To be sure, use **Transaction SICF** in System B to verify that the corresponding service is active. This service allows you to call remote-enabled function modules as web services.

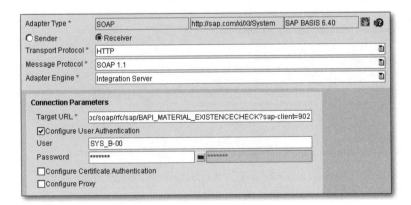

Figure 4.42 Setting up the SOAP Receiver Channel for System B

In the details window of the communication channel, enable the **Configure User Authentication** option. Fields for user and password are displayed. Enter the data of your user **SYS_B-##** (see Figure 4.42), and save the communication channel.

Using the Configuration Wizard

After the final piece for the configuration has been created, start the Configuration Wizard from the menu bar **Tools • Configuration Wizard** or by clicking the **Configuration Wizard** icon. The integration scenario you are implementing belongs to the **Internal Communication** category. The sender is the **Business System A**, which sends data using the message interface **MI_ABAP_PROXY_MAT_EXIST_##_Sync_Out**. The adapter is of the **XI** type and should already be set (see Figure 4.43).

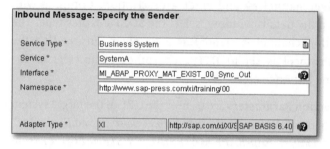

Figure 4.43 Settings of the Sender in the Configuration Wizard of the ABAP-Proxy-to-SOAP Exercise

The receiver is the **Business System B** that receives information via the **SOAP** adapter type. The used message interface is **MI_ws_bapi_material_existencecheck_Sync_In** (see Figure 4.44).

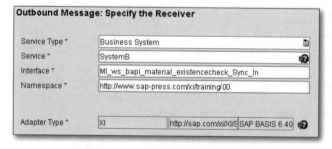

Figure 4.44 Settings of the Receiver in the Configuration Wizard of the ABAP-Proxy-to-SOAP Exercise

In the next step, you won't need to create a sender agreement because no conversion takes place. The next screen informs you that the receiver determination **SystemA | MI_ABAP_PROXY_MAT_ EXIST_##_Sync_Out** is created for this scenario. The interface determination shown in the next step should already display the appropriate interface mapping for the target interface **MI_ws_bapi_material_ existencecheck_Sync_In**. Continue with the next step.

The receiver agreement **| SystemA | | SystemB | MI_ws_bapi_ material_existencecheck_Sync_In** should refer to the communication channel you just created, **SOAP_Receiverchannel_##**. Make sure that the new objects are added to your scenario **XI_Training_##** and finish the Wizard. Activate all new and changed configuration objects in your change list.

4.3.4 Process and Monitoring

In this scenario, the proxy class with the **EXECUTE_SYNCHRONOUS** method must be integrated in an ABAP program. Log in to the client of System A as user **SYS_A-##** and call **Transaction SE38** or **SE80**. You can create the program for calling the proxy method yourself or import the corresponding transport from the web site for this book. If you develop the transport yourself, you will find the sample source code of the Z_MATERIAL_EXISTENCECHECK_## program in the Appendix of this book. You can partially use the data types of the **BAPI_ MATERIAL_EXISTENCECHECK** BAPI, which you can view using the Function Builder in **Transaction SE37**.

Creating a calling ABAP program

Most variables correspond to the structures that have been generated together with the ABAP class. The ABAP class must be referenced via an object so the **EXECUTE_SYNCHRONOUS** method can be called. Additionally, for the **wa_input** response structure note that the structure contains **wa_return** and is therefore detached in a separate step.

Test the program after you have checked and activated it. Specify the **XI_BOOK-##** material created in Exercise 2 and run the program. You should receive the return code **000** and the message "The material is available," as shown in Figure 4.45.

In contrast to asynchronous scenarios, a synchronous scenario usually does not leave any marks. Only asynchronous messages are stored in the persistence layer of SAP XI to enable a later analysis.

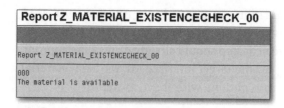

Report Z_MATERIAL_EXISTENCECHECK_00

Report Z_MATERIAL_EXISTENCECHECK_00

000
The material is available

Figure 4.45 Successful Availability Check of a Material

4.4 Exercise 4: Business Process Management

Course of the exercise The last exercise deals with the simple scenario that a department manager or a material manager must be informed about the successful creation of materials. On the sending side, notification is sent using the RFC adapter while the result is stored as a file in System B.

The important part of this process is that notifications are collected and sorted by creating users. If three messages have been created by one user, those three messages are merged into one and transferred to the material manager. This is controlled using an integration process.

As such, the focus of this exercise does not lie on using new adapters but on the introduction of SAP XI *Business Process Management* (BPM). You will deal with the corresponding tools in the Integration Repository as well as the representation in the Integration Directory.

Figure 4.46 contains a rough overview of this scenario.

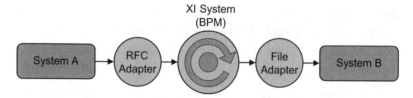

Figure 4.46 Scheme of Exercise 4: Business Process Management

4.4.1 Basics

Basics of BPM Business Process Management (BPM) is mainly about integrating processes that can be implemented within one company or across several different companies. For that purpose, a *Business Process Engine* (BPE) is used to merge individual transformations to a business process that were implemented using the Adapter Engine and the Integration Engine.

The *Business Process Execution Language* (BPEL) is used to describe the business processes. Process models are created via a graphical editor that is introduced in the following section.

In contrast to the SAP Business Workflow, the BPE communicates with applications on backend systems exclusively using messages.[3] It cannot access processes within applications, the user, or organization management on backend systems. Therefore, the following applies:

▸ The BPE doesn't control processes within applications. However, you can use messages to integrate applications in cross-system processes.

▸ The BPE doesn't control user interactions as they can only be controlled on the backend systems.

The BPM itself does not provide any cross-system monitoring for business documents processed within an integration process. Within the technical monitoring, however, you can display the log of an integration process and the corresponding messages.

Before you start working on this exercise, it's important to look at the steps taking place within the business process. At first, the business process records all messages of a specific interface and sorts them by their creators. A loop is opened for each creator name that collects messages of this type until a number of three has been reached. As soon as three identical messages from the same creator have been collected, the loop ends. These three individual messages are merged into a single message in a new format and then sent. How these considerations are implemented in the BPM of SAP XI is explained in the course of the design phase.

Internal procedure of the integration process

As in Exercise 1, the RFC call starting the integration process is made using the program Z_PROG_MATERIALINFO_##, which calls the remote-enabled function module **Z_RFM_MATERIALINFO_##**. The module only works with the three parameters of the material number, the creator name, and the creation date. Again, the source code can be

---

3 More information about this topic can be found in the SAP Help Portal under *http://help.sap.com/saphelp_nw2004s/helpdata/de/3c/831620a4f1044dba38b370f77 835cc/content.htm*.

found in the Appendix and the corresponding transport can be downloaded from this book's web page.

4.4.2 Design

We first want to deal with the design objects of this exercise before you put the individual objects together to form an integration process.

Creating the Design Objects

Particular aspects of the design phase

In the context of using business processes, you will get to know a new category of message interfaces: *abstract interfaces*. The important thing to know about abstract interfaces is that they don't have a direction. This means they aren't assigned to the **Inbound** or **Outbound** category, and can be used in both directions. The only exception is that abstract interfaces may only be used in integration processes.

This property requires them to be declared separately as interfaces of the **Abstract** category, even for imported objects. However, if the abstract interfaces are used for receiving or sending messages within a process, you need a counterpart in the defined direction.

Communication between an abstract and a direction-related interface does not require a mapping as long as the same message type is used. The mapping objects in this exercise are solely used for generating a single message from the three collected messages. You will deal with the particular aspect of mappings that can have several messages on one side. Because the target format of the integration process needs to be created, the required design objects are listed in Table 4.10.

Object Type	Sender Side	Integration Process/ Receiver
Message interface	**MI_RFM_MATINFO_##_ Async_Abstract**	► **MI_MatInfo_List_Async_ Abstract** ► **MI_MatInfo_List_Async_In**

Table 4.10 Elements in the Integration Repository for the BPM Exercise

Object Type	Sender Side	Integration Process/ Receiver
Message type	Z_RFM_MATERIALINFO_ ##	▸ MT_MatInfo_List
Data type		▸ DT_MatInfo_List
		▸ DT_MatInfo
Interface mapping	MM_RFM_MATINFO_##_Async_Abstract_to_MT_MatInfo_List_Async_Abstract	
Message mapping	MM_RFM_MATINFO_##_to_MT_MatInfo_List	
Integration process	IP_MatInfo_##	

Table 4.10 Elements in the Integration Repository for the BPM Exercise (cont.)

First, import the definition of the RFC function module **Z_RFM_MATERIALINFO_##** from business system A. In the directory **Imported Objects**, use the menu and log in as user **SYS_A-##**. Based on the **Z_RFM_MATERIALINFO_##** message of this imported interface, create the message interface **MI_RFM_MATINFO_##_Async_Abstract**. Make sure that you set the category to **Abstract**. Creating the objects for the sender side

By selecting this option, the name of the message used changes from **Input** or **Output Message** to just **Message** (see Figure 4.47). This interface is **Asynchronous**. After saving the interface, you will have created all objects on the sender side.

Figure 4.47 Definition of the Abstract Interface MI_RFM_MATINFO_##_Async_Abstract

The message type containing the collected notifications at the end of the process is based on a multilevel file type. That means that there is an atomic data type **DT_MatInfo** which can contain the contents of one notification. For several messages to be merged into one, the Creating the data types

179

atomic data type must be integrated in a parent type. For this example, the parent data type is **DT_MatInfo_List**.

Start by creating the **DT_MatInfo** data type, and add three elements containing the **materialnumber**, the **creator**, and the **creationdate**. The first two values are of the **xsd:string** type, while the **creationdate** is of the **xsd:date** type. Save these data types.

Next, create the data type **DT_MatInfo_List** so it only contains a single element. This element **MatInfo** is of the **DT_MatInfo** type, which you can select using the search help. Once you have created a nested structure, you can now record a notification.

To convert the data type into a list, though, you need to change the occurrence of this element. When you double-click in the **Occurrence** column of the element, a new window opens. From the input help of the **MaxOccurs** field, select the **unbounded** entry so an unlimited number of notifications can be recorded. Confirm your selection and save the data type. The data type should now be structured as shown in Figure 4.48.

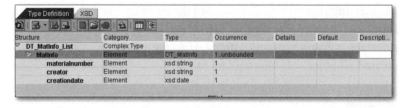

Figure 4.48 Structure of the DT_MatInfo_List Data Type

Creating the
remaining objects
on the receiver
side Create the message type **MT_MatInfo_List** and base it on the **DT_MatInfo_List** data type. Integrate this new message type in the message interface **MI_MatInfo_List_Async_Abstract**, which you later use in the integration process. The message interface belongs to the **Abstract** category and the **Asynchronous** mode. Save the abstract interface.

Sending a message via this interface requires a counterpart in the form of an interface belonging to the **Inbound** category. Therefore, create a message interface **MI_MatInfo_List_Async_In** that uses the **MT_MatInfo_List** message type as well. However, this interface is used as an **Inbound** interface for asynchronous communication. Save this interface object. You have now created all objects for the receiver side.

Mapping isn't required for connecting abstract and direction-related interfaces of the same message type. However, for converting the three notifications into a single message, a mapping is required at the message and interface level.

Start by creating the message mapping **MM_RFM_MATINFO_##_to_MT_MatInfo_List**. The outbound message is **Z_RFM_MATERIALINFO_##** of the RFC interface of the same name. The target message is the **MT_MatInfo_List** type you just created.

As you can see, the mapping does not present much of a challenge with regard to its contents. However, its characteristics show that several outbound messages are transformed into a target message. To realize this navigate to the **Messages** tab where the two used messages can be found, including their occurrences. For the outbound message, set an occurrence of **0..unbounded**, and then return to the **Design** tab (see Figure 4.49).

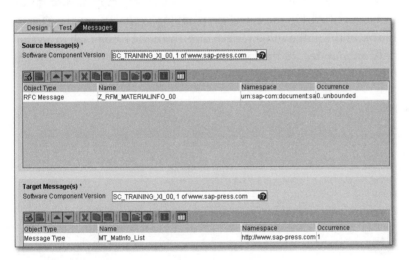

Figure 4.49 Setting the Occurrence in the Message Mapping

Now map the three fields to one another and connect the node **Z_RFC_MATERIALINFO_##** on the outbound side to the target node **MatInfo**, as shown in Figure 4.50. Save the mapping and test it by duplicating the subtree **Z_RFM_MATERIALINFO_##** on the outbound side using the menu and populating it with data.

Figure 4.50 Message Mapping of the BPM Exercise

Creating the Inter-
face Mapping

This message mapping still needs to be integrated in an appropriate interface mapping. The special thing about this mapping is that both the sending and the receiving interface belong to the **Abstract** type. Still, you can handle and map these interfaces as usual.

Create the interface mapping **MM_RFM_MATINFO_##_Async_Abstract_to_MT_MatInfo_List_Async_Abstract** and use **MI_RFM_MATINFO_##_Async_Abstract** as the outbound interface. The target interface is of the **MI_MatInfo_List_Async_Abstract** type. The occurrence setting you just specified for the message mapping also needs to be specified for the interface mapping. You can set the **Occurrences** of the outbound interface directly in the **Design** tab to a value of **0..unbounded**. In the lower area, import the interfaces and select the message mapping you just created (see Figure 4.51).

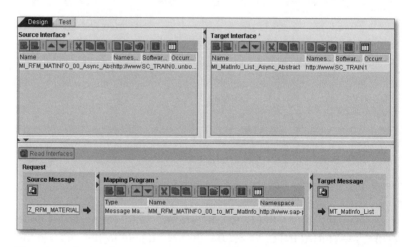

Figure 4.51 Setting the Occurrence in the Interface Mapping

Creating the Integration Process

Creating the inte-
gration process

You have now created all of the objects you will use during the integration process. Within the namespace, navigate to the directory **Inte-**

gration Scenarios & Integration Processes. Use the context menu to create the new integration process **IP_MatInfo_##**. For this object, it is necessary to assign the participant number because your process will later be visible in the entire SAP NetWeaver Exchange Infrastructure.

By creating the object, you get to the details window which is a graphical BPM editor. Detach the window and hide the header to have as much space as possible (see Figure 4.52).

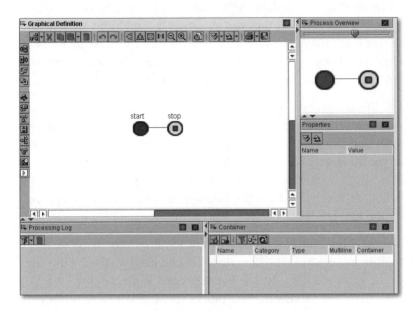

Figure 4.52 Structure of the Graphical BPM Editor

The editor itself is divided into several areas. The most obvious element is the graphical work area where you can add objects by dragging and dropping them from the list on the left side. You will find functions for controlling the view at the top of the work area.

Structure of the BPM editor

The space to the right of the work area is divided into two parts: The upper area contains an overview for particularly large integration processes. The slider lets you set the zoom. Below the Process Overview section, the Properties section shows the elements selected in the work area. In the bottom-left section of the editor is the Processing Log that displays error messages and annotations. To the right of the log is a list of the Container elements. These containers are the process-internal representation of interfaces or variables you can create for internal use.

All of the panes provide additional alternative functions, which you can select using the list icon next to the name of the pane. In this exercise, you will only get to know the work area and container panes in another function when you create a correlation.

Let's start by creating the container elements: As mentioned earlier, the container elements contain objects that are only used within the process. In the case of messages, however, these internal objects equal an abstract interface. A particular aspect of these message container elements is that they can also exist in a multiline format. This means that a list of messages can be addressed with a single element. However, these multiline containers can only exist within the process; they can't be sent in their original format.

For this integration process, you will need three message container elements. The first container, called **MatInfo**, belongs to the **Abstract Interface** category and uses the interface **MI_RFM_MATINFO_##_ Async_Abstract**. You can find this entry in the input help that only lists abstract interfaces of your software component version. This container always contains the message currently sent to the process by the RFC sender.

Note that the **Multiline** column can be used to make this container a multiline container. The **Container** column displays the validity area of the elements. Usually, the entire process is the validity area. You can restrict the validity of these blocks only if you insert the blocks in the work area.

According to the same pattern, create the **MatInfoContainer** element that belongs to the same category and type, but is a multiline element. This element stores **MatInfo** messages until they are sent in a single message. Before being sent, however, this element must be converted due to its multiline character: The target element of this conversion is **MatInfo_List**, which also belongs to the **Abstract Interface** category but references the **MI_MatInfo_List_Async_Abstract** type.

Last but not least, you need a variable that counts how many times the loop runs. This variable is to be named **Counter**, and should be of the simple **xsd:integer** type.

The list of your container elements should now correspond to the one shown in Figure 4.53.

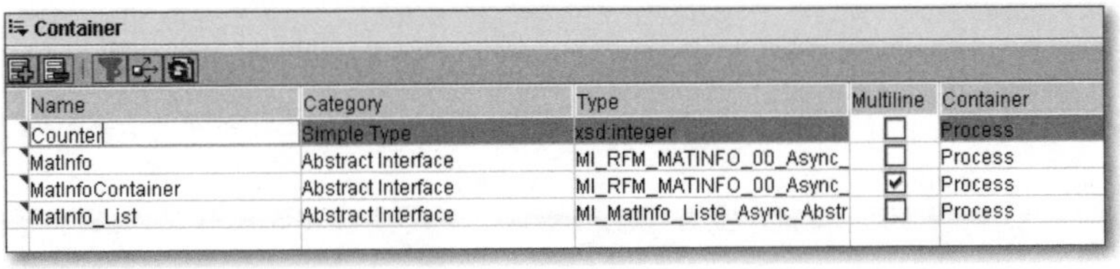

Figure 4.53 Container Elements of the Integration Process

Before you get to the graphical modeling, you need to create a *corre-*   Creating the
lation. Using this correlation, the process can identify related mes-   correlation
sages by their content. In this exercise, the process must also map
and collect messages from the same creator. Thus, the correlation
consists of the **creator** field contents of the incoming messages.

To create a correlation, click the **Switch Editor** icon, and select the
alternative function **Correlation Editor** of the **Container** pane. Enter
the name **MatInfo** for the correlation. Highlight the new entry and
click on the **Details** icon above the list. The graphical work area
changes into the **Correlation Editor** view.

In the upper area of this view, the newly created correlation is
already selected. The area below it is divided into three parts:

▶ In the left, you can see the correlation containers of the correlation fields.

▶ The center part lets you select involved messages.

▶ The right area lets you specify the actual fields.

In the left area, specify the name **creator** and maintain the type of
xsd:string. The message to which the correlation should apply is of
the type **MI_RFM_MATINFO_##_Async_Abstract**, which can be specified in the center area. By selecting the interface, it is also displayed
in the right area, which up to now wasn't available for input. Open
the input help next to the **Creator** field and select the **ERNAM** element from the displayed message. For this, you first need to activate
the option **InterfaceVariable** (see Figure 4.54).

Accept the selection. You are then brought back to the correlation
editor, as shown in Figure 4.55.

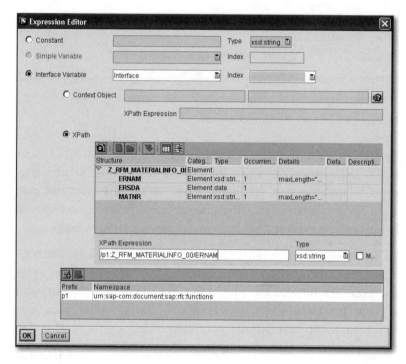

Figure 4.54 Expression Editor in the Correlation Editor

Correlation Container		Involved Messages		Properties	
Name	Type	Name	Namespace	Name	Value
creator	xsd:string	MI_RFM_MATINFO_...	http://www.sap-pres...	▽ **MI_RFM_MATINFO**	
				creator	Interface./p1:Z_RFB...

Figure 4.55 Correlation Editor

Click the **Switch Editor** icon on the top-left of the correlation editor to change back to the view **Graphical Definition**. You can now begin with the graphical modeling of the business process. Table 4.11 gives you an overview of all available objects (or step types) in the BPM editor. However, you will only use a few of them in this exercise.

Icon	Step Type
	Receive step
	Send step

Table 4.11 Step Types in the BPM Editor

Icon	Step Type
	Receiver Determination step
	Transformation step
	Switch
	Container Operation
	Control
	Block
	Fork
	Loop
	Wait
	Undefined

Table 4.11 Step Types in the BPM Editor (cont.)

The first step in a business process must always be a **Receive step**. It can either be situated at the very beginning or be integrated in a loop. Because this process receives exactly three messages, the most obvious procedure is to use a loop.

Creating the receive loop

Drag a loop from the left toolbar to the work area between the **start** and **stop** objects. The place where you can drop the loop is indicated by yellow parentheses. The new loop element is automatically highlighted, and its properties are displayed to the right of the work area. Name this object **Receiving_Notification**. The **Condition** field specifies how long this loop is supposed to run, therefore making it a WHILE loop.

Click on the white area displaying a red question mark, and open the input help; the condition editor is displayed. Set the loop so it runs as long as the **Counter** variable is not **3**. For this, click on the input help of the field in the **Left Operand** column and select the simple **Counter** variable by activating the corresponding option. Accept the selection. Set the operator between the two operands as **unequal** (≠). The **Right Operand** is the constant **3** of the type **xsd:integer** (see Figure 4.56). Accept the condition; it is now displayed in the appropriate field within the properties.

Figure 4.56 Condition of the Receive Loop

Inserting the
loop steps

Now insert a **Receive** step in the loop and call it **Receive Notification**. Because this is the first receive step in the process, the **Start Process** property is automatically set for this object. In the properties, set the container element **MatInfo** as the **Message**. The receive step then expects a message of this type. Specify the **MatInfo** correlation as the used and activated correlation. Incoming messages are then sorted using this correlation.

An incoming message is now to be appended to the **MatInfoContainer** container element. This is accomplished by adding a **Container Operation** step. This step allows you to make changes to containers, such as setting variables or appending messages to lists. Add the new object after you have received it and name it **Add Message**. The target of this operation is the **MatInfoContainer** container element to which the **MatInfo** container element is appended. Note that the operation must be **Append**, not **Assign**.

The last object in the loop is another **Container Operation** which increases the variable counter by one; name the Container Operation, **Increase Counter**. The target of this operation is the **Counter** container element. This time, the **Assign** operation can remain. As the first expression, reselect the **Counter** container element. The operator for the addition is a **plus sign** (+). The second expression is a constant of the type **xsd:integer** with a value of **1**. The property values of this object result in the mathematical expression **Counter = Counter +1**.

Conversion and
delivery of the out-
bound message

The two missing steps merge the multiline container element into a single message before sending the message. Before the loop, insert a **Transformation** object and call it **Create MatInfo_List**. Transformation objects allow you to convert messages to a different format. For this, specify the interface mapping **MM_RFM_MATINFO_##_Async_ Abstract_to_MT_MatInfo_List_Async_Abstract**. At process execution time, the source messages reside in the **MatInfoContainer** container element. In this transformation, the target message is passed to the **MatInfo_List** element.

As the name suggests, the last step **Send Message** is a **Send step**. The container element **MatInfo_List** is sent asynchronously.

The entire structure of the integration process is illustrated in Figure 4.57. Save the process and verify it using the menu option **Integration Process • Check**. If the process is successful, you should only get a note that **MatInfo** is initialized but not used. If there are no more errors you can activate all new objects.

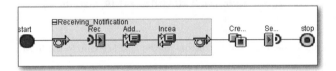

Figure 4.57 Structure of the Integration Process

4.4.3 Configuration

Message processing is configured in two steps, because an integration process is equal to a business system with regard to configuration. The RFC call must be forwarded to the process; for this, use the RFC sender channel you created in Exercise 1. Integration processes don't need any adapters because they run using SAP XI. You also need to configure how outbound messages from the process are sent to System B. So you will need to create two configuration scenarios.

Overview of the configuration scenarios

Before you can use the integration process during the configuration phase you must declare it in the Integration Directory. In the Integration Directory for the **XI_Training_##** project, choose **Service Without Party • Integration Process**. Create a new process that represents your **IP_MatInfo_##** object from the Integration Repository. In the third step of the definition wizard, you can specify a different name for your process. To keep things simple, use the same name you used in the Integration Repository, **IP_MatInfo_##**. After completing the wizard, the scenario now shows up in your process.

Creating the Integration Process in the Integration Directory

Delivery of the inbound messages to the integration process

Table 4.12 provides an overview of all configuration objects for delivering the creation notification to the integration process. Communication channels identified by an asterisk (*) were created in Section 4.1.3 and will be reused here.

Object Type	Sender Side: System A	Receiver Side: Integration process IP_MatInfo_##
Communication channel	RFC_SenderChannel_## *	
Sender agreement	| SystemA | Z_RFM_ MATERIALINFO_##|*|*	
Receiver determination	| SystemA | Z_RFM_MATERIALINFO_##	
Interface determination	|SystemA|Z_RFM_MATERIALINFO_##||IP_MatInfo_##	

Table 4.12 Elements in the Integration Directory for the First Scenario in the BPM Exercise

Calling the Configuration Wizard for the first scenario

Call the Configuration Wizard and select the **Internal Communication** option. The sender is the **Business System A**, which sends data using the RFC adapter with the RFC interface, **Z_RFM_MATERIAL-INFO_##**. The receiver is the **IP_MatInfo_##** integration process, which is addressed with the **XI** adapter. When you open the input help of the interface, only the interface **MI_RFM_MATINFO_##_ Async_Abstract** is displayed; this is used for the receive step to start the process (see Figure 4.58).

Figure 4.58 Receiver Settings in the Configuration Wizard of the First Scenario

The following sender agreement **|SystemA|Z_RFM_MATERIAL-INFO_##|*|*** uses the existing communication channel **RFC_ SenderChannel_##** of Exercise 1. The screen for creating the receiver determination **| SystemA | Z_RFM_MATERIALINFO_##** is of purely informative nature.

The interface determination **|SystemA|Z_RFM_MATERIALINFO_ ##||IP_MatInfo_##** in the next step displays the interface **MI_RFM_ MATINFO_##_Async_Abstract** as the target, but does not seem to find an interface mapping. This is not necessary because both the sending and the receiving interface use the same message type. A receiver agreement is not required because the receiver is integrated with the XI adapter.

Assign all objects to your **XI_Training_##** scenario and quit the Wizard. In general, you could already test the integration process after it has been activated, but the outbound message would not be delivered. Before testing the project, you should wait until the delivery of the outbound message has been configured.

Delivery of the Outbound Message of the Integration Process

Delivery of the outbound message can be arranged in a similar way like the first configuration scenario of this exercise. The existing communication channel **File_ReceiverChannel_##** that was created in Exercise 1 is used for the receiver.

Table 4.13 provides an overview of all configuration objects used in this scenario.

Object Type	Sender Side: Integration Process IP_MatInfo_##	Receiver Side: System B
Communication channel		File_ReceiverChannel_##*
Receiver agreement	|IP_MatInfo_##||SystemB|MI_ MatInfo_List_Async_In	
Receiver determination	|IP_MatInfo_##|MI_MatInfo_List_Async_Abstract	
Interface determination	|IP_MatInfo_##|MI_MatInfo_List_Async_Abstract|| SystemB	

Table 4.13 Elements in the Integration Directory for the First Scenario in the BPM Exercise

Calling the Config-
uration Wizard for
the first scenario Call the Configuration Wizard once more and select **Internal Communication**. The sender of this scenario is the integration process **IP_
MatInfo_##** which uses the adapter type **XI**. Help is restricted again
because only the interfaces used are displayed when sending messages from the process. In this case, only one message is sent so only
one interface is displayed (see Figure 4.59).

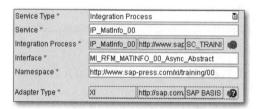

Service Type *	Integration Process	
Service *	IP_MatInfo_00	
Integration Process *	IP_MatInfo_00	http://www.sar SC_TRAINI
Interface *	MI_RFM_MATINFO_00_Async_Abstract	
Namespace *	http://www.sap-press.com/xi/training/00	
Adapter Type *	XI	http://sap.com. SAP BASIS

Figure 4.59 Sender Settings in the Configuration Wizard of the Second Scenario

The outbound message receiver is a **File** adapter of **Business System
B**, which responds to the **MI_MatInfo_List_Async_In** interface. This
interface is the direction-related counterpart to the abstract interface
of the outbound message. A sender agreement isn't used because the
sending process runs in SAP XI.

The receiver determination step informs you that System B is
integrated in the object **|IP_MatInfo_##|MI_MatInfo_List_Async_
Abstract**. As with the first scenario, the interface determination **|IP_
MatInfo_##|MI_MatInfo_List_Async_Abstract||SystemB** doesn't re-
quire an interface mapping since it uses the same message type. The
receiver agreement **|IP_MatInfo_##||SystemB|MI_MatInfo_List_
Async_In** uses the existing communication channel **File_Receiver-
Channel_##**.

Add all new objects to your scenario and finish the wizard. You can
now activate all new configuration objects. Now that you've finished
the fourth exercise, test the process.

4.4.4 Process and Monitoring

The process of this integration scenario starts in System A. As such,
log in as user **SYS_A-##** and call **Transaction SA38**.

Run the program Z_PROG_MATERIALINFO_##. Within the program you
can only specify a material number. Information about the creator,
including the creation date, are sent along automatically. The mate-

rial you specify isn't important at this point. Simply enter a name and run the program. You will see a message notifying you that the function module was successfully called, but that does not imply that the message was actually received; it only informs you that the proxy method has been called without any errors.

Now change to the XI system and call **Transaction SXMB_MONI**. You can see that your message came in and has been successfully processed. If you scroll the display a bit to the right, you can see that the **Outbound status** column (next to the Outbound column) displays a clock symbol (see Figure 4.60). This means that the message is currently being sent. This display remains unchanged until three message of the same creator have come in and the outbound message can be created.

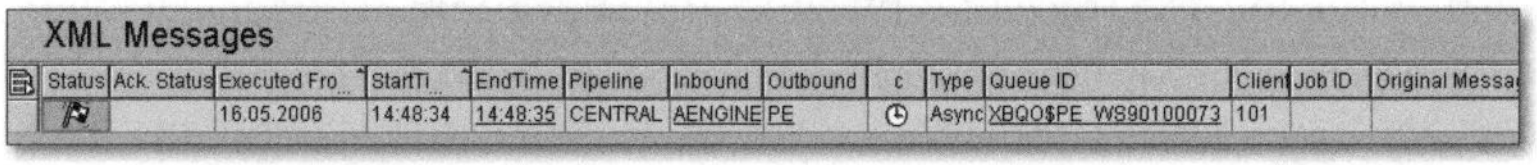

XML Messages

	Status	Ack. Status	Executed Fro	StartTi	EndTime	Pipeline	Inbound	Outbound	c	Type	Queue ID	Clien	Job ID	Original Messa
			16.05.2006	14:48:34	14:48:35	CENTRAL	AENGINE	PE	⏱	Async	XBQO$PE_WS90100073	101		

Figure 4.60 Message Monitoring After the First Message

Call the program for notifying the material manager twice more and return to the monitoring. You should now see the three incoming notifications as well as a fourth message. The outbound status of the first three messages now displays a black-and-white checkered flag (see Figure 4.61), which lets you know that the process has completed. Call **Transaction AL11** or the provided file tool on the XI system to see if a file containing the corresponding message has been created.

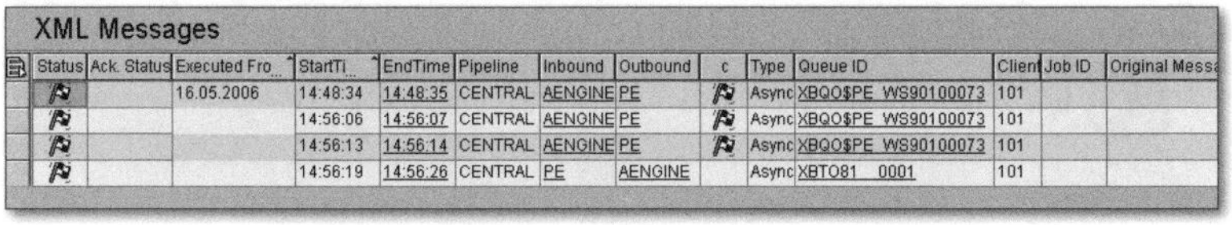

XML Messages

	Status	Ack. Status	Executed Fro	StartTi	EndTime	Pipeline	Inbound	Outbound	c	Type	Queue ID	Clien	Job ID	Original Mess
			16.05.2006	14:48:34	14:48:35	CENTRAL	AENGINE	PE		Async	XBQO$PE_WS90100073	101		
				14:56:06	14:56:07	CENTRAL	AENGINE	PE		Async	XBQO$PE_WS90100073	101		
				14:56:13	14:56:14	CENTRAL	AENGINE	PE		Async	XBQO$PE_WS90100073	101		
				14:56:19	14:56:26	CENTRAL	PE	AENGINE		Async	XBTO81_0001	101		

Figure 4.61 Message Monitoring After Three Messages

If the fourth message is not displayed in the monitoring, look at the monitoring of business processes. In the XI system, call **Transaction SXMB_MONI_BPE** and double-click on the **Process Selection** entry. In the selection mask of the **Service** field, enter your integration process **IP_MatInfo_##** and run the query. The work items belonging to your process are now displayed as well. Double-click on the corresponding row. You are now presented with an overview of the individual steps of the process (see Figure 4.62).

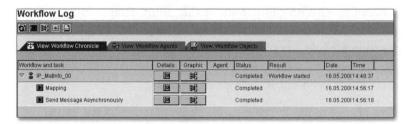

Figure 4.62 Display of the Workflow Log

Click on one of the buttons in the **Graphic** column. This brings you to the graphical display of the business process (see Figure 4.63). The green arrows allow you to trace the process to see which processes have run. If a problem has occurred, double-click on the relevant object to display the log and trace files by choosing **Workitem • Object • Display**.

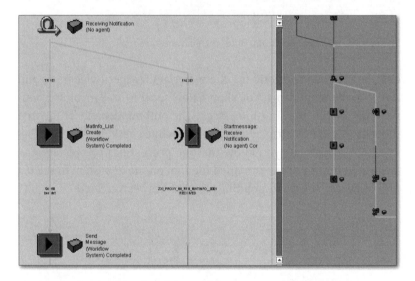

Figure 4.63 Graphical Display of the Workflow Log

4.5 More Adapters

Despite the variety of integration examples, not all of the adapters can be discussed in the presented exercises. The following case study provides an overview of the omitted, but still frequently used, adapter types. The focus lies on particular aspects of their real-life usage. The mail adapter is not considered here because it is implemented in the case study in Chapter 5.

4.5.1 JDBC Adapters

The *Java Database Connectivity* (JDBC) adapter allows you to directly access database tables; it can be used both in reading and writing. Data exchange can be synchronous or asynchronous.

Before JDBC is used, you need to install vendor-dependent drivers. The individual JAR files can be downloaded from the website of the database vendor. These JAR files must be merged into another JAR file, named *aii_af_jmsproviderlib.sda*, so they can be imported via the *Software Deployment Manager* (SDM). The SDA file extension stands for *Software Deployment Archive*. An exact instruction for merging driver files and for their deployment can be found either in the *SAP XI Configuration Guide*, or in the separate guide *How To Install and Configure External Drivers* on the SAP pages.[4]

Driver installation

If the JDBC adapter is configured as a sender, a SQL query specified in the communication channel is issued to determine the corresponding data. The results are converted to a message type that must exist as a design object. After selecting and converting, a SQL update can be performed. This is often used for marking the read rows with the appropriate flag in a specific column. This prevents the rows from being re-read in the next query.

Configuration of the JDBC adapter

The receiving JDBC adapter performs various actions on the rows of a table. These actions include UPDATE, INSERT, DELETE, SELECT, and UPDATE_INSERT, which is equivalent to MODIFY. Additionally, stored procedures can be executed to directly transfer more complex SQL statements. The table and the action to be performed are determined using the message type of the receiving side.

4.5.2 JMS Adapter

The *Java Message Service* (JMS) adapter is mainly used for exchanging data with other EAI and messaging systems, such as IBM WebSphere MQ or SonicMQ. In contrast to other adapters, the JMS adapter only allows asynchronous communication.

Application areas of the JMS adapter

---

4 The instructions can be found in the SAP Service Marketplace under *https://service.sap.com/netweaver* in the directory **SAP NetWeaver • SAP NetWeaver 2004 – Release Specific Information • How-to Guides • Exchange Infrastructure**. There you will also find a list of other useful documents.

As with the JDBC adapter, JMS also requires vendor-dependent drivers to be deployed. The drivers can be obtained from the vendors of the integrated EAI systems, and set up the same way as the JDBC drivers. Since the queues of other products are read or written to when using this adapter, you also need to configure the connected EAI product as well as the SAP XI communication settings.

Configuration of the JMS adapter

When configuring the JMS adapter both as a sender and a receiver, SAP provides additional transport protocols, some of which are product-specific. The settings of the sending JMS adapter lets you to establish correlations based on different criteria. Additionally, you can choose whether the JMS payload is transferred as an entire message or as a message payload. For asynchronous communication, there are two qualities of service: Exactly Once and Exactly-Once-in-Order.

In its role as a receiver, the JMS adapter allows you to return the parameters and to specify the validity period and the priority of the JMS message for the receiving system. Additionally, you can set whether data is transferred in a transactional JMS session. Depending on your choice of the integrated EAI system (and thus the transport protocol), configuration options will vary significantly and might include additional parameters.

4.5.3 SAP Business Connector Adapter

Application area of the SAP BC adapter

The SAP Business Connector adapter (SAP BC) allows for communication with the SAP Business Connector. As such, it is particularly useful for integration scenarios to be partially replaced with SAP XI.

A prerequisite for integrating SAP Business Connector is that it must be at least version 4.7. The SAP BC adapter can process RFC and IDoc XML documents. The adapter calls, however, are stateless. This means that transactional sessions are not possible, and the EOIO quality of service is not available. Additionally, it cannot process attachments.

Configuration of the SAP BC adapter

As the sender, the adapter settings are very few, especially because the majority of these are done in SAP BC. As a sender, the SAP BC adapter provides three parameters: storage period, repeat interval, and timeout. The message protocol setting determines if RFC or IDoc documents are received. In the SAP Business Connector itself, however, it is specified that the transport takes place as XML in the SAP XML dialect. Additionally, the URL of the BC adapter is specified, which is structured according to the scheme *http://<xi-host-name>:<j2ee-port>/MessagingSystem/receive/BcAdapter/BC*. In addition to the parameters mentioned earlier, using the BC adapter in the receiver role requires the URL of the receiving SAP Business Connector and the corresponding access data.

4.5.4 Plain HTTP Adapter

The SAP XI plain HTTP adapter allows you to receive and send data in pure HTTP format. This is important when integrating business systems that cannot create or process SOAP documents. The receiving HTTP adapter is addressed using the URL *http://<xi-host-name>:<abap-port>/sap/xi/adapter_plain?<query-string>*. The query string contains control data (such as the sender service, namespace, and interface) which allows it to be identified and assigned to an appropriate receiver agreement. The payload itself is sent in an HTTP post as an XML document using UTF-8. Security settings, such as the use of HTTPS, can be set in the communication channel.

Using the plain HTTP adapter

The plain HTTP adapter supports all qualities of service. When used in synchronous mode, the HTTP adapter can return feedback about errors or success using the HTTP return code.

The case study of the fictitious trading company SARIDIS is used at several universities teaching SAP-related topics, and is used in this chapter as a template for the implementation of classic sales and distribution processes based on the SAP NetWeaver Exchange Infrastructure (XI). In this technical project, you will implement the steps involved in a traditional sales and distribution process using SAP XI.

5   SARIDIS Case Study in Sales and Distribution

Now that you have been introduced to the different adapters and learned how to use the components of SAP XI, this chapter shows you how to implement a technically and contextually consistent business process that integrates several different scenarios. For a better understanding, the individual processes have been simplified in such a way that numerous special characteristics and details that occur in practice have been ignored here.

SARIDIS case study as a basis

In addition to the elements you are already familiar with, you will learn how to use some new techniques and aspects. You will work on a portion of the SARIDIS case study, which is widely used at universities for teaching SAP-related topics. Experience has shown that the content of the materials used in the SARIDIS case study is close enough to real life to be relevant, and also, that the simplification of some of the facts adds to a better understanding of cross company business processes.

You can use the case study without any further adjustment in existing IDES training systems. Other training systems that contain configured SD and FI areas can also be used with some slight changes. However, in both cases you must configure the basic settings described in Chapter 3. Moreover, you should first work through the exercises in the preceding chapter.

Prerequisites for the case study

Technically speaking, business system A is used as the ERP system of the SARIDIS company. To keep the scenario simple, business system B represents all external systems, particularly those of the fictitious customer, Hitech AG.

The sample scenario

In the case study, the fictitious label, SARIDIS, is used by the IDES enterprise to market the computer and accessories trade. It is part of the corporate group in this case study and uses the group's customer relationships and logistical facilities within the ERP system.

One of their major customers, Hitech AG, is restructuring its IT infrastructure and wants to automate ordering processes with its suppliers. For this purpose, the company has integrated SAP XI into its system landscape and now wants to automate the ordering process at SARIDIS as a reference implementation. As a prerequisite for its cooperation in this integration project, SARIDIS assumes that the existing processes in its SAP system will not have to undergo any significant changes. For this reason, the integration scenarios are integrated into the existing processes using IDocs. You are now contracted by Hitech AG as an in-house SAP XI development consultant to implement the integration process and to test the result on the basis of a purchase order for computer monitors.

> **Note**
>
> The case study is completely mapped via the German subsidiary of IDES (company code 1000) as this leaves the door open for proprietary extensions. However, it can also be reconstructed in other international subsidiaries, provided the training landscape is maintained accordingly.

Dividing the case study into several steps

In the context of the automation process, we want to map a total of four integration scenarios. The first step consists of an inquiry at SARIDIS. Based on an inquiry in a file that's created by the retailing system of Hitech AG, we will create an inquiry in the SAP system at SARIDIS (see Section 5.1). The second step uses the inquery to create a quote which is sent back to the customer. At this point, Hitech AG wants to obtain a quote from their supplier, Sunny Electronics. For this, they want to use an existing web service to automatically obtain quotes from the second supplier. This entire process is supposed to run automatically in a business process that transports both quotes (see Section 5.2). If SARIDIS submits a better quotation, the purchase order should be transmitted automatically. On the side of Hitech AG this integration step is implemented by extending an existing Java solution (see Section 5.3). Once the goods have been shipped, SARI-DIS is automatically sends an invoice to Hitech AG for fast entry (see Section 5.4).

Figure 5.1 provides an overview of all integration scenarios within the case study.

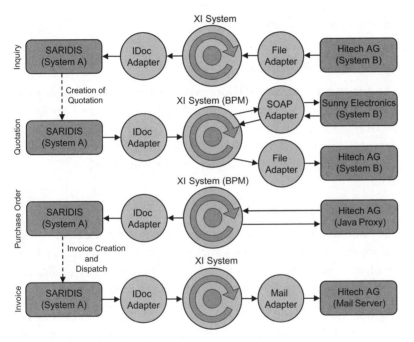

Figure 5.1 Flow of the Case Study

5.1 Creating the Query

The first step to be carried out using SAP XI is to create and submit queries to the supplier, SARIDIS. The original query is generated as a file in a legacy system at Hitech AG and is submitted as an IDoc. The IDoc is then automatically processed in the SARIDIS system (see Figure 5.2).

The first step

If you completed the exercises in Chapter 4, you may remember a similar example in the second exercise. In contrast to that exercise, however, the IDoc can accept several query items. In the exercise you worked on in Section 4.1 and 4.2, the IDoc **MATMAS02** merely contained one material master record in a flat data structure.

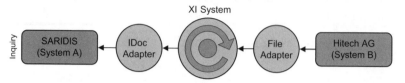

Figure 5.2 The Flow of Step 1

5.1.1 Basic Principles

Overview of the preparatory steps

The dispatch and receipt of IDocs in this step requires some preparation. In Section 4.2, you already configured a partner profile to receive an IDoc. It is possible that Hitech AG uses different material descriptions that SARIDIS. To ensure that all documents refer to the same material, make the corresponding assignments.[1]

Maintaining Partner Profiles

Creating the partner profile for System B

The information on the settings that you can make in the partner profile for the processing of IDocs originates from the SAP Service Marketplace.[2] There you can also find documentation on EDI application scenarios and listings for automatic inbound processing of IDocs.

Login to System A and call **Transaction WE20**. Then select **Partners • Create** from the menu bar or click the **Create** icon to create a new partner profile. As partner number, enter the number of the logical system of System B, which is structured according to the schema, **<SID>CLNT<Client>**. Select the item **LS—Logical System** as partner type and make sure that the partner status value is set to **A** (which stands for "active") in the **Classification** tab.

Configuring the inbound parameters

You now want to specify that IDocs of the **REQOTE** (inquiry) type are automatically processed according to a specific pattern when received. For this, save the partner profile, go to the **Inbound parameters** section and click the **Create inbound parameter** icon.

---

1 These two basic steps can be carried out only once in System A. In the context of a training course, the instructor should demonstrate these activities.

2 You can find a list of all IDocs including the necessary settings for the partner agreement at the following address: *https://websmp110.sap-ag.de/~form/sap-net?FRAME=CONTAINER&_OBJECT=011000358700004380801999D*

In the next step, you must set the **REQOTE** message type (see Figure 5.3). Below the **Inbound options** tab, select the predefined process code, **REQO**. This process code ensures that the inbound IDoc is processed automatically in such a way that it generates an inquery. We want it to be processed immediately by the function module. Save these settings and exit the transaction.

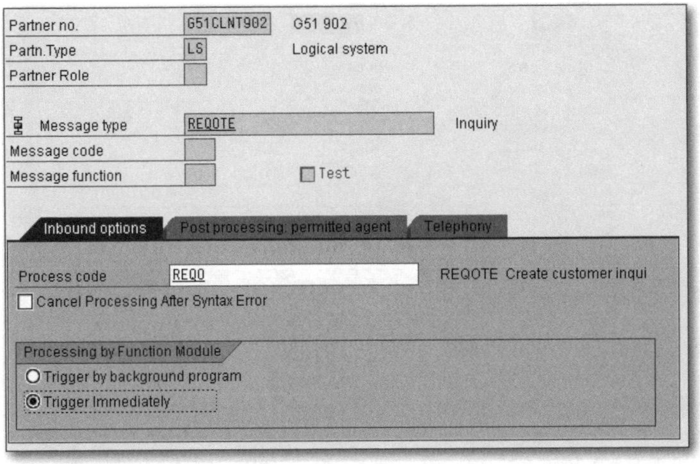

Figure 5.3 Maintaining Inbound Parameters for the REQOTE IDoc

Assigning Material Descriptions in the Supplier System

In reality, the material descriptions used by the customer often differ from those used by the supplier. For this reason, it is necessary to map the material descriptions used on the customer's side with those used on the supplier's side to allow automatic processing of sales documents—even if the materials bear the same names, both in the source and target systems, as in this case study.

Mapping customer and supplier master data

In business system A (SARIDIS), go to **Transaction VD51**. Enter **Customer Number 1171** for Hitech AG as well as **Sales Organization 1000** and **Distribution Channel 10**; confirm your entries by pressing **Enter**.

In the assignment table that displays next (see Figure 5.4), enter the materials **M-01** through **M-20** both in the **Material number** and **Customer material** columns, and confirm your entries by pressing **Enter**. The **Description** column then displays the names of the materials contained in the **Material number** column. Every student can enter 20 different materials to order their own material or monitor type, respectively. Save these assignments and exit the transaction.

Customer	1171	Hitech AG
Sales Organization	1000	Germany Frankfurt
Distribution Channel	10	Final customer sales

Material no.	Description	Cust. material	RdPr	UM	Tex
M-01	Sunny Sunny 01	M-01			
M-02	Sunny Xa1	M-02			
M-03	Sunny Tetra l3	M-03			
M-04	Sunny Extreme	M-04			
M-05	Flatscreen LE 50 P	M-05			
M-06	Flatscreen MS 1460 P	M-06			
M-07	Flatscreen LE 64P	M-07			
M-08	Flatscreen MS 1575P	M-08			
M-09	Flatscreen MS 1585	M-09			
M-10	Flatscreen MS 1775P	M-10			
M-11	Flatscreen MS 1785P	M-11			
M-12	MAG DX 15F/Fe	M-12			
M-13	MAG DX 17F	M-13			
M-14	MAG PA/DX 175	M-14			

Figure 5.4 Assigning Material Descriptions in the Supplier System

> **Note**
>
> The IDES system does not provide the **M-00** material for the instructor, so you will need to create that material item in System A. To do so, call **Transaction MM01**, go to industry sector **Retail** and then to material type **Finished product (FERT)**. To create the material here, you can use material **M-01** from the same sales area as a template. Moreover, you should add the sales conditions in **Transaction VK31** by double-clicking on the **Prices • Material Price** directory. Next, click in the row on the right that contains the variable key, **CnTy Sorg. DChl Material ReST** in the **Selection** on the icon that represents an empty sheet. Define the sales price for material **M-00** in the new table. Save the settings and include the new material in the assignment described earlier.

5.1.2 Design

Configuring classification objects for the case study

Because the exercises and the case study involve a large number of design elements that make it difficult not to lose one's overview, it is useful to use at least one separate namespace per student in the case study. As described in the course-specific preparations in Section 3.6, you can also create new software components. Regardless of whether you create only namespaces or software components, you should not carry out this step until the actual implementation of the case study begins. Otherwise you may run the risk of students storing objects from the exercises in the namespace or software component that is reserved for the case study.

You can create new namespaces in the details window of the software component version. Assign a name to the namespace according to the following schema: `http://www.sap-press.com/xi/case-study/##`. New software components should be created in the SLD according to the schema **SC_CASESTUDY_##**.

To dispatch the inquiry, use nested data types on the sender's side to account for the IDoc structure. The smallest data type will be the inquiry item, which can be contained multiple times in the inquiry. In addition to the individual items, the inquiry itself contains header data.

Overview of design objects

At this stage, as in the following steps of the case study, you will need to familiarize yourself with the processing of nested messages. Let's take a closer look at the message mapping for this step. Table 5.1 provides an overview of all design objects involved in this step.

Type of object	Sender side	Receiver side
Message interface	MI_Inquiry_Async_Out	REQOTE.ORDERS01
Message type	MT_Inquiry	
Data type	▸ DT_Inquiry ▸ DT_InquiryItem	
Interface mapping	IM_MI_Inquiry_Async_Out_to_REQOTE_ORDERS01	
Message mapping	MM_MT_Inquiry_to_REQOTE_ORDERS01	

Table 5.1 Design Objects for Step 1 of the Case Study

Login to the integration repository and navigate to the software component of the case study. Import the IDoc interface, **REQOTE.ORDERS01**, in the relevant subdirectory, **Imported Objects**. This import contains everything you need for the receiver side.

Importing the IDoc for the receiver side

Go to the new namespace, `http://www.sap-press.com/xi/case-study/##`, and create data type **DT_InquiryItem**. This data type contains information on individual items within an inquiry. It represents a simplified version of the segments to be used later on in the IDoc.

Creating data type DT_InquiryItem

As shown in Figure 5.5, create the following elements in this data type and save it: **ItemNumber**, **MaterialNumber**, **Description**, **Quantity**, **MaterialGroup**, **NetWeight**, **GrossWeight**, **WeightUnit**, and **DeliveryDate**.

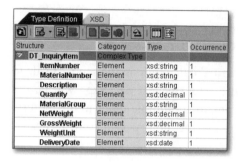

Figure 5.5 Structure of Data Type DT_Inquiry_Item

The **Description**, **Net Weight**, and **GrossWeight** elements contain values provided by the customer and can therefore deviate from the values of the supplier. When in doubt, use them to clearly identify a material. The **DeliveryDate** element does not contain the final delivery date, but rather a requested date from the sold-to-party. This does not need to match the delivery date that will be offered in the quote.

Creating data type DT_Inquiry

The **DT_InquiryItem** data type must now be integrated in the **DT_Inquiry** data type, which allows you to store multiple inquiry items in this format.

For this, create the **DT_Inquiry** data type and generate the elements shown in Figure 5.6: **Customer**, **DocumentNumber**, **CreationDate**, **CreationTime**, **CollectiveNumber**, **Vendor**, **ValidTo**, and **InquiryItem**. The **InquiryItem** element is not assigned to a built-in type; it is rather based on the **DT_InquiryItem** data type, which was just created.

Once you have selected this data type via the input help, you will see that this type's elements are grayed out. The gray text indicates that these elements cannot be changed because they don't originate with this data type. Because an inquiry item can occur multiple times in an inquiry, you must change the occurrence of the **InquiryItem** correspondingly. To do this, double-click in the **Occurrence** column of the **InquiryItem** element. This opens a new window in which you can specify both the minimum and maximum occurrence of the element. Open the input help for the maximum occurrence and select **Unbounded** (which indicates that no limit has been set), and save the data type.

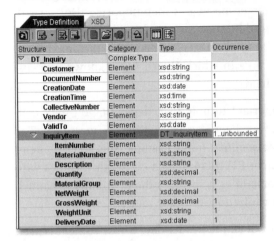

Figure 5.6 Structure of Data Type DT_Inquiry

The **DocumentNumber** and **CollectiveNumber** elements make it easier for the customer to assign the future quotation to the relevant inquiry that has been sent. The **Vendor** element contains the number of SARIDIS in the Hitech AG's system. The **ValidTo** element specifies the period in which the quotation created by SARIDIS will be valid.

The next step is to integrate the **DT_Inquiry** data type in the new message type **MT_Inquiry**, and save the object. At this point, you should review the structure of the data type being used. Create a new message interface, called **MI_Inquiry_Async_Out**, and base it on message type **MT_Inquiry**. This interface is later used to send the inquiry from the file adapter on the customer's side. As you can gather by its name, the message interface belongs to the **Outbound** category and the **Asynchronous** mode. Copy **MT_Inquiry** as output an message type and save the object.

Creating message type and message interface

Since an IDoc is used, the message mapping for this step, **MM_MT_Inquiry_to_REQOTE_ORDERS01**, becomes a little more complicated and sheds light on a new aspect of message processing. Where the assignment of individual elements to each other is more or less self-explanatory, you must separately consider the occurrence of subor-

Mapping the inquiry header data

dinate elements. For this reason, message mapping development is divided into two parts which represent different hierarchy levels.

First, you must assign the header data of the inquiry to the IDoc. To do this, select message type **MT_Inquiry** as a source message from your namespace. The target message is then imported IDoc format, **REQOTE.ORDERS01**. In addition to the data provided by the message type **MT_Inquiry**, different constants are necessary in some places. For example, the sales area in which Hitech AG is known as a customer must be maintained.

At this point, it is important to note that, depending on their contents, the segments of an IDoc can have different meanings. The meaning is defined by a *qualifier*. In the example, this is clearly demonstrated by the segment **E1EDK14**, which occurs three times with different meanings: sometimes it specifies the distribution channel, sometimes the sales organization, or other values.

Table 5.2 provides a list of all the header data whose content is used in the case study. In addition, each target segment and the underlying **SEGMENT** element listed in Table 5.2 must be assigned the **MT_Inquiry** node. This way, you can define that the used segments are created as long as the **MT_Inquiry** node exists in the outbound message. In other words, once.

Data element of MT_Inquiry or constants	Data element of REQOTE.ORDERS01	Segment of REQOTE.ORDERS01
Constant: 1	BEGIN	None (IDOC)
Constant: IN (Inquiry)	BSART	E1EDK01
DocumentNumber	BELNR	E1EDK01
Vendor	RECIPNT_NO	E1EDK01
Constant: 006 (Division)	QUALF	E1EDK14(1)
Constant: 00	ORGID	E1EDK14(1)
Constant: 007 (Distribution Channel)	QUALF	E1EDK14(2)
Constant: 10	ORGID	E1EDK14(2)
Constant: 008 (Sales Organization)	QUALF	E1EDK14(3)

Table 5.2 Assigning the Header Data in the Message Mapping of Step 1

Data element of MT_Inquiry or constants	Data element of REQOTE.ORDERS01	Segment of REQOTE.ORDERS01
Constant: 1000	ORGID	E1EDK14(3)
Constant: 004 (Valid To)	IDDAT	E1EDK03(1)
ValidTo	DATUM	E1EDK03(1)
Constant: 012 (Creation Date)	IDDAT	E1EDK03(2)
CreationDate	DATUM	E1EDK03(2)
Constant: AG (Sold-to-Party)	PARVW	E1EDKA1
Customer	PARTN	E1EDKA1
Constant: 003 (Original document data)	QUALF	E1EDK02(1)
DocumentNumber	BELNR	E1EDK02(1)
CreationDate	DATUM	E1EDK02(1)
CreationTime	UZEIT	E1EDK02(1)
Constant: 007 (Collective Number)	QUALF	E1EDK02(2)
CollectiveNumber	BELNR	E1EDK02(2)

Table 5.2 Assigning the Header Data in the Message Mapping of Step 1 (cont.)

Maintain the header data assignments described and deactivate all non-used segments of the IDoc for the time being. Note that you can duplicate the segments that are used several times, such as **E1EDK14**, using the **Duplicate Subtree** option in the menu of the relevant segment. Within the table, the different subtrees are distinguished with an index that is not explicitly displayed in the mapping. The sequence of the duplicates does not play any role.

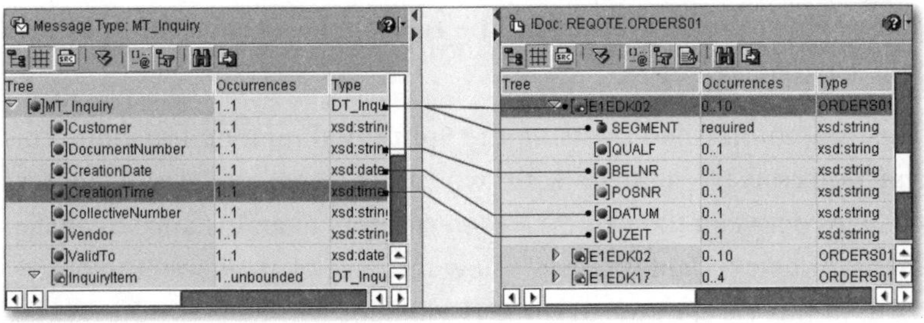

Figure 5.7 Assigning the IDoc Segment E1EDK02

Creation of the **CollectiveNumber** enables Hitech AG to bundle several inquiries logically. For this reason, the value must be returned later when the quote is created. Figure 5.7 displays a sample assignment of the elements within segment **E1EDK02**.

Testing the header data mapping

Now test the part of the mapping we have described up to this point. To test the mapping, load an already existing file in the inquiry format in the **Test** tab by clicking the **Load Test Instance** icon. You can also click the **Source Text View** icon to change and save the structure of the file once again. The test should create a document on the target side which contains all segments used up to this point, including the respective values.

Deriving item mapping

Now that the header data mapping has been completed successfully, you can take care of the item data. When assigning data types and segments, it's important to note that individual inquiry items can occur in an almost unlimited number within an inquiry.

Let's first think about the mapping, and imagine that the inquiry file contains several items; for example, that the embedded **DT_Inquiry-Item** data type occurs several times. The data of each item must be stored in segment **E1EDP01**. As such, the segment will be created as many times as inquiry items exist in the file. Now imagine that the file contains two items, which means that the **InquiryItem** node exists twice. Since segment **E1EDP01** can occur an unlimited number of times, it isn't a problem to create two segments. This clarifies the assignment of the **InquiryItem** node to **E1EDP01**.

Now let's look at the **SEGMENT** element below **E1EDP01**, which must occur exactly once in each segment. This means assigning the **InquiryItem** node to this element poses a problem if several items exist. To return to the example of the two items, SAP XI cannot assign a row with two items to an element that can only contain one value. Thus, the two values in the row or queue must be split into two separate values.

This is accomplished by using the **SplitByValue** node function. This function converts a queue with two values into a queue with context changes between the values. A *context* refers to an instance of an element. A *context change* causes a new instance of an element to be created; in this case, of the **SEGMENT** element.

Figure 5.8 illustrates the mapping for target element **SEGMENT** within IDoc segment **E1EDP01**. The original queue of the **Inquiry-Item** node contains two items that are enclosed by context changes. A context change occurs at the beginning and end of each queue. This context change is displayed in gray text. Due to the use of the **SplitByValue** node function, a context change is inserted after each value, as you can see in the second queue. This way, the two values are assigned to two different instances of the element.

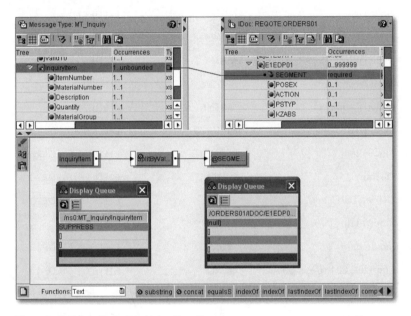

Figure 5.8 Using the SplitByValue Function

However, you can also set the parameters of the function so it generates a context change; for instance, only if the values are changed or if the contents are blank. Before you do this, you should extend the mapping, as shown in Table 5.3. Target elements marked with an asterisk (*) require the **SplitByValue** in the mapping.

Data element of MT_Inquiry/InquiryItem or constants	Data element of REQOTE.ORDERS01/ E1EDP01	Segment of R EQOTE.ORDERS01/ E1EDP01
InquiryItem	E1EDP01	None (IDOC)
InquiryItem	SEGMENT *	E1EDP01

Table 5.3 Assigning the Item Data in the Message Mapping of Step 1

Data element of MT_ Inquiry/InquiryItem or constants	Data element of REQOTE.ORDERS01/ E1EDP01	Segment of R EQOTE.ORDERS01/ E1EDP01
Itemnumber	POSEX	E1EDP01
Constant: 001 (Create)	ACTION	E1EDP01
Quantity	MENGE	E1EDP01
Constant: PCE (Quantity unit)	MENEE	E1EDP01
NetWeight	NTGEW	E1EDP01
WeightUnit	GEWEI	E1EDP01
MaterialGroup	MATKL	E1EDP01
GrossWeight	BRGEW	E1EDP01
MaterialNumber	MATNR	E1EDP01
InquiryItem	E1EDP20 *	E1EDP01
InquiryItem	SEGMENT *	E1EDP01/E1EDP20
Quantity	WMENG	E1EDP01/E1EDP20
DeliveryDate	EDATU	E1EDP01/E1EDP20
InquiryItem	E1EDP19 *	E1EDP01
InquiryItem	SEGMENT *	E1EDP01/E1EDP19
Constant: 001 (Description)	QUALF	E1EDP01/E1EDP19
MaterialNumber	IDTNR	E1EDP01/E1EDP19
Description	KTEXT	E1EDP01/E1EDP19

Table 5.3 Assigning the Item Data in the Message Mapping of Step 1 (cont.)

With the two segments, **E1EDP19** and **E1EDP20**, the target structure has an additional hierarchy level; however, this level isn't discussed in this example. Basically, you could specify the delivery of the material in different batches or enter a more detailed description of the material by using several instances of the segments.

Note

You can save frequently used mappings (or parts of mappings) using the two icons, **Create Template Based on Mapping** or **Show Suitable Templates**, which allow you to integrate them quickly. Templates are saved in the **Mapping Templates** directory and can be edited and tested like real mappings.

Save your message mapping and go to the test mode. Expand the **MT_Inquiry** node and duplicate the **InquiryItem** subtree at least once. Fill in the fields of the header data and of the two items. You can still use any value at this stage. Start the transformation by clicking the icon in the bottom-left of the screen and see whether the target structure contains the correct number of all segments. The structure should correspond to the one shown in Figure 5.9. The figure displays the segments of the IDoc. Note that some segment types can occur several times, depending on the specific requirements. Segment **E1EDP01** contains the details of the items as well as other segments.

Testing the message mapping

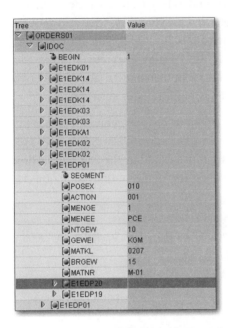

Figure 5.9 Structure of the Target Structure in Step 1 of the Case Study

Now return to the **Design** tab and select an element that uses the **SplitByValue** function in the mapping. Open the menu of the source element in the work area and select the **Display Queue** option. Repeat this step for the source element. The system should now display a screen that looks similar to the one shown in Figure 5.8.

The last object to be created in the design phase is interface mapping **IM_MI_Inquiry_Async_Out_to_REQOTE_ORDERS01**. The source interface **MI_Inquiry_Async_Out** is converted into target interface **REQOTE.ORDERS01** by using the message mapping we just created.

Interface mapping

Due to its origin, you can find the target interface in the **Imported Objects • IDocs** directory. Save the interface mapping and test it.

You activate all design objects and exit the integration repository.

5.1.3   Configuration

Creating another configuration scenario

As in the integration repository, it will also be difficult to keep your overview in the integration directory, given the number of objects it contains. For this reason, create a new logical section in the form of an additional configuration scenario.

Go to the integration directory and select **Object • New** from the menu to create a scenario named **XI_CaseStudy_##**. Save and activate the new scenario. In the **Scenarios** tab, be sure to adjust the display to the new scenario by clicking the **Display Previous Subtree** and **Only Display Selected Subtree** icons. In the **Objects** tab, add the two business systems (SystemA and SystemB) to your scenario.

Overview of configuration objects

As with the last exercise of the previous chapter, you will create the delivery of an inquiry using the Configuration Wizard. The only pre-requisites for using the wizard are represented by the communication channels. Table 5.4 provides an overview of all configuration objects.

Type of object	Receiver side: System A	Sender side: System B
Communication channel	IDoc_ReceiverChannel	File_SenderChannel_##
Sender agreement	| SystemB | MI_Inquiry_Async_Out | |	
Receiver agreement		| SystemB | | SystemA | REQUOTE.ORDERS01
Receiver determination	| SystemB | MI_Inquiry_Async_Out	
Interface determination	| SystemB | MI_Inquiry_Async_Out | | SystemA	

Table 5.4 Elements in the Integration Directory of Step 1 in the Case Study

Creating the IDoc receiver channel

The IDoc receiver channel of System A should only be created once by the instructor. To do this, go to the integration directory and create the channel **IDoc_ReceiverChannel** using the context menu of the communication channels for System A. Select the adapter type **IDoc** and set the direction to **Receiver**. You don't need to change the details for the protocols or the adapter engine.

As **RFC Destination** you can use the **SystemA_IDoc** connection you created in Section 3.5.3 when preparing for the technical exercises. Depending on the connected system, the interface version should have **SAP Release 4.0 or Higher**. Moreover, you should also use the **SAP<SIDA>** port you created when preparing for the exercises. Note that **SIDA** stands for the system ID of System A. The **SAP Release** being used depends on the connected system. In the case of SAP ECC 5.0, the SAP Release number is **500** (see Figure 5.10).

Adapter Type *	IDoc		http://sap.com/xi/XI/System	SAP BASIS 6.40	
○ Sender	● Receiver				
Transport Protocol *	IDoc				
Message Protocol *	IDoc				
Adapter Engine *	Integration Server				
RFC Destination *	SystemA_IDoc				
Segment Version					
Interface Version *	SAP Release 4.0 or Higher				
Port *	SAPG50				
SAP Release *	500				

Figure 5.10 Creating the IDoc Receiver Channel for System A

Like all other objects not directly related to an IDoc, the **File Sender Channel** of System B can be created by every student. Go to the integration directory, open the context menu of the communication channels of System B, and create the entry, **File_SenderChannel_##**. Select the **File** adapter type and the **Sender** direction in the detail window. Again, you can use the */tmp* as the source directory on Unix systems, and *C:\temp* for Windows systems. The file name of the file to be imported should be structured according to the schema, *inquiry_##.dat*. Leave the **Quality-of-Service** setting at **Exactly Once**.

Creating the file sender channel

Set the **Poll Interval** to between three and five minutes. The **Processing Mode** can be freely selected, depending on the scope of rights you have at file level and whether or not an archive directory exists. If your rights are restricted and you don't have complete access to the relevant file, activate the **Process Read-Only Files** option (see Figure 5.11).

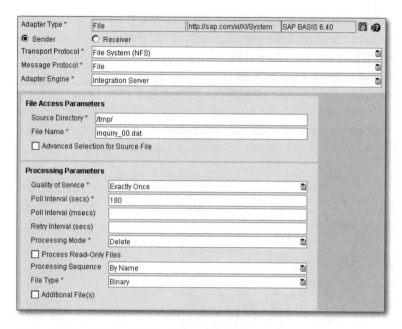

Figure 5.11 Creating the File Sender Channel for System B

Starting the Configuration Wizard Two communication channels are the last two objects needed to call the configuration wizard. Start the wizard by selecting **Tools • Configuration Wizard** from the menu, or click the corresponding icon. You will create this example as internal communication, although from the point of view of its content, it is a partner communication. However, because you are still using business systems for communication, this selection will simplify your work.

The sending **service** is **business system B**, which uses the **file adapter** to send data records via the **MI_Inquiry_Async_Out** interface. When selecting the message interface, select the object from your own software component (see Figure 5.12).

Service Type *	Business System		
Service *	SystemB		
Interface *	MI_Inquiry_Async_Out		
Namespace *	http://www.sap-press.com/xi/casestudy/00		
Adapter Type *	File	http://sap.com,	SAP BASIS

Figure 5.12 Sender Settings in the Configuration Wizard for Step 1

The message receiver is **business system A**, which uses adapter type **IDoc**. The **interface** is the definition of the **REQOTE.ORDERS01** IDoc, which is contained in your software component (see Figure 5.13).

Service Type *	Business System	
Service *	SystemA	
Interface *	REQOTE.ORDERS01	
Namespace *	urn:sap-com:document:sap:idoc:messages	
Adapter Type *	IDoc	http://sap.com SAP BASIS

Figure 5.13 Receiver Settings in the Configuration Wizard for Step 1

For the sender agreement you should use communication channel **File_SenderChannel_##** of System B, which you have just created. The screen template used for the receiver determination, **|SystemB|MI_Inquiry_Async_Out**, is only supposed to provide you with information, particularly since no message have yet been sent from System B via this interface and therefore no adjustment is needed.

In the next step that determines the interface **|SystemB|MI_Inquiry_Async_Out||SystemA**, make sure that the appropriate interface mapping, **IM_MI_Inquiry_Async_Out_to_REQOTE_ORDERS01**, is displayed. The new receiver agreement, **|SystemB||SystemA|REQOTE.ORDERS01**, uses communication channel **IDoc_ReceiverChannel** of System A that has been created by the instructor.

In the final step, add all objects to your new scenario, **XI_CaseStudy_##**, and quit the Wizard. Activate your change list in the integration directory.

At this point we want to draw your attention to a specific option that's contained in recent support packages, which allows you to simulate a configuration. Before you can do this, however, the **sap/xi/simulation** service in Transaction SICF of the XI system must be released.

Using the configuration test

To do that, select **Tools · Test Configuration** from the menu of the integration directory. In the input fields, specify the **Sender** and the **Interface** to be used for sending. Click the **Run** icon in the flow control. SAP XI now locates the objects of the message path as in a real run. You can use the log to identify and troubleshoot errors (see Figure 5.14). Note, however, that some objects cannot be identified correctly without a corresponding message.

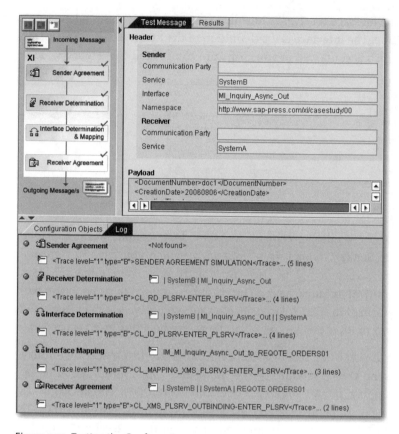

Figure 5.14 Testing the Configuration

5.1.4 Process and Monitoring

Controlling
IDoc processing

The process of Step 1 of the case study starts with the creation of file *inquiry_##.dat* in the corresponding directory of the file sender adapter, **File_SenderChannel_##**. You can find a sample of this file in the Appendix of this book. Apart from that, you can also enter data in the test mode of the message mapping and then save the source code of this test data as a file. Regardless, make sure that the **DocumentNumber** is structured according to the schema, **Inquiry-##**, which allows you to find the document again at a later stage. Furthermore, you should structure the name of the **CollectiveNumber** according to the schema, **SUBMI_##**, because this entry is used to select a receiver in the next step of the case study.

If the message sends successfully, it is displayed in SAP XI's message monitoring, which you can access via Transactions **SXMB_MONI** or

SXI_MONITOR. Within business system A, you can monitor the receipt of the IDoc in **Transaction BD87**. In this transaction, you should view all IDocs and consider the rows in the section **IDoc in inbound processing**, whereby only **IDoc REQOTE** is relevant. You can see whether or not the IDoc has arrived, or if problems occurred during processing.

If you double-click on an error or success message, the system displays a detailed message which tells you the exact error that occurred. Most errors are caused by incorrectly structured original files or by errors in the message mapping. If necessary, you should examine the behavior of the mapping once again using the content of the imported file. You can also double-click on the detailed error message to go directly into the IDoc that has arrived.

The actual goal of this step, however, was not just the dispatch of an IDoc containing inquiry data, but also to automatically create an inquiry. **Transaction VA13** allows you to verify that. You can find this transaction in the SAP Easy Access Menu which you can call using the following path: **Logistics • Sales and Distribution • Sales • Inquiry • Display**. The functions to display and create inquiries are not only available in the sales and distribution area. Similarly, SARIDIS can send inquiries to another company. This type of inquiry is located in the purchasing area and must not be confused with the inquiry in the sales area.

Checking the incoming inquiry

Once you have changed to **Transaction VA13**, you won't be able to find the number of your inquiry. For this, go to **Transaction BD87** and navigate to the success message and memorize the number, or you can use the search function of the **Inquiry** input field. To do this, press F4 (help) in the field and select the **Sales document by customer** tab. Enter partner **1171** (Hitech AG) as well as the partner function **SP** (Sold-to-Party). In particular, you should keep the document number **(Inquiry-##)** of your inquiry in the **Purchase order no.** field.

If your inquiry is displayed in the list, run the query. Double-click on the inquiry to copy the inquiry number. Confirm your entries by pressing **Enter**, and go to the inquiry view (see Figure 5.15). You should now see the data of your inquiry, which means you have successfully completed the first step of the case study.

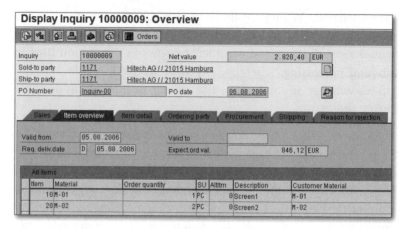

Figure 5.15 Displaying the Inquiry of Hitech AG

5.2 Submitting the Quotations

The process of the second step

Now that the inquiry of Hitech AG has been received by SARIDIS, the next step is to assume the role of the responsible person on the receiving side and create a quote based on the inquiry. The quote is automatically sent as an IDoc from the system and submitted to Hitech AG. Once the quote has arrived in Hitech AG's XI system, a web service of Sunny Electronics is used to obtain an alternate quote for the products. Results from the two inquiries with SARIDIS and Sunny Electronics are then compiled and submitted to Hitech AG.

Figure 5.16 roughly illustrates this process.

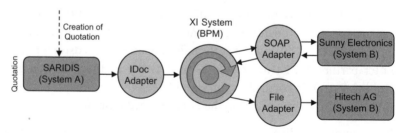

Figure 5.16 The Flow of Step 2

5.2.1 Basic Principles

Overview of all preparatory activities

Before you start working on this comprehensive step, you must prepare two things: First, as is the case regarding the receipt of an IDoc, you must also establish the integration into existing processes to be able to dispatch an IDoc. This can be done by using a corresponding *partner profile*. In addition, you will address a web service within the business process that you can create or import by yourself.[3]

Maintaining the Partner Profiles

Login to System A and call **Transaction WE20** to maintain the partner profiles. Create a new partner profile for **partner type KU** and partner **1171** (Hitech AG) and save the profile. Below the empty list of Outbound Parameters, click the **Create outbound parameter** button.

Maintaining the outbound parameters for customer Hitech AG

Then select partner Sold-to Party role (SP) from the detail window that opens next (see Figure 5.17). This means that the outbound parameter is only valid if an IDoc is sent to Hitech AG as the sold-to-party. Select the **QUOTES** message type, which contains the inquiries. Go to the **Outbound Options** tab in the lower area and configure receiver port **XI_SYSTEM**. This port was already created during the preparations for the technical exercises (see Chapter 3), and refers to an RFC connection to the XI system. Select the output mode, **Transfer IDoc Immediately**, and enter the basic type, **ORDERS01**. The selection of this basic type ensures that when you confirm your entries, the package size is set to 1, which means that only one IDoc is collected in a package before it is dispatched. The basic type **ORDERS01** represents the basic structure of the IDocs used in purchasing, sales, and distribution, which allows them to be used many different ways.

Next, go to the **Message Control** tab to start the integration into the sales and distribution transactions. Click the **Insert Row** icon to add a new row to the end of the list and select the V1 (Sales) item in the **Application** column (see Figure 5.18). Since integration is supposed to be limited to the dispatch of quotations at first, you must select the **AN00** (Quotation) option in the Message type column. Finally, apply the **SD12** entry in the **Process code** column using the input help and confirm your entries.

Check the values once more using the summary directly above the list. While working through this step, you will see the effects of this integration as you create the quote.

---

3 Because both steps can be carried out only once, they should be implemented by the instructor.

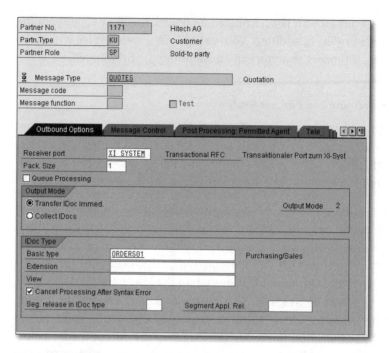

Figure 5.17 Outbound Options of the Outbound Parameter for Customer Hitech AG

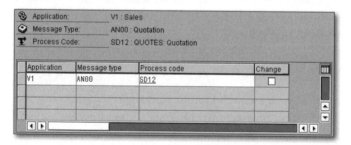

Figure 5.18 Message Control of the Outbound Parameter for Customer Hitech AG

Setting up the Web Service at Sunny Electronics

Source of web service

To avoid having to extend the training landscape even further, the web service of Sunny Electronics is provided by System B. Similar to Exercise 3 in the previous chapter, an RFC-enabled ABAP function module is used by all course participants to provide the web service. You can find the source code of this function module in Appendix A, or you can download it from the book's web site. For now, though, let's take a closer look at the structure and process of the web service.

The web service receives a quote's header data along with an unlimited number of quotes. Technically speaking, this is implemented by a table that's used to transfer the parameters. To use this table, a data structure must be created for the web service in the data dictionary. You can also import this structure using the transport, or you can create it by yourself according to the instructions provided in Appendix A. Header data, as well as the majority of item data, is left unchanged during the transfer.

Structure of the web service

The only information that changes are the quotation and validity dates, as well as all pricing details. This allows you to forward the quote from SARIDIS to Sunny Electronics later as both of them quote their prices identically. Sunny Electronics' monitor prices match those from SARIDIS; however, they are changed slightly using a certain multiplication factor. By default, the goods of Sunny Electronics cost 110 percent of the price offered by SARIDIS. (If there wasn't a variance, you would be able to continue with the entire case study from this point.)

5.2.2 Design

In contrast to how we proceeded in the design and configuration phases up to now, this step first requires you to examine the entire scenario and then work through it part by part. Each individual part contains an overview of the objects used.

Creating the Business Process Structure

Because this second step of the case study is affected by the business process, we will start with it. This makes it easier for you to understand which actions are necessary and how to divide the flow into three different blocks.

Flow of the integration process

First open the integration repository and navigate to your software component version, and then to the namespace of the case study. Go to the **Integration Scenarios & Integration Processes • Integration Processes** directory and create the new integration process, **IP_Quotation_##**, where ## represents your participant number. Detach the detail window by clicking the Detach Window icon in the top left-hand corner and hide the header area to obtain as much space as possible. Insert three blocks and assign the following names to them in sequence: **IDoc Processing**, **Web Service Call**, and **List Processing**.

Next, insert a Receive step in the first block and call it **Receive IDoc**. Add a Transformation step after that and call it **Transform IDoc**. This step converts the IDoc into a simplified quotation format for additional processing. The simplified quotation format is identical to the response format of the web service from Sunny Electronics. The last step involves a container operation, called **Append SARIDIS Quotation**. During this operation, the simplified SARIDIS quote is included in a list of quotes.

The second block begins by converting the SARIDIS quote into the format of the web service request. This step is called **Create WS Request**. It is followed by a synchronous sending step called **Call Web Service**. In this step, the web service is called to obtain the alternate quote. Note, you must select the Synchronous mode from the properties for this element. The container operation **Append Sunny Quotation** at the end of the block also inserts the alternative quote into the list of quotes. This is possible without using a transformation because the response from the web service is identical to the simplified quote format.

The third block consists of only two elements. The first element is a transformation element, called **Transform Quotation list**, which converts the quotation list that consists of several rows into a simple message containing all quotations. The final step, **Send Quotations**, dispatches the newly created message in an asynchronous sending step.

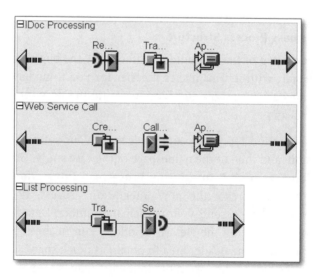

Figure 5.19 Structure of the Business Process Blocks

The three blocks should now have the structure shown in Figure 5.19. In the following steps, you will fill the business process structure with data.

Design Objects of the First Block

From the design phase point of view, the most important part of the first block in the integration process is converting the IDoc into the simplified quotation format. First of all, you must create both the simplified quotation format and a corresponding message mapping. This message mapping requires you to take a closer look at how mappings are used to handle contexts. The interface mapping has the special characteristic that both interfaces are abstract because they are used in a business process. For this reason, it is also necessary to create an abstract interface for IDoc **QUOTES.ORDERS01**. Table 5.5 provides an overview of all objects used in this part.

Overview of design objects in the first block

Type of object	Sender side	Receiver side
Message interface	▸ **QUOTES.ORDERS01** ▸ **MI_QUOTES_ORDERS01_Async_Abstract**	**MI_ws_sunny_response_Async_Abstract**
Message type Data type	**QUOTES.ORDERS01**	**Z_SUNNY_QUOTATION-Output**
Interface mapping	**IM_QUOTES_ORDERS01_Async_Abstract_to_MI_ws_sunny_response_Async_Abstract**	
Message mapping	**MM_QUOTES_ORDERS01_to_Z_SUNNY_QUOTATION-Output**	

Table 5.5 Design Objects for the First BP Block of Step 2 of the Case Study

You should begin with the elements on the sender side: First import the IDoc definition **QUOTES.ORDERS01** from System A. Then create message interface **MI_QUOTES_ORDERS01_Async_Abstract** on the basis of this imported object. This unusual step is necessary because the interface declaration must be declared as being abstract so it can be converted into an integration process. Therefore, select the category **Abstract** as well as the **Asynchronous** mode.

Creating the objects on the sender side

Both the data and message types of the simplified quotation format match the response format of the web service at Sunny Electronics.

Creating the objects on the receiver side

Thus, you do not need to create these two elements manually. Instead, you can obtain them by importing the WSDL description of the corresponding web service.

Call the web service repository of System B via the following URL: *http://<Host SystemB>:<Port 80XX>/sap/bc/bsp/sap/webservicebrowser/ search.html?sap-client=<Client>*. Login as the user, **SYS_B-##**. Search for the **Z_SUNNY_QUOTATION** web service and save the WSDL description by clicking on the **wsdl** entry next to the corresponding row. If necessary, you can save the description in the source text view of the web browser and store the definition as **Z_SUNNY_ QUOTATION_SystemB.wsdl** in your frontend.

Create the external definition, **ws_sunny_quotation**, in your case study namespace on the basis of the WSDL file. Once you have imported the file, you must check if the two messages, **Z_SUNNY_ QUOTATIONInput** and **Z_SUNNY_QUOTATIONOutput**, exist in the Messages tab.

Creating the message interface

Now you must create the message interface **MI_ws_sunny_response_ Async_Abstract** for the receiver side. For this, use the message type **Z_SUNNY_QUOTATIONOutput**. Because this interface is also used in the business process, its category must be set to Abstract and its mode to Asynchronous.

Creating the message mapping

Now that you have created the objects for the sender and receiver sides, you can move on to create the mapping objects. To do this, you should first create the message mapping, **MM_QUOTES_ ORDERS01_to_Z_SUNNY_QUOTATIONOutput**. Select the IDoc type **QUOTES.ORDERS01** as outbound message and **Z_SUNNY_QUOTA- TIONOutput** from the external definition, **ws_sunny_quotation**, as the target message.

Note that the target message is structured in an unusual way. The **ITEMS** substructure that contains multiple quotation items is not located at the end of the message, but included in alphabetical order. Detach this window as well so there's enough space for you to work on the mapping.

Start mapping the header data; this shouldn't a problem if you use the information provided in Table 5.6. For the time being, you should skip those target elements that originate from more than one source element.

Segment of QUOTES.ORDERS01	Data element of QUOTES.ORDERS01	Data element of Z_SUNNY_QUOTATIONOutput
E1EDK01	RECIPNT_NO	CUSTOMER
E1EDK01	BELNR	DOCUMENTNUMBER
E1EDK03	IDDAT (025) DATUM	QUOTATIONDATE
E1EDK03	IDDAT (006) DATUM	VALIDTO
E1EDK04	MSATZ	TAXRATE
E1EDK04	MWSBT	TAXAMOUNT
E1EDK02	QUALF (007) BELNR	COLLECTIVENUMBER
E1EDS01	SUMID (002) SUMME	NETPRICE
E1EDS01	SUMID (002) SUNIT	CURRENCY
	Constant: SARIDIS	VENDOR

Table 5.6 Assigning the Header Data in the Message Mapping of the First Block of Step 2

Now consider the target elements that are created on the basis of more than one element, such as **QUOTATIONDATE** and **VALIDTO**. Both elements are created on the basis of the same data of segment **E1EDK03**, although they can assume different values. The reason for this is that the IDDAT element within the segment indicates what type of data is contained in a specific instance of the segment. A quotation IDoc sent from System A contains several instances of this segment with different contents in the IDDAT field.

To get a better picture of this, skip ahead to Section 5.2.4, create a quotation, and dispatch it as an IDoc. At that point, the IDoc has been created, but not delivered. **Transaction BD87** in System A allows you to view the exact structure of the IDoc. The structure looks similar to the one displayed in Figure 5.20. As you can see in the figure, segment **E1EDK03** occurs five times. To the right of the segment name, you can see the contents of the **IDDAT** field, which exactly identifies the individual instances.

It is now necessary to query the contents of the **IDDAT** element and to decide whether or not the target element should be filled with data, depending on the respective contents. You can do that using the graphical function, **IfWithoutElse**, in the area of **Boolean** functions. You can select the functional area below the work area. The individual

Header data mapping for several identical IDoc segments

functions are then displayed to the right of the work area. Compare the contents of **IDDAT** with a corresponding constant whose contents you can also obtain from Table 5.6. If the two values are identical, the target element is assigned the value of the **DATUM** field.

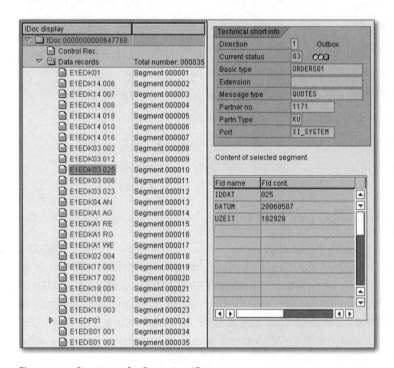

Figure 5.20 Structure of a Quotation IDoc

Since you want to compare two string variables with each other, use the equals function from the Text area. In the mapping's test area, fill in the corresponding segments with sample data, but don't run the test yet. Make sure you enter several items and that segments that can occur several times do actually occur several times. If necessary, you can use the IDoc you just sent from System A. In the message monitoring module of the XI system, copy the exact XML structure. This is necessary so data will appear in the queue display.

Next, use the menu bar to display the queues of the `if` function. From the mapping you worked on in the first step, you may remember that each gray-colored field represents a context change, which corresponds to a new instance of an element. This means that four instances of the target element would be created according to the output queue of the `if` function. However, because the target element is only set to 1, this causes an error. You must remove all unnecessary context changes.

The **removeContexts** function (in the **Node Functions** area) removes all contexts of a queue except for the start and end contexts. Insert this function between the `if` function and the target element and view your queue again. You should now see that there's only one source element instead of the four you had previously seen (see Figure 5.21). Complete the mapping for the remaining header data according to this procedure. Note, however, that the **COLLECTIVE-NUMBER** target element represents another exception.

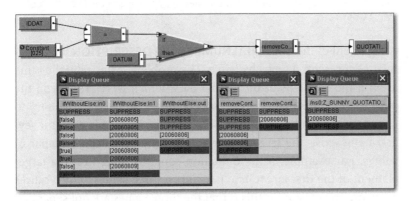

Figure 5.21 Header Data Mapping for Several Identical IDoc Segments

With the exception of two elements (**MATERIALNUMBER** and **DESCRIPTION**), continue by mapping item elements according to the details shown in Table 5.7.

Mapping the item elements

Segment of QUOTES.ORDERS01	Data element of QUOTES.ORDERS01	Data element of Z_SUNNY_ QUOTATIONOutput
None (IDoc)	E1EDP01	Item
E1EDP01	POSEX	ITEM
E1EDP01	MENGE	QUANTITY
E1EDP01	NTGEW	NETWEIGHT
E1EDP01	GEWEI	WEIGHTUNIT
E1EDP01	CURCY	CURRENCY

Table 5.7 Assigning the Item Data in the Message Mapping of the First Block of Step 2

Segment of QUOTES.ORDERS01	Data element of QUOTES.ORDERS01	Data element of Z_SUNNY_QUOTATIONOutput
E1EDP01	MATKL	MATERIALGROUP
E1EDP01	BRGEW	GROSSWEIGHT
E1EDP01/E1EDP05	BETRG	AMOUNT
E1EDP01/E1EDP20	EDATU	DELIVERYDATE
E1EDP01/E1EDP19	QUALF (002) IDTNR	MATERIALNUMBER
E1EDP01/E1EDP19	QUALF (002) KTEXT	DESCRIPTION

Table 5.7 Assigning the Item Data in the Message Mapping of the First Block of Step 2 (cont.)

Distributing values to different items

Assignment of the **MATERIALNUMBER** and **DESCRIPTION** target elements represents a new challenge. The problem is basically the same as with the elements of the header data, which were created on the basis of segments that occurred several times. However, if you try to use the same solution, you will see in the queue displays that if several items exist, the target element is assigned the same number of values. For example, if the quotation contains three items, a target element of the first target item is assigned three values, which causes an error. The reason for this is that the three values are not separated by contexts.

You solved a similar problem in Step 1 of the case study by using the **SplitByValue** graphical function from the **Node functions** area. This function inserts a context change after each value, thus distributing the three values to three different items.

The mapping process first compares the contents of queue **QUALF** with the constant until the defined value is found. The corresponding value of the queue **IDTNR** is copied. The resulting queue contains as many entries as materials have been transferred, but it still contains too many context changes. To correct the number of context changes, you must first remove all contexts. In a separate step, a new context change is inserted for each value that is obtained. Implement the solution shown in Figure 5.22 for the two target elements, **MATERIALNUMBER** and **DESCRIPTION**.

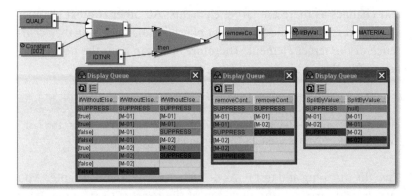

Figure 5.22 Item Data Mapping for Several Identical IDoc Segments

Let's look at another option as an alternative to the previous solution. This alternative involves checking the context view while mapping the **MATERIALNUMBER** target element.

Other mapping options

The context changes of the two source elements, **QUALF** and **IDTNR**, are defined by the total number of segments **E1EDP01/E1EDP19** (i.e., these segments are viewed as the same segment type). However, you can change this level by selecting the menu of the corresponding source element and using the **Context** option to change from **E1DP19** to **E1EDP01**.

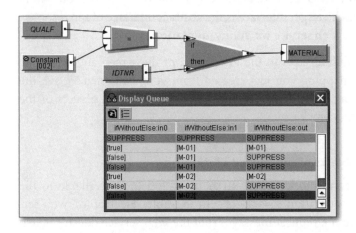

Figure 5.23 Changing the Context View for Source Elements

If you display the queues for these two elements once again, the entries of the queues change because a context change is only carried out after a new **E1EDP19** segment. Thus, there are only as many context changes as there are target elements. All other context changes are suppressed, and they no longer play any role regarding the occurrence of the target element. Therefore, you can omit the node functions after the `if` block (see Figure 5.23).

Note

If a queue contains fewer values than there are target elements, the last value of the queue is used for the remaining target elements.

Testing the message interface	Save the mapping and test it. As described earlier in this chapter, you can already carry out the first step of the process to create an IDoc quotation. You can then view the structure of the XML document in the message monitoring module of the XI system and save it as an XML file for the test. However, make sure that you only save the source code of the display, otherwise the minus signs won't be interpreted. If the test is successful, save the outbound message because it can be used for testing purposes with a second block.
Creating the interface mapping	For the final step of the design phase of the first block, you will create the interface mapping, **IM_QUOTES_ORDERS01_Async_Abstract_ to_MI_ws_sunny_response_Async_Abstract**. For this, you must create a new interface mapping and use the abstract interface of IDoc definition **MI_QUOTES_ORDERS01_Async_Abstract** as the outbound interface. The target interface is the abstract interface of the response message of web service **ws_sunny_quotation**.

Import the interfaces in the lower area of the screen and select the message mapping you just created from your namespace. Save the interface mapping. You have now created all design objects of the first process block.

Design Objects of the Second Block

Overview of the design objects of the second block	In the second block, the SARIDIS quotation (now available in the simplified quotation format) is sent to Sunny Electronics' web service. Since the request message from the web service doesn't match the simplified quotation format, you will need to create a simple message mapping. Since both the request and response messages need to be processed separately with abstract interfaces, you will need two appropriate abstract interfaces.

For the response message, use the abstract interface from the first block. When the web service is called, an abstract synchronous message interface is used to send messages. However, the receiving counterpart outside the business process requires a normal synchronous Inbound interface.

Table 5.8 lists all design objects used for this second block. Note that the confusing names of the two mappings originate from the fact that the simplified quotation format is identical to the response format of the web service. Here, an asterisk (*) means that the mentioned object was created in a previous step.

Type of object	Sender side	Receiver side
Message interface	MI_ws_sunny_request_Async_Abstract	MI_ws_sunny_response_Async_Abstract*
	▸ MI_ws_sunny_quotation_Sync_Abstract ▸ MI_ws_sunny_ quotation _Sync_In	
Message type Data type	Z_SUNNY_QUOTATIONInput*	Z_SUNNY_QUOTATION-Output*
Interface mapping	IM_ws_sunny_response_Async_Abstract_to_ws_sunny_request_Async_Abstract	
Message mapping	MM_Z_SUNNY_QUOTATIONOutput_to_Z_SUNNY_QUOTATIONInput	

Table 5.8 Design Objects for the Second BP Block of Step 2 of the Case Study

First, begin with the interfaces that you will need to process the web service request and response. Create the message interface **MI_ws_sunny_request_Async_Abstract**, which is used for calling the web service. This interface represents the **Z_SUNNY_QUOTATIONInput** message from your namespace. Its category is set to **Abstract** and its mode is **Asynchronous**. Save the interface.

Creating the message interfaces

Since Sunny Electronics' web service is called in synchronous mode, you must create an abstract synchronous interface for the integration process. Moreover, a synchronous Inbound interface is needed for the external counterpart.

Start by creating the abstract interface, **MI_ws_sunny_quotation_Sync_Abstract** (see Figure 5.24). As the name suggests, it is an abstract interface that works in Synchronous mode. Because this interface is used by the integration process, the type of the output message is **Z_SUNNY_QUOTATIONInput**, which is taken from the external definition, **ws_sunny_quotation**. Note, from the web service's point of view, the messages have now been assigned names. The type of the input message is **Z_SUNNY_QUOTATIONOutput**. After entering its settings, save the message interface.

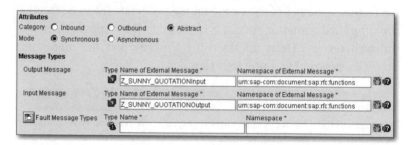

Figure 5.24 Abstract Interface for Synchronous Web Service Call

The category of the **Inbound** interface (**MI_ws_sunny_quotation_ Sync_In** for the synchronous processing of the web service call) is **Inbound** and its mode is **Synchronous**. Because this interface is used by the web service, the message descriptions are now correct. Thus, the input message type is **Z_SUNNY_QUOTATIONInput**, and the output message type is **Z_SUNNY_QUOTATIONOutput**. You can find both messages below the external definition, **ws_sunny_quotation**. Save this message interface.

Next, continue with the message mapping **MM_Z_SUNNY_QUOTA- TIONOutput_to_Z_SUNNY_ANGEBOTInput**, which is used to convert the simplified SARIDIS quotation into a web service request. Use output message **Z_SUNNY_QUOTATIONOutput** of the external definition, **ws_sunny_quotation**, as the outbound message. The target message is **Z_SUNNY_QUOTATIONInput**, which originates from the same external definition. Begin with the header data and assign the source elements, **CUSTOMER**, **VENDOR**, and **COLLECTIVENUMBER** to the corresponding counterparts. As the remaining source header data won't be used any further in this mapping, you can leave them unchanged.

Select the **ITEMS** on both sides and click the **Map Selected Fields and Substructures if Names Are Identical** icon. This automatically maps all fields with each other (see Figure 5.25), and you can save the mapping.

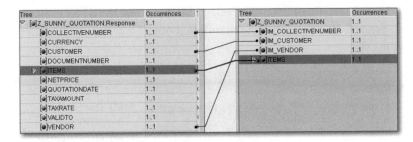

Figure 5.25 Message Mapping in the Second Block of Step 2

Test the mapping using data from the mapping in the first block. If errors occur at this point, you must check the mapping again and, if necessary, also the mapping in the first block.

Now create interface mapping **IM_ws_sunny_response_Async_Abstract_to_ws_sunny_request_Async_Abstract** on the basis of the message mapping. Use **MI_ws_sunny_response_Async_Abstract** from your case study namespace as the outbound interface. The type of the target interface is **MI_ws_sunny_request_Async_Abstract**. Import the two interfaces in the lower part of the screen and assign them the message mapping **MM_Z_SUNNY_QUOTATIONOutput_to_Z_SUNNY_QUOTATIONInput**, created earlier. Save this object. You have now created all design objects for the second block.

Creating the interface mapping

Design Objects of the Third Block

In the third block, convert the multiline container that stores quotations during the integration process into a format that can accommodate several quotations in one message. This is necessary because multiline container objects only exist within an integration process and cannot be dispatched directly.

Overview of design objects

Therefore, you must create a corresponding data and message type that is represented by an abstract interface. Unfortunately, the data type cannot reference the messages of the external definition, which is why you must reproduce the data types of the web service response. In addition, you need a message mapping that is able to transfer the individual quotations into the list. Accordingly, you must use an appropriate interface mapping.

Table 5.9 contains a list of all design objects for the third block. Here, an asterisk (*) means that the mentioned object was created in a previous step.

Type of object	Sender side	Receiver side
Message interface	**MI_ws_sunny_response_Async_Abstract***	▸ **MI_QuotationList_Async_Abstract** ▸ **MI_QuotationList_Async_In**
Message type	**Z_SUNNY_QUOTATIONOutput***	**MT_QuotationList**
Data type		▸ **DT_QuotationList** ▸ **DT_Quotation** ▸ **DT_QuotationItem**
Interface mapping	**IM_ws_sunny_response_Async_Abstract_to_MI_QuotationList_Async_Abstract**	
Message mapping	**MM_Z_SUNNY_QUOTATIONOutput_to_MT_QuotationList**	

Table 5.9 Design Objects for the Third BP Block of Step 2 of the Case Study

Creating the data types

The structure of data type **DT_QuotationItem** corresponds to the **ITEMS** substructure of the web service's response message. Create the data type, as shown in Figure 5.26.

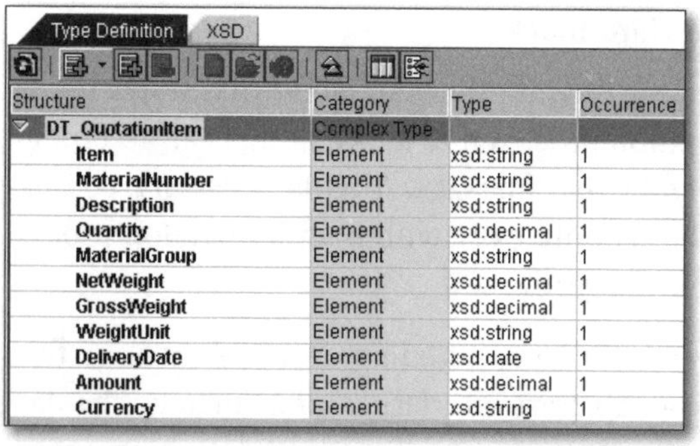

Structure	Category	Type	Occurrence
DT_QuotationItem	Complex Type		
Item	Element	xsd:string	1
MaterialNumber	Element	xsd:string	1
Description	Element	xsd:string	1
Quantity	Element	xsd:decimal	1
MaterialGroup	Element	xsd:string	1
NetWeight	Element	xsd:decimal	1
GrossWeight	Element	xsd:decimal	1
WeightUnit	Element	xsd:string	1
DeliveryDate	Element	xsd:date	1
Amount	Element	xsd:decimal	1
Currency	Element	xsd:string	1

Figure 5.26 Structure of Data Type DT_QuotationItem

Data type **DT_Quotation** contains both header data that occurs only once per quotation and an unlimited number of quotation items. You must create the header data in the new data type. Quotation items can be created by referencing the newly created data type. Figure 5.27 displays the complete structure. You should also note that the **QuotationItem** element can occur an unlimited number of times in the quotation. Save the data type.

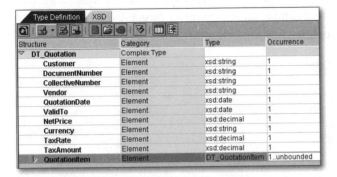

Figure 5.27 Structure of Data Type DT_Quotation

To integrate a quotation list in a message, it is necessary to include the data type **DT_Quotation** an unlimited number of times in the data type **DT_QuotationList**. As such, create the data type **DT_QuotationList** and add to it an element called **Quotation**. This element is of type **DT_Quotation** and has the occurrence **1..unbounded**. When you save this last data type, creation of the quotation list is complete.

Creating the elements on the receiver side

Now integrate the data type **DT_QuotationList** into the new message type **MT_QuotationList** and save the new message type. Next, create a new message interface, called **MI_QuotationList_Async_Abstract**. This interface belongs to category **Abstract** and to the **Asynchronous** mode. Use data type **MT_QuotationList** as a message and save the interface. In addition, you must create the message interface **MI_QuotationList_Async_In** for the receiving system B. This message interface also uses the **MT_QuotationList** message type. It belongs to the Inbound category and uses Asynchronous mode to receive messages.

You have now created all objects for the receiver side of this block. Since the objects of the sender side are reused from previous blocks, you can continue with the mappings.

First, create the message mapping, **MM_Z_SUNNY_QUOTATIONOutput_to_MT_QuotationList**. The outbound message type is **Z_SUNNY_QUOTATIONOutput**, which corresponds to the simplified quotation format. The target message is message type **MT_QuotationList**, which you have just created.

Creating the mapping objects

Before you begin the actual mapping process, go to the **Messages** tab and set the occurrence value for the outbound message to **0..unbounded** (see Figure 5.28). This way you can make sure that several messages can be converted into a target message in the integration process.

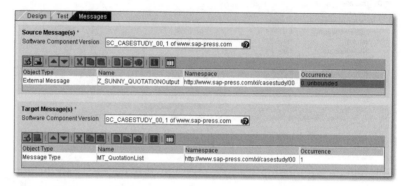

Figure 5.28 Setting the Occurrence of the Outbound Message

The mapping process itself is not difficult at all, especially because you only need to assign elements with identical names to each other. Note that the Quotation target element represents an exception in this case, as it must be assigned the root element, **Z_SUNNY_QUOTATION.Response**, from the source message to convert every message into a quotation in the quotation list. The target element, **QuotationItem**, is assigned the source element, **item**, from the **ITEMS** substructure.

Because the element names are case sensitive, you cannot use the automatic assignment function here. Figure 5.29 provides a complete overview of the message mapping. Save the message mapping and test it with the result of the message mapping from the first block.

Tree	Occurrences		Tree	Occurrences
▽ [●]Messages	1..1		▽ [●]Messages	1..1
▽ [●]Message1	1..1		▽ [●]Message1	1..1
▽ [◁]Z_SUNNY_QUOTATION.Response	0..unbounded ■		▽ [●]MT_QuotationList	1..1
[●]COLLECTIVENUMBER	1..1	●	◁[●]Quotation	1..unbounded
[●]CURRENCY	1..1	●	●[●]Customer	1..1
[●]CUSTOMER	1..1	●	●[●]DocumentNumber	1..1
[●]DOCUMENTNUMBER	1..1	●	●[●]CollectiveNumber	1..1
▷ [●]ITEMS	1..1	●	●[●]Vendor	1..1
[●]NETPRICE	1..1	●	●[●]QuotationDate	1..1
[●]QUOTATIONDATE	1..1	●	●[●]ValidTo	1..1
[●]TAXAMOUNT	1..1	●	●[●]NetPrice	1..1
[●]TAXRATE	1..1	●	●[●]Currency	1..1
[●]VALIDTO	1..1	●	●[●]TaxRate	1..1
[●]VENDOR	1..1	●	●[●]TaxAmount	1..1
			▷ ●[●]QuotationItem	1..unbounded

Figure 5.29 Message Mapping in the Third Block of Step 2

The final step in this block consists of creating the interface mapping, **IM_ws_sunny_response_Async_Abstract_to_MI_QuotationList_Async_ Abstract**. In this step, you must link the outbound message **MI_ws_ sunny_response_Async_Abstract** from the external definition **ws_ sunny_quotation** with target interface **MI_QuotationList_Async_ Abstract**. Make sure that the occurrence of the outbound interface is set to **0..unbounded** (see Figure 5.30). This setting must be made in both the message and interface mapping for it to take effect. Import the two interfaces and select the message mapping you just created using the input help. Save and test the interface mapping.

Creating the inter-face mapping

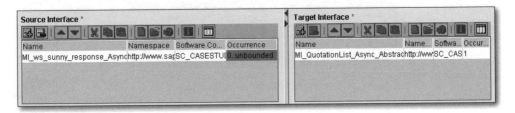

Figure 5.30 Setting the Occurrence of the Outbound Interface

Integrating all Design Objects in the BP Structure

You have now created all design objects required to implement inte-gration process **IP_Quotation_##**. Table 5.10 lists all abstract inter-faces that you have already created during the course of this step, which you'll now put to use. Here, an asterisk (*) indicates that the object was created in a previous step.

Overview of container elements used

	Abstract Message Interfaces
First Block	► MI_QUOTES_ORDERS01_Async_Abstract ► MI_ws_sunny_response_Async_Abstract
Second Block	► MI_ws_sunny_request_Async_Abstract ► MI_ws_sunny_response_Async_Abstract* ► MI_ws_sunny_quotation_Sync_Abstract ► MI_ws_sunny_aquotation_Sync_In
Third Block	► MI_ws_sunny_response_Async_Abstract* ► MI_QuotationList_Async_Abstract

Table 5.10 Abstract Interfaces in Step 2 of the Case Study

Open the integration process and detach the window so your work area is as big as possible. First, go to the container area and create the necessary containers. The container elements are based on abstract interfaces and are used to reference messages that occur in the integration process. Figure 5.31 provides an overview of all elements used. When creating the elements, make sure that they all refer to the Process container so they are usable throughout the entire integration process. The **QuotationContainer** is a multiline element and must be marked as such when created.

Name	Category	Type	Multiline	Container
QuotationContainer	Abstract Interface	MI_ws_sunny_response_Async_Abstract	☑	Process
QuotationList	Abstract Interface	MI_QuotationList_Async_Abstract	☐	Process
SARIDIS_IDoc	Abstract Interface	MI_QUOTES_ORDERS01_Async_Abstract	☐	Process
SARIDIS_Quotation	Abstract Interface	MI_ws_sunny_response_Async_Abstract	☐	Process
Sunny_Request	Abstract Interface	MI_ws_sunny_request_Async_Abstract	☐	Process
Sunny_Response	Abstract Interface	MI_ws_sunny_response_Async_Abstract	☐	Process

Figure 5.31 Overview of Container Elements Used

Assigning the container elements to the process

First you must use the **SARIDIS_IDoc** element to reference the IDoc received by the first block. This IDoc is then converted into the simplified quotation format and used as **SARIDIS_Quotation** from that point forward. This message type is included in the multiline **QuotationContainer**, while the message itself is converted into the **Sunny_Request** format. Based on the incoming IDoc data the **Sunny_Request** format is used to call the web service of Sunny Electronics. The response of the **Sunny_Response** web service is also transferred into the quotation container once the web service has been called. Finally, the quotation container is transferred to the **QuotationList Format** and dispatched.

Settings used in the first block

Navigate to the first block and click **Receive IDoc**. The system displays the settings of this step on the right side of the window. In the list of settings, you can see a question mark next to the Message field, which indicates that information is missing at this point. Open the input help and select the **SARIDIS_IDoc** container element. At this point, you must also make sure that the **Start Process** option is checked, otherwise no starting point will be defined.

Click on the next step, **Transform IDoc**. The IDoc format is now converted into the simplified quotation format. For this, you must select the interface mapping **IM_QUOTES_ORDERS01_Async_Abstract_to_ MI_ws_sunny_response_Async_Abstract** and specify the **SARIDIS_**

IDoc container element as the source element. The target message is **SARIDIS_Quotation**.

Once you have selected the two messages, the red rectangles around the input fields should disappear. If they don't, an error exists. Click the next step, **Append SARIDIS Quotation**. Select the **QuotationContainer** as the target which is assigned the content of interface variable **SARIDIS_Quotation** with the **Append** operation (see Figure 5.32).

Properties	
Name	**Value**
Step Name	Append SARIDIS Quotation
Target	QuotationContainer
Operation	Append
Expression	SARIDIS_Quotation

Figure 5.32 Properties of the Process Step for Appending the SARIDIS Quotation

Navigate forward to the **Web Service Call** block and click on the first step, **Create WS Request**. The conversion of the SARIDIS quotation into the web service request is carried out using interface mapping **IM_ws_sunny_response_Async_Abstract_to_ws_sunny_request_Async_Abstract**. The source message is **SARIDIS_Quotation**, while the target message is **Sunny_Request**.

Settings used in the second block

Continue with the **Call Web Service** step. It should already have been stored in the settings that this is a synchronous sending call. Specify the synchronous, abstract interface, **MI_ws_sunny_quotation_Sync_Abstract**. The request message is **Sunny_Request**, while the response is stored in **Sunny_Response**. Finally this message is appended with the SARIDIS quotation to the Quotation Container list in the **Append Sunny Quotation** step of this block.

The **Transform Quotation list** step at the beginning of the third block converts the **QuotationContainer** into the **QuotationList** message. For this purpose, interface mapping **IM_ws_sunny_response_Async_Abstract_to_MI_QuotationList_Async_Abstract** is used (see Figure 5.33).

Settings used in the third block

The final step of the integration process consists of dispatching the **QuotationList** message that contains both quotations.

Save and check the process. Make sure that no red error messages are displayed. You can ignore the notification that the **Sunny_Response** container element has been initialized but isn't used. Finally, activate all design objects of this step.

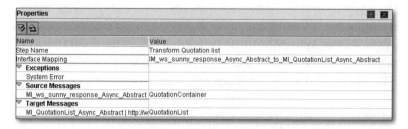

Name	Value
Step Name	Transform Quotation list
Interface Mapping	IM_ws_sunny_response_Async_Abstract_to_MI_QuotationList_Async_Abstract
▽ Exceptions	
System Error	
▽ Source Messages	
MI_ws_sunny_response_Async_Abstract	QuotationContainer
▽ Target Messages	
MI_QuotationList_Async_Abstract	http://w	QuotationList

Figure 5.33 Properties of the Process Step for Converting Quotation Container

5.2.3 Configuration

Overview of the preparatory steps

Before you can use the configuration objects for the integration scenario, you need some new objects. To transfer the integration process from the integration repository into the integration directory so that the process can act as a sender or receiver, you need several communication channels. You must first send an IDoc from System A. The integration process itself also communicates with a web service in synchronous mode. Finally, Hitech AG's quotation list is delivered with a file adapter.

Preparing the Configuration

Declaring the integration process

Let's begin with the integration process. In the integration directory, create a new integration process in case study scenario **XI_Case-study_##**. A wizard opens telling you that you can copy integration processes from the integration repository. Continue with the next step and select the **IP_Quotation_##** process from the list. Proceed to the next screen and enter the same name again. This way, you ensure that the name of the integration process is **IP_Quotation_##**, both in the repository and in the directory.

Creation of the IDoc sender channel by the instructor

Due to its nature, the instructor should create the IDoc sender channel of System A. Creation of IDoc sender channels is rather unusual because they aren't needed for the technical process. However, the existence of such a channel allows you to use the configuration wizard.

Create the entry, **IDoc_SenderChannel**, under the **Communication Channel** directory of business system A. Select adapter type **IDoc** and the **Sender** direction (see Figure 5.34). You will see that these are the only settings you can make. Save the channel. Students should copy this channel from the **Objects** tab into their scenario.

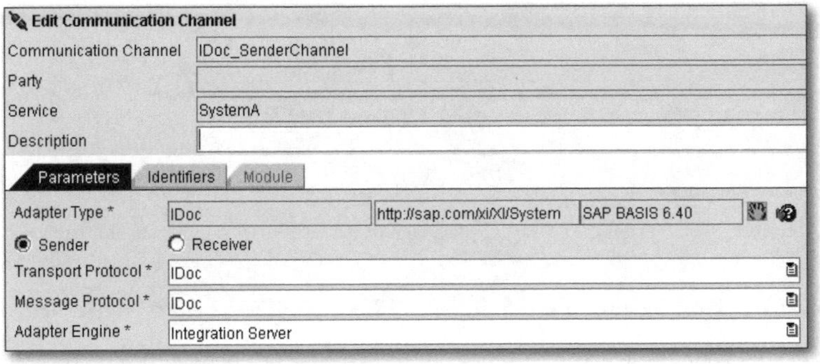

Figure 5.34 Creating the IDoc Sender Channel for System A

You will need a SOAP receiver channel to call Sunny Electronics' web service. Since all students will use the same web service, it doesn't matter (from a technical viewpoint) if you create the communication channel only once or several times. However, Sunny Electronics' web service will be used as a basis for you to deal with business services. For this reason, each student should carry out the following step.

Creating a business service and a SOAP receiver channel

Create a new business service called **Sunny_Quotation_##** in your scenario. Select the **Receiver** tab in the detail window of the new service. There you can specify all interfaces known by the new service. At the moment this is only one single interface, namely **MI_ws_sunny_quotation_Sync_In**, which you have created in the design phase of the web service call. Select this interface (see Figure 5.35) and save the business service.

Creating a business service

Navigate to the newly created business service and expand the respective directory. You will see that the business service can contain its own communication channels. At this point you must create communication channel **SOAP_Receiver_Quotation_##**, including adapter type **SOAP** and direction **Receiver**. Set HTTP as the transport protocol and leave all other values unchanged (see Figure 5.36). The **Target URL** of the web service is *http://<host SystemB>:80XX/sap/bc/soap/rfc/sap/Z_SUNNY_QUOTATION?sap-client=<Client>*. Click the **Configure User Authentication** option and enter your user **SYS_B-##** and the password.

Creating the SOAP communication channel

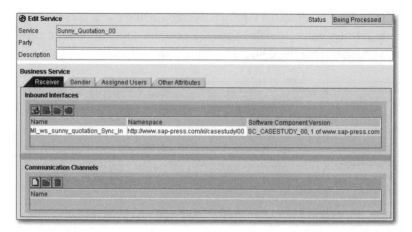

Figure 5.35 Editing a Business Service

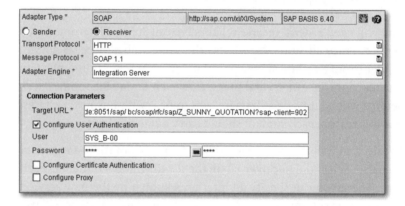

Figure 5.36 Setting the SOAP Receiver Channel for the Business Service

Using the file communication channel

For the third communication channel, which writes the quotation list into a file at the end of the process, you can use the **File_Receiver-Channel_##** channel from the first exercise in Chapter 4. If you haven't created that channel yet, or if you want to change the file name, create a new channel according to the description in Section 4.1.

Three-way division of the configuration

As in the design phase, the configuration phase is also divided into three parts. Whereas the division of the design phase was based on logical aspects, the configuration phase must be subdivided for technical reasons. Strictly speaking, this step of the case study contains three configuration scenarios:

- The IDoc is delivered to the integration process.
- Sunny Electronics' the web service is called, which also requires a separate configuration.
- The quotation list is dispatched to System B.

Transferring the IDoc to the Integration Process

All three steps are carried out using the configuration wizard because the number of new objects is rather large. Table 5.11 lists the configuration objects used in this scenario.

Configuration objects of the first block

Type of object	Sender side: System A	Receiver side: IP_Quotation_##
Communication channel 1	IDoc_SenderChannel	
Sender agreement	| SystemA | QUOTES. ORDERS01 | * | *	
Receiver determination	| SystemA | QUOTES.ORDERS01	
Interface determination	| SystemA | QUOTES.ORDERS01 | | IP_Quotation_##	

Table 5.11 Configuration Objects for the First Block of Step 2 of the Case Study

Start the wizard from the menu or by clicking on its icon. Because the two business systems A and B are regarded as internal systems, the current scenario can be referred to as an internal communication. Define **Business System A** as the sender with adapter type **IDoc**. The interface used here is **QUOTES.ORDERS01**.

The receiver is integration process **IP_Quotation_##**, while the **Adapter type** should be left as **XI**. The input help for the interface contains only the value **MI_QUOTES_ORDERS01_Async_Abstract**. This is because the value corresponds to the interface used to provide the initial reception step with the data (see Figure 5.37).

The sender agreement **| SystemA | QUOTES.ORDERS01 | * | *** uses communication channel **IDoc_SenderChannel**. The receiver determination **| SystemA | QUOTES.ORDERS01** is created for the first participant, while all other participants can only extend it. You shouldn't worry too much about the notification message regarding the receiver agreement as you will manually edit the receiver determination at a later stage anyway.

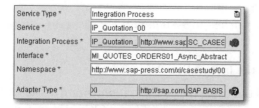

Figure 5.37 Settings for the Receiver when Using the Process

In contrast to the usual procedure, the interface determination | **SystemA | QUOTES.ORDERS01 | | IP_Quotation_##** doesn't display an interface mapping (see Figure 5.38). This is because no interface mapping is needed. Both the sending and the receiving interface use the same structure, namely IDoc type **QUOTES.ORDERS01**.

Figure 5.38 Interface Determination for Delivery to the Integration Process

A receiver agreement isn't needed because adapter type XI has been selected as the receiver. Add the newly created configuration objects to your scenario and complete the wizard. Activate the newly created objects in the change list.

Adjusting the receiver determination

At this point, if you used the IDoc from system A the IDoc would be sent to all integration processes. To avoid that and to make sure that each IDoc is sent to only one process, you must manually adjust the receiver determination, **SystemA | REQUOTE.ORDERS01**. However, the lock mechanism of SAP XI ensures that not all course participants can process this object at the same time; you should therefore coordinate the different access times.

Editing the conditions

Figure 5.39 shows that only one receiver has been configured so far. To link the delivery with a specific connection, specify a corresponding expression in the first column of the receivers list. The goal is to define a receiver that matches the contents of the collective number entry.

You already entered the **SUBMI_##** entry in the corresponding field during the creation of the inquiry in the previous step. Accordingly, the receiver must be selected on the basis of the collective number.

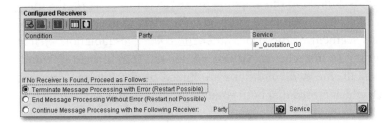

Figure 5.39 Post-Editing the Receiver Determination

Click in the **Condition** column to open the input help. This opens a window in which you can create conditions. Next, open the input help in the Left Operand column. This opens the Expression Editor (see Figure 5.40). The **XPath** option allows you to select a field from the structure of the inbound IDoc. Select the field, **/ORDERS01/ IDOC/E1EDK02/QUALF**, and copy the value.

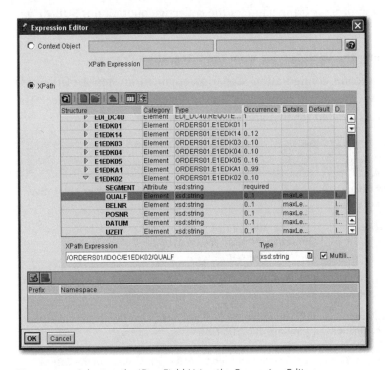

Figure 5.40 Selecting the IDoc Field Using the Expression Editor

Insert a new row in the condition overview and repeat the selection of an IDoc field by selecting **/ORDERS01/IDOC/E1EDK02/BELNR**.

Once both fields are transferred, assign concrete values to the right operands. Similar to the mapping in the first process block, the qualifier must also contain the value **007** if it refers to the collective quotations segment of the IDoc. Enter the collective quotation's name according to the schema, **SUBMI_##**, for the second right operand. By default, the two conditions are linked by the Boolean operator AND, which means that both conditions must be met for it to be true (see Figure 5.41).

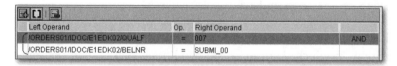

Left Operand	Op.	Right Operand	
/ORDERS01/IDOC/E1EDK02/QUALF	=	007	AND
/ORDERS01/IDOC/E1EDK02/BELNR	=	SUBMI_00	

Figure 5.41 Condition Overview in the Receiver Determination

Save the modified receiver determination which, in the future, will only forward IDocs of the **REQUOTE.ORDERS01** type to your integration process if the name of the collective quotation is **SUBMI_##**.

Calling the Web Service from the Integration Process

Configuration objects of the second block

The second configuration scenario contained in Step 2 of the case study consists of calling the Sunny Electronics' web service. The objects needed for that are listed in Table 5.12.

Type of object	Sender side: IP_Quotation_##	Receiver side: Sunny_Quotation_##
Communica- tion channel		SOAP_Receiver_Quotation_ ##
Receiver agreement	| IP_Quotation_## | | Sunny_ Quotation_## | MI_ws_sunny_ quotation_Sync_In	
Receiver determination	| IP_Quotation_## | MI_ws_sunny_Auotation_Sync_Abstract	
Interface determination	| IP_Quotation_## | MI_ws_sunny_auotation_Sync_Abstract | | Sunny_Quotation_##	

Table 5.12 Configuration Objects for the Second Block of Step 2 of the Case Study

Call the Configuration Wizard and select the **Internal Communication** option. Define integration process **IP_Quotation_##** with adapter type **XI** as the sender. If you open the input of the interface, it displays two values because the process can be sent to two different places. The web service call can be synchronous or it can be an asynchronous dispatch of the quotation list. To run the Wizard, select the interface **MI_ws_sunny_quotation_Sync_Abstract** (see Figure 5.42).

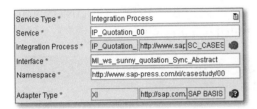

Figure 5.42 Sender Settings in the Configuration Wizard of the Web Service Call

The receiver of the web service call is business service **Sunny_Quotation_##**, which you created earlier. Communication with this service runs through the SOAP adapter. Select **MI_ws_sunny_quotation_Sync_In**, which is the only interface you have stored on the side of this business service (see Figure 5.43).

Figure 5.43 Receiver Settings in the Configuration Wizard of the Web Service Call

Due to the XI adapter, you don't need a sender agreement. The next screen displays information about the creation of the new receiver determination, **| IP_Quotation_## | MI_ws_sunny_quotation_Sync_ Abstract**. The interface determination, **| IP_Quotation_## | MI_ws_ sunny_quotation_Sync_Abstract | | Sunny_Quotation_##**, does not use any interface mapping because the message types of the sender and receiver are identical, as is the case in the configuration of the IDoc delivery. The receiver agreement, **|IP_Quotation_##||Sunny_ Quotation_##|MI_ws_sunny_quotation_Sync_In**, uses communication channel **SOAP_Receiver_Quotation_##**, which you created during your preparations for the configuration phase. Add the new objects to your scenario and close the wizard.

Sending the Quotation List to System B

Configuration objects of the third block

The last configuration step consists of sending the final quotation list to the file adapter of business system B, which does not involve any special characteristics regarding the configuration. Table 5.13 provides a list of all configuration objects used. Here, an asterisk (*) indicates that the object was created in a previous step.

Type of object	Sender side: IP_Quotation_##	Receiver side: System B
Communication channel		File_ReceiverChannel_##*
Receiver agreement	|IP_Quotation_##||SystemB|MI_QuotationList_Async_In	
Receiver determination	|IP_Quotation_##|MI_QuotationList_Async_Abstract	
Interface determination	|IP_Quotation_##|MI_QuotationList_Async_Abstract||SystemB	

Table 5.13 Configuration Objects for the Third Block of Step 2 of the Case Study

Again, call the Configuration Wizard and select the **Internal Communication** option. The sender is integration process **IP_Quotation_##**, which exchanges data via adapter type **XI**. Select interface **MI_QuotationList_Async_Abstract** for sending purposes. The receiver is **Business System B**, which receives data using a file adapter with interface **MI_QuotationList_Async_In**. Due to the adapter type used, the sender agreement isn't necessary.

The next screen informs you about the creation of the receiver determination, **\|IP_Quotation_##\|MI_QuotationList_Async_Abstract**. Like all configuration scenarios that include integration processes, interface determination **\|IP_Quotation_##\|MI_QuotationList_Async_Abstract\|\|SystemB** doesn't require interface mapping. The receiver determination, **\|IP_Quotation_##\|\|SystemB\|MI_QuotationList_Async_In** reuses communication channel **File_ReceiverChannel_##** from the first technical exercise.

Add the new objects to your scenario and close the wizard. You have now created all configuration objects for Step 2 of the case study. Activate all changes in the **Change Lists** tab.

5.2.4 Process and Monitoring

Now that you have created a large number of design and configuration objects in this step of the case study, it is time to see how the step is processed.

Flow of the Step

The process begins by creating a quotation. In our case, this quotation is based on the inquiry of Hitech AG, but it could also be created without such a prior inquiry.

Creating the quotation

Login to business system A as the user, **SYS_A-##**, and call **Transaction VA21**, which allows you to create quotations. Because you already received an inquiry that contains all relevant data, you will refer to this inquiry in your quotation. To do this, you must specify quotation type **QT** (quotation), and then select **Sales document · Create with Reference** from the menu to select the respective inquiry.

The new window should already display the Inquiry tab. Open the input help of the Inquiry input field. In the search help, navigate to the **Sales document by customer** tab and enter the document number of Hitech AG in the **Purchase order number** field according to the schema, **Inquiry-##**. This allows you to find the inquiry; select it by double-clicking on the name.

Confirm the inquiry number. This opens the item overview of the quotation. Please note that both the **Sold-to party** and the **Ship-to party** are represented by customer **1171** (Hitech AG). Enter a date within a week in the **Valid to** field of the **Item overview** tab. The prices for the requested items are determined and displayed automatically (see Figure 5.44).

To ensure that the quotation is automatically sent as an IDoc when saved, you must make two more settings: Select **Extras · Output · Header · Edit** from the menu and choose the line that shows partner 1171 (Hitech AG) from the list of messages. Next, change the medium to **6 EDI** so the quotation is sent as an electronic document using the partner agreement (see Figure 5.45).

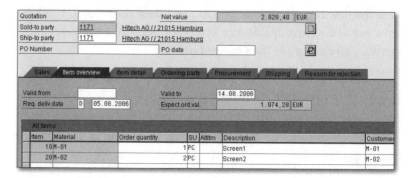

Figure 5.44 Display of the Quotation Items

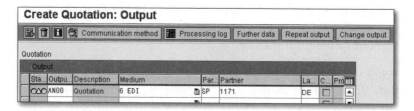

Figure 5.45 Selecting the Message Medium

Highlight the selected line and then select **Edit • Further data** from the menu, and then click the **Further data** button. Select the dispatch time **Send immediately (when saving the application)** in the **Requested Processing** section (see Figure 5.46). This ensures that no messages are collected prior to being sent.

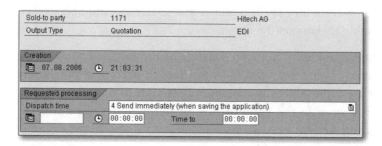

Figure 5.46 Setting Further Data for the Message Control

Now return to the item overview and save the quotation. When you save the quotation, a message is automatically generated and dispatched as an IDoc.

If no inquiry exists, you can also create a quotation without any reference. To do this, select quotation type **QT** (quotation) in the initial screen of **Transaction VA21**, as well as sales organization **1000**, distribution channel **10**, and division **00**. Confirm your entries by pressing **Enter**. Next, select customer **1171** as both the sold-to-party and ship-to-party.

After that, select **Goto · Header · Purchase order data** from the menu and maintain the collective request for quotation with an entry according to the schema, **SUBMI_##**. Return to the item overview and enter the relevant materials and their respective quantities according to the schema **M-##**. From this point forward, all subsequent steps are identical to the steps in the inquiry-based quotation process.

Creation without inquiry

Monitoring the Process

As a result of this scenario, you should obtain a file that contains both the quotation from SARIDIS and that from Sunny Electronics. You can check this via **Transaction AL11** in SAP XI or by using the file tool, which you can download from the web site for this book. In addition, you can use the message monitoring function in SAP XI to see if the data is being processed correctly.

Tracking the message path

In the present case, you should see two messages: one that contains the message that was sent with the IDoc to the integration process, and the message containing the quotation list sent from the integration process. Due to its synchronous nature, you won't be able to find the web service call in the message monitoring.

If no message is displayed in the message monitoring module, you can call **Transaction BD87** in System A to see whether the IDoc was created at all. If the IDoc wasn't created, the reason can often be found in the partner agreement containing errors, or in the fact that the two settings are not made when the quotation is created. If the IDoc contains an error, it is probably caused by the use of incorrect logon data in RFC destination **XI_System** or in the transactional RFC port.

If a notification is displayed in the message monitoring, it means that the business process has not been completely processed. In that case, you can call **Transaction SXMB_MONI** in SAP XI and search for the **PE** (process engine) entry in the first message. When you find the entry, click on it. **Transaction SXMB_MONI_BPE** provides generic

Monitoring the business process

access to this display. In any case, you will navigate to the display of the individual process steps and their status (see Figure 5.47).

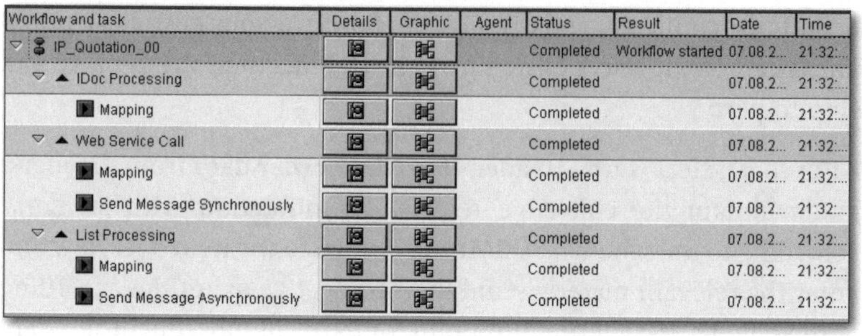

Workflow and task	Details	Graphic	Agent	Status	Result	Date	Time
▽ 👤 IP_Quotation_00	🖻	🖳		Completed	Workflow started	07.08.2...	21:32:...
▽ ▲ IDoc Processing	🖻	🖳		Completed		07.08.2...	21:32:
▶ Mapping	🖻	🖳		Completed		07.08.2...	21:32:...
▽ ▲ Web Service Call	🖻	🖳		Completed		07.08.2...	21:32:...
▶ Mapping	🖻	🖳		Completed		07.08.2...	21:32:...
▶ Send Message Synchronously	🖻	🖳		Completed		07.08.2...	21:32:...
▽ ▲ List Processing	🖻	🖳		Completed		07.08.2...	21:32:...
▶ Mapping	🖻	🖳		Completed		07.08.2...	21:32:...
▶ Send Message Asynchronously	🖻	🖳		Completed		07.08.2...	21:32:...

Figure 5.47 Workflow Log for Step 2 of the Case Study

You can see the sequence of steps arranged by the different blocks and you can obtain a graphical display of the same information by clicking on a button in the Graphic column. The graphical display allows you to easily identify the cause of the error. If you double-click on a workflow item, the system displays the corresponding detail view. There you can view the log files for the individual operations by selecting **Work item • Object • Display** from the menu.

5.3 Entering a Sales Order

Flow of the Step

Because of the unbeatable prices offered by SARIDIS, Hitech AG decided to choose SARIDIS as their supplier. The third step of the case study consists of submitting a purchase order for different types of monitors from Hitech AG to SARIDIS. The purchase order is submitted as an IDoc for which we'll use the basic type **ORDERS01**, which you have already come across in the first two steps of the case study.

The special characteristic of this scenario is that it requires the creation of a Java standalone proxy, used for sending the data after it has been called by a program in SAP NetWeaver Developer Studio. Thus, you need SAP NetWeaver Developer Studio on your system to be able to implement this scenario.

Another challenge is that the Java standalone proxy can only communicate in synchronous mode. This means we'll have to transform the synchronous interface into an asynchronous one. To do this, we'll use the *sync-async-bridge*.

In the previous step, you did the exact opposite: You used an *asnyc-sync-bridge* to create a synchronous web service call from an asynchronous message. However, the problem of a *sync-async-bridge* is that the connection must be kept active until the asynchronous message has been sent. Business process management contains a predefined option to implement such a solution.

Figure 5.48 illustrates the flow of this step.

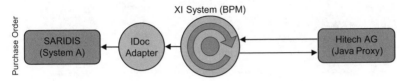

Figure 5.48 The Flow of Step 3

5.3.1 Basic Principles

The preparation for this step mainly consists of extending the partner agreement in System A, which allows you to automatically process incoming purchase orders. This extension can be carried out only once.

Configuring the partner agreement

To do this, login to System A and call **Transaction WE20** to edit the partner agreements. In the **Partner Type LS** directory, select the entry with the logical System name of System B, which you created in Step 1. Next, specify that incoming IDocs of the **ORDERS** (purchase order/order) type are automatically processed according to a specific pattern. For this, click the **Create inbound parameter** icon in the **Inbound parameters** section and set value for the message type to **ORDERS**.

Below the **Inbound options** tab, select the predefined process code, **ORDE** (see Figure 5.49). This process code ensures that the inbound IDoc is processed automatically in such a way that it generates an order. We want it to be processed immediately by the function module. Save these settings and finish this transaction.

> **Note**
>
> The IDoc type, **ORDERS**, is used for both purchase and sales orders. The determination of a concrete IDoc is based on a specific identifier in **E1EDK01**.

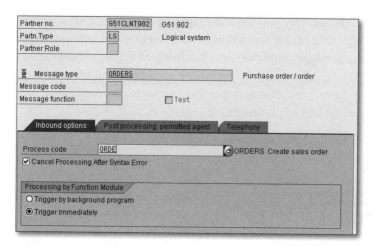

Figure 5.49 Maintaining Inbound Options for the ORDERS IDoc

5.3.2 Design

Subdividing the
design phase

Because the *sync-async-bridge* is used as an integration process, you'll need to create two separate design scenarios and the integration process. We'll work through these two tasks separately. As the integration process is not too complex, we can first go through it mentally:

The process begins with the reception of the synchronous message, which indicates the starting point for the *sync-async-bridge*. As long as this bridge is active, the connection to the sending Java proxy is also kept active. The next step in this process consists of transforming the inbound message into an order IDoc. The IDoc is then delivered in a later step. Once the asynchronous communication has been completed, the synchronous communication can be terminated as well. For this, we'll generate an appropriate response message for the incoming purchase order. In our example, the response message is kept rather simple as we'll merely return a return code and a message to confirm that the received purchase order has been successfully forwarded. Since the response message can appear "out of nowhere," it is generated in a mapping from the incoming purchase order. The concluding dispatch of the response message to the synchronous call terminates the *sync-async-bridge*.

Design Elements Used for Synchronous Processing

During the design phase of this substep, you will create separate data and message types to be used on the sender side for creating the purchase order and the response. Because the structure and the majority of the order elements correspond to those used in the previous steps of the case study, you can create these elements by copying most of the existing objects. The proxies will occur as part of System B. The message interfaces of the Java proxy contain the participant number, which allows the sending proxy to be clearly identified at a later stage. This is the only way you can assign an inbound message to the appropriate integration process. Alternatively, you could create separate business services.

Overview of the design objects

Table 5.14 provides an overview of all design objects.

Type of object	Sender side	Receiver side
Message interface	MI_SalesOrder_Sync_Out_##	▸ MI_SalesOrder_Sync_Abstract ▸ MI_SalesOrder_Async_Abstract ▸ MI_Response_Async_Abstract
Message type	▸ MT_SalesOrder ▸ MT_Response	
Data type	▸ DT_SalesOrder ▸ DT_SalesOrderItem ▸ DT_Response	
Interface mapping	IM_MI_SalesOrder_Async_Abstract_to_MI_Response_Async_Abstract	
Message mapping	MM_MT_SalesOrder_to_MT_Response	

Table 5.14 Design Objects for Asynchronous Processing in Step 3 of the Case Study

To facilitate the work a little, you can copy most of the data types of the inquiry scenario and use them for the order. To do this, go to the namespace of the case study in your software component version and select the data type, **DT_InquiryItem**. Open the context menu of this object and select the **Copy Object** option; this allows you to create the new **DT_SalesOrderItem** object. You can leave all elements

Design elements of the order

unchanged. Repeat this operation to create **DT_SalesOrder** on the basis of **DT_Inquiry**.

Next, open the new data type for editing, rename the **InquiryItem** element to **SalesOrderItem**, and assign it the type **DT_SalesOrder-Item**. Your new data type should now be structured, as shown in Figure 5.50.

Now create message type **MT_SalesOrder** on the basis of data type **DT_SalesOrder**.

Structure	Category	Type	Occurrence
▽ MT_SalesOrder	Element	DT_SalesOrder	
Customer	Element	xsd:string	1
DocumentNumbe	Element	xsd:string	1
CreationDate	Element	xsd:date	1
CreationTime	Element	xsd:time	1
CollectiveNumbe	Element	xsd:string	1
Vendor	Element	xsd:string	1
ValidTo	Element	xsd:date	1
▽ SalesOrderItem	Element	DT_SalesOrderItem	1..unbounded
ItemNumber	Element	xsd:string	1
MaterialNumb	Element	xsd:string	1
Description	Element	xsd:string	1
Quantity	Element	xsd:decimal	1
MaterialGroup	Element	xsd:string	1
NetWeight	Element	xsd:decimal	1
GrossWeight	Element	xsd:decimal	1
WeightUnit	Element	xsd:string	1
DeliveryDate	Element	xsd:date	1

Figure 5.50 Structure of Data Type DT_SalesOrder

Design elements of the response

The design elements of the response must be created from scratch. Start with data type **DT_Response** in your namespace. This data type contains the two elements, **Type** and **Message** (see Figure 5.51). The Type element contains a return code which will simply be **OK** in the case of success, while the Message element contains a corresponding success message and the purchase order number. The type of both fields is **xsd:string**. Save the object once you have created the elements.

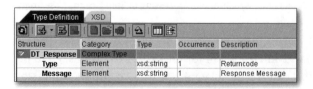

Structure	Category	Type	Occurrence	Description
▽ DT_Response	Complex Type			
Type	Element	xsd:string	1	Returncode
Message	Element	xsd:string	1	Response Message

Figure 5.51 Structure of Data Type DT_Response

Now create message type **MT_Response** on the basis of this data type.

The message interface **MI_SalesOrder_Sync_Out_##** contains both the sending and the receiving message type for the synchronous communication. First, set the **Outbound** category and the **Synchronous** mode. Use **MT_SalesOrder** as the output message and **MT_Response** as input message. You don't need an interface mapping that uses this interface because the abstract interfaces in the integration process use the same message types.

Creating the message interface

The counterpart of this message interface in the integration process is a synchronous interface that is split into two asynchronous, abstract messages upon receipt. Create message interface **MI_SalesOrder_Sync_Abstract** with category **Abstract** and **Synchronous** mode (see Figure 5.52). Use **MT_SalesOrder** as the output message and **MT_Response** as input message. These settings are thus identical to those of the corresponding **Outbound** interface.

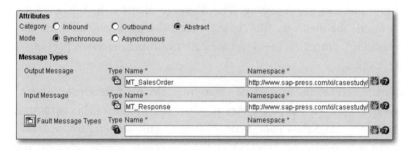

Figure 5.52 Settings for the Synchronous Outbound Message Interface

Before you can process the two messages of the synchronous interface separately within the integration process, you need an abstract interface for each message type. First, the create message interface **MI_SalesOrder_Async_Abstract**, which contains message type **MT_SalesOrder** and belongs to category **Abstract** and the **Asynchronous** mode. The second interface, **MI_Response_Async_Abstract**, uses the **MT_Response** message and its category and mode are also **Abstract** and **Asynchronous**, respectively.

To terminate the *sync-async-bridge* at the end of the integration process, the response message must be generated based on the order. For this, you need a message mapping and an interface mapping between the two abstract interfaces.

Creating the mapping elements

You should at least create the message mapping **MM_MT_SalesOrder_to_MT_Response** and assign it the output message **MT_**

SalesOrder. The type of the target message is **MT_Response**. Assign the source node **MT_SalesOrder** to the **MT_Response** node. The **Type** element must be assigned the **OK** constant.

We want the **Message** element to contain a success message and the purchase order number. You can implement this using constants, the **DocumentNumber** source element, and the **concat** text function, as shown in Figure 5.53.

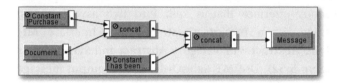

Figure 5.53 Message Mapping for the Response Message

Save and test the mapping. The **Message** element in this example contains the message, "Purchase Order 1234 has been delivered successfully". Note that the purchase order number merely represents a test value.

Next, create the interface mapping **IM_MI_SalesOrder_Async_Abstract_to_MI_Response_Async_Abstract**; this links the outbound interface **MI_SalesOrder_Sync_Abstract** with target interface **MI_Response_Async_Abstract**. Once the objects are selected, import the interfaces in the lower part of the screen and assign it the newly created message mapping. You have now created all design objects you need to map the synchronous communication between the Java proxy and the integration process.

Design Elements Used for Asynchronous Processing

Overview of design objects
In this scenario, the design elements needed for asynchronous processing ensure that the integration process can send the purchase order as an IDoc. The sender side reuses the objects that were also used for synchronous processing. When sending the IDoc, the interface is used as an abstract interface in the integration process. The design objects used are listed in Table 5.15. Here, an asterisk (*) indicates that the object was created in a previous step.

Type of object	Sender side	Receiver side
Message interface	MI_SalesOrder_Async_Abstract*	▸ MI_ORDERS_ ORDERS_Asnyc_ Abstract ▸ ORDER.ORDERS01
Message type	MT_SalesOrder*	ORDER.ORDERS01
Interface mapping	IM_MI_SalesOrder_Async_Abstract_to_MI_ORDERS_ ORDERS_Asnyc_Abstract	
Message mapping	MM_MT_SalesOrder_to_ORDERS_ORDERS01	

Table 5.15 Design Objects for Asynchronous Processing in Step 3 of the Case Study

First, import the **ORDERS.ORDERS01** IDoc in business system A. Create the message interface **MI_ORDERS_ORDERS_Asnyc_Abstract** based on this IDoc. The interface is abstract and is used for asynchronous communication.

The incoming purchase order from Hitech AG must be converted into the order IDoc in this process. For this, you need a message mapping and an interface mapping between the two abstract interfaces.

Mapping the header data

Accordingly, you must map the output message **MT_SalesOrder** to the **ORDERS.ORDERS01** IDoc in message mapping **MM_MT_SalesOrder_ to_ORDERS_ORDERS01**. You can assign the header data elements according to the following mapping table (see Table 5.16). Here, an asterisk (*) indicates that the object was created in a previous step.

Data element of MT_Sales-Order or constants	Data element of ORDERS.ORDERS01	Segment of ORDERS.ORDERS01
Constant: 1	BEGIN	None (IDOC)
Constant: TA (Standard order)	BSART	E1EDK01
DocumentNumber	BELNR	E1EDK01
Vendor	RECIPNT_NO	E1EDK01
Constant: 006 (Division)	QUALF	E1EDK14(1)
Constant: 00	ORGID	E1EDK14(1)
Constant: 007 (Distribution Channel)	QUALF	E1EDK14(2)

Table 5.16 Assigning the Header Data in the Message Mapping of Step 3

Data element of MT_Sales-Order or constants	Data element of ORDERS.ORDERS01	Segment of ORDERS.ORDERS01
Constant: 10	ORGID	E1EDK14(2)
Constant: 008 (Sales Organization)	QUALF	E1EDK14(3)
Constant: 1000	ORGID	E1EDK14(3)
Constant: 004 (Quotation Deadline)	IDDAT	E1EDK03(1)
ValidTo	DATUM *	E1EDK03(1)
Constant: 012 (Creation Date)	IDDAT	E1EDK03(2)
CreationDate	DATUM *	E1EDK03(2)
Constant: AG (Sold-to-party)	PARVW	E1EDKA1
Customer	PARTN	E1EDKA1
Constant: 003 (Original document data)	QUALF	E1EDK02(1)
DocumentNumber	BELNR	E1EDK02(1)
CreationDate	DATUM *	E1EDK02(1)
CreationTime	UZEIT *	E1EDK02(1)
Constant: 007 (Collective Number)	QUALF	E1EDK02(2)
CollectiveNumber	BELNR	E1EDK02(2)

Table 5.16 Assigning the Header Data in the Message Mapping of Step 3 (cont.)

The **ValidTo** and **CollectiveNumber** elements are optional in this case, but they can be used for a better orientation on the customer and supplier side. In addition to the mappings shown in Table 5.16, you must link each segment to be used, including its **SEGMENT** element on the target side, with the **MT_SalesOrder** node on the source side. Deactivate the non-mapped target segment **EDI_DC40** in the menu and duplicate the target segments that are used several times using the menu.

One special characteristic of the data to be transferred through this mapping is the date and time data. The Java program you will create later fills this data using the standard Java date and time format. Date information contains data for the time zone as well as time data in terms of milliseconds. For example, a date could look like this: 2006 - 05 - 16+01:00, whereas the time could be represented in the following way: 10:41:44.796. However, the structure of these formats can cause problems when they are received in an IDoc.

Although you can solve this problem directly in the Java proxy, you can use the **DateTrans** mapping function that's contained in the functional area, **Date**. It concerns the mappings of source elements **CreationDate**, **CreationTime**, and **ValidTo**, which are marked with an asterisk (*) in Table 5.16.

In the work area, move the **DateTrans** function between the source and target elements and double-click on it to set the parameters. First, enter the format of the source date: **yyyy-MM-dd** (see Figure 5.54). Now the question is how we want to map the time zone. However, due to the way this function works, we don't need to map the time zone at all. The **DateTrans** function works in such a way that it fills only the placeholders contained in the source format and ignores everything else. The target format is supposed to be structured according to the schema, **yyyyMMdd**. Moreover, go to the advanced extensions section and ensure that the calendar is lenient.

Figure 5.54 Parameters of Mapping Function DateTrans

Proceed in the same way for source element **CreationDate**, where you should convert the source format (**hh:mm:ss**) into the target format (**hhmmss**).

Item data mapping occurs according to Table 5.17. Note the elements marked with an asterisk (*); this indicates that the object was created in a previous step. To create as many element instances as items exist, you must insert the node function **SplitByValue** between the source and target elements. Because the source element **Delivery-Date** also exists in Java, you must convert this element as described earlier using the **DateTrans** function.

Data element of MT_SalesOrder/Sales-OrderItem or constants	Data element of ORDERS.ORDERS01/ E1EDP01	Segment of ORDERS.ORDERS01/ E1EDP01
SalesOrderItem	E1EDP01	None (IDOC)
SalesOrderItem	SEGMENT *	E1EDP01
ItemNumber	POSEX	E1EDP01
Constant: 001 (Create)	ACTION	E1EDP01
Quantity	MENGE	E1EDP01
Constant: PCE (Unit of quantity: Piece)	MENEE	E1EDP01
NetWeight	NTGEW	E1EDP01
WeightUnit	GEWEI	E1EDP01
MaterialGroup	MATKL	E1EDP01
GrossWeight	BRGEW	E1EDP01
MaterialNumber	MATNR	E1EDP01
SalesOrderItem	E1EDP20 *	E1EDP01
SalesOrderItem	SEGMENT *	E1EDP01/ E1EDP20
Quantity	WMENG	E1EDP01/ E1EDP20
DeliveryDate	EDATU	E1EDP01/ E1EDP20
SalesOrderItem	E1EDP19 *	E1EDP01
SalesOrderItem	SEGMENT *	E1EDP01/E1EDP19
Constant: 001 (Description)	QUALF	E1EDP01/E1EDP19
MaterialNumber	IDTNR	E1EDP01/E1EDP19
Description	KTEXT	E1EDP01/E1EDP19

Table 5.17 Assigning the Item Data in the Message Mapping of Step 1

Test the mapping using at least two different order items by duplicating the node element using the menu in the **Test** tab. When doing this, you should also use the Java date and time formats. Save the mapping if the test is successful.

Based on this message mapping, create the corresponding interface mapping, **IM_MI_SalesOrder_Async_Abstract_to_MI_ORDERS_ORDERS_Asnyc_Abstract**. As the outbound interface, include the type **MI_SalesOrder_Async_Abstract** and use the **MI_ORDERS_ORDERS_Asnyc_Abstract** interface as the target type. Finally, import the interfaces and assign it the message mapping **MM_MT_SalesOrder_to_ORDERS_ORDERS01** you just created.

Creating the Integration Process

You have now created all design objects required for the integration process. Next, create the integration process **IP_SalesOrder_##** and ensure you have enough space on your screen for editing it.

Creating the container elements

First, create the following three container elements (see Figure 5.55):

- **SalesOrder**, belongs to the abstract interface category and uses the **MI_SalesOrder_Async_Abstract** type. Once it has been called by the Java proxy, it will contain the order message in the purchase order.

- **Response**, is also an abstract interface and uses the **MI_Response_Async_Abstract** type.

- **IDoc_SalesOrder**, is also an abstract interface and uses the **MI_ORDERS_ORDERS01_Async_Abstract** type to send the order as a purchase order.

Name	Category	Type	Multili...	Container
SalesOrder	Abstract Interface	MI_SalesOrder_Async_Abstract	☐	Process
Response	Abstract Interface	MI_Response_Async_Abstract	☐	Process
IDoc_SalesOrder	Abstract Interface	MI_QUOTES_ORDERS01_Async_Abstract	☐	Process

Figure 5.55 Container Elements of Step 3 of the Case Study

You may be surprised now that we haven't created a container element of the abstract interface type, **MI_SalesOrder_Sync_Abstract**. The reason is because messages received by the synchronous interface aren't explicitly used within the integration process. However, you will see now why you have created the corresponding message interface.

Insert the first step for receiving the message in the process and call it **Receive ProxyCall**. This step is used to open the *sync-async-bridge*. Correspondingly, you must select the **Opens S/A Bridge** mode from the properties. This allows you to specify the synchronous interface, **MI_SalesOrder_Sync_Abstract**. However, the **Message** field does not expect any container element of a synchronous interface. Instead, it expects the message in which the input part (from the point of view of the process) of the synchronous interface is to be stored. In our case, that's the **SalesOrder** container element.

Figure 5.56 displays the settings for the first step in the integration process.

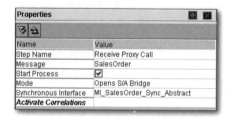

Figure 5.56 Settings for the Synchronous Reception Step

The next steps in the process consist of transforming the order into the IDoc and dispatching the IDoc. For this, you must insert a transformation step, called **Create IDoc**. Assign the source message as **SalesOrder** and the target message as **IDoc_SalesOrder** to the interface mapping **IM_MI_SalesOrder_Async_Abstract_to_MI_ORDERS_ORDERS_Asnyc_Abstract**. This mapping copies the order into the IDoc. After that, insert the **Send IDoc** step, as you want to send the **IDoc_SalesOrder** message in asynchronous mode.

To close the open *sync-async-bridge*, you must generate and deliver the response message. To do this, you must include another transformation step at the end of the process. This step, **Create Response**, uses the interface mapping **IM_MI_SalesOrder_Async_Abstract_to_MI_Response_Async_Abstract**. After that, assign **SalesOrder** as the source message and **Response** as the target message to the step.

The final step to be carried out in the integration process is the sending step, which actually delivers the response. For this, you must attach a sending step to the end of the process and call it **Close Bridge** (see Figure 5.57). Select the **Closes S/A Bridge** mode, which changes all other input fields, then select the **Response** message that is to be sent at this point. You can now specify the step that opened the bridge in the **Opened By** field. The input help contains the only existing reception step, **Receive Proxy Call**, which you must select as well.

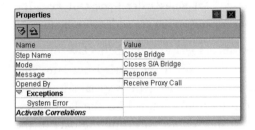

Name	Value
Step Name	Close Bridge
Mode	Closes S/A Bridge
Message	Response
Opened By	Receive Proxy Call
▽ **Exceptions**	
System Error	
Activate Correlations	

Figure 5.57 Properties of the Closing Send Step

Save the integration process and check it using the corresponding option from the menu. If there aren't any errors, you can activate all design objects for this step of the case study via the change list.

5.3.3 Configuration

Due to the two send steps of the integration process the configuration phase is divided into two parts:

Dividing the configuration into two parts

▶ You must configure message delivery from the Java proxy to the integration process. Message delivery is a synchronous process, even though the two parts of the interface are processed separately.

▶ The second configuration scenario handles delivery of the IDoc to System A.

Before you can begin with the two scenarios you must declare the integration process in the integration directory. To do this, open the integration directory and navigate to your scenario, **XI_CaseStudy_##**. Create the new integration process, **IP_SalesOrder_##,** and import the process of the same name from the integration repository.

Declaring the integration process

Defining the Java-
proxy web service

The Java proxy later uses information contained in a WSDL file to determine to which XI server it must connect with which interface. You can create this WSDL file in the integration directory. To do this, open the wizard by selecting **Tools • Define Web Service**.

Read through the first step and continue to the next screen. In that screen you must specify the URL through which the XI system receives SOAP requests. Click the **Propose URL** button to enter data from the current SAP XI system. Proceed to the next step, open the input help, and select message interface **MI_SalesOrder_Sync_Out_##**. The namespace and software component version are added automatically.

In the subsequent step you must specify as what the Java proxy is described. For configuration purposes to be carried out later, the Java proxy must be identified as a service with a specific interface. Because this kind of data can be freely defined for the Java proxy, you should enter **SystemB** as the service and copy the data of the message interface created in the previous step. The Back and Continue buttons allow you to navigate forward and backwards without losing any data. Once you have copied all the data, the wizard should look as shown in Figure 5.58. This data presupposes that System B does not use the specified message interface for sending purposes in any another configuration as that would raise confusion about the sender. Finally, close the Wizard.

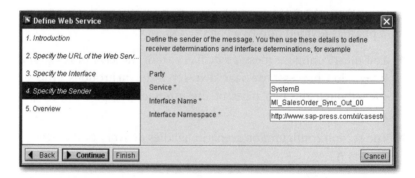

Figure 5.58 Sender Data for the Web Service Definition

When you close the wizard, the system generates the required WSDL file, which you should save as *MI_SalesOrder_Sync_Out_##.wsdl*.

> **Note**
>
> The WSDL file does not correspond to the WSDL display of the message interface in the integration repository. The description in the design phase lacks the concrete details on the XI server so it cannot be used directly in a Java proxy.

Configuring the Synchronous Communication

Table 5.18 provides an overview of all configuration objects used in this scenario.

Configuring the Java proxy integration

Type of object	Sender side: System B/ Java Proxy	Receiver side: IP_SalesOrder_##
Receiver determination	|SystemB|MI_SalesOrder_Sync_Out_##	
Interface determination	|SystemB|MI_SalesOrder_Sync_Out_##||IP_SalesOrder_##	

Table 5.18 Configuration Objects for Synchronous Communication in Step 3 of the Case Study

The Java proxy later appears as part of System B, which is why you can consider the proxy as an equal counterpart of System B in the following configuration steps. Open the Configuration Wizard and create an **Internal Communication**. The sender is business system B with the XI adapter. Like the ABAP proxy, the Java proxy uses the XI format to communicate with the central integration engine. Select interface **MI_SalesOrder_Sync_Out_##** from your namespace; the Java proxy will send data through this interface (see Figure 5.59).

Service Type *	Business System
Service *	SystemB
Interface *	MI_SalesOrder_Sync_Out_00
Namespace *	http://www.sap-press.com/xi/casestudy/00
Adapter Type *	XI — http://sap.com, SAP BASIS

Figure 5.59 Settings for the Java Proxy as a Sender

The message receiver is integration process **IP_SalesOrder_##**, which can only receive data via interface **MI_SalesOrder_Sync_Abstract**. Due to the integration process, the adapter type used here is XI. You

269

won't need a sender or receiver agreement. Note the creation of receiver determination **|SystemB|MI_SalesOrder_Sync_Out_##**, displayed in the subsequent step. The interface determination **|SystemB|MI_SalesOrder_Sync_Out_##||IP_SalesOrder_##** displayed in the screen that follows next does not display an interface mapping because both the interface being used and its abstract counterpart use the same messages in the integration process. As such, you won't need to carry out any assignments. Finally, add all objects to your scenario, **XI_CaseStudy_##**, and close the wizard.

Configuring the Asynchronous Communication

Configuration objects for the IDoc delivery The second configuration scenario is also created using the Configuration Wizard. Table 5.19 provides an overview of the objects created or reused in this process. Here, an asterisk (*) indicates that the object was created in a previous step.

Type of object	Sender side: IP_SalesOrder_##	Receiver side: System A
Communication channel		IDoc_ReceiverChannel*
Receiver agreement		|IP_SalesOrder_##||SystemA| ORDERS.ORDERS01
Receiver determination	|IP_SalesOrder_##|MI_ORDERS_ORDERS01_Async_ Abstract	
Interface determination	|IP_SalesOrder_##|MI_ORDERS_ORDERS01_Async_ Abstract||SystemA	

Table 5.19 Configuration Objects for Asynchronous Communication in Step 3 of the Case Study

Open the Configuration Wizard to create another internal communication. The message with interface **MI_ORDERS_ORDERS01_Async_Abstract** is sent by integration process **IP_SalesOrder_##** using the XI adapter. The IDoc receiver is business system A, which receives messages through the IDoc adapter in the **ORDERS.ORDERS01** interface. Because of the integration process, you don't need to create a sender agreement.

Details for creating the receiver determination **|IP_SalesOrder_##|MI_ORDERS_ORDERS01_Async_Abstract** are only used for information. The interface determination **|IP_SalesOrder_##|MI_ ORDERS_ORDERS01_Async_Abstract||SystemA** will not determine any mapping because the sending and receiving interfaces use the same message type. The receiver agreement **|IP_SalesOrder_ ##||SystemA|ORDERS.ORDERS01** integrates communication channel **IDoc_ReceiverChannel** into the scenario. Finally, save the configuration objects in your scenario.

If you completed this step of the case study using the configuration as presented up to this point, the IDoc can't be sent to System A later on because SAP XI cannot deliver an IDoc from an integration process without further configuration. The reason is that the sender service **IP_SalesOrder_##** cannot be converted into a logical system for ALE communication.

Manual maintenance of the receiver determination

To avoid this problem, you must adjust the receiver agreement **|IP_ SalesOrder_##||SystemA|ORDERS.ORDERS01**. Open the relevant object for editing, select the **Sender Service** option in the **Header Mapping** section, and then select business system B (see Figure 5.60).

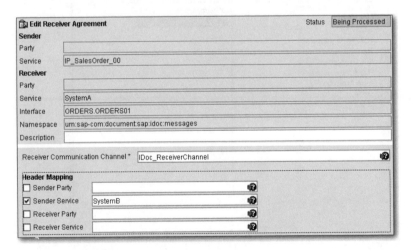

Figure 5.60 Manual Maintenance of the Receiver Agreement

This way you can make sure that IDocs being sent from the integration process are treated as if they were sent from System B. This makes it possible for System A to process the order on the basis of the existing partner agreement.

Save the modified receiver agreement and use the change list to activate all elements that have changed.

5.3.4 Process and Monitoring

Creating a stand-
alone-proxy
project Delivery of the purchase order starts by calling the Java proxy in a
Java program. To implement both the proxy and the Java program,
you need SAP NetWeaver Developer Studio and the WSDL file you
generated during the configuration phase.

Open Developer Studio and create a new **Web Services** project.
Make sure that the **Standalone Proxy Project** subcategory is selected
on the right-hand side (see Figure 5.61).

The other variant, **Deployable Proxy Project**, is an application which
you can deploy and operate on an SAP J2EE engine. In this step,
however, you are introduced to the standalone variant that can be
called from any Java application.

Figure 5.61 Creating a Standalone Proxy Project

Click **Next** to continue and enter the name **ProxyCall** for the project.
Now you can complete the project.

Creating the Java
proxy Use menu to open your **ProxyCall** project and select **New • Client
Proxy Definition**. Specify the package **sap.press.com.xi** and enter

JavaProxy as the name of the proxy. In addition, select the WSDL source, **Local File System or URL** (see Figure 5.62), and continue.

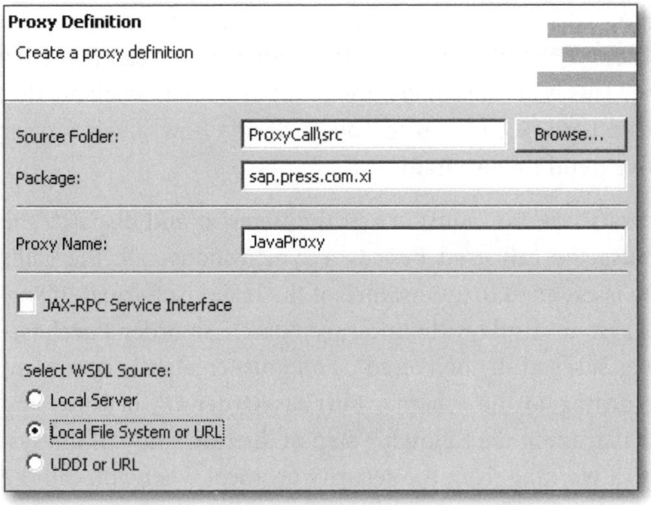

Figure 5.62 Creating the Java Proxy

In the next step, select the file *MI_SalesOrder_Sync_Out_##.wsdl*. Go to the next step and close the Wizard without entering any changes.

Select **Window • Open Perspective • Resource** from the menu or click on the corresponding **Resource Perspective** icon in the upper-left side of the screen to go to the resource perspective of the project. Navigate to your project and open the context menu of path **ProxyCall • src • sap • press • com • xi**. Select **New • File** from the menu and enter the new file name, *SendJavaProxy.java*, in the window that opens. This is the file in which you will do the actual development work.[4]

Creating the Java program

While importing the WSDL definition, classes and methods were created which will be used for calling the proxy and for using the data types in interface **MI_SalesOrder_Async_Out_##**. These classes are imported in the source code. In addition, the system uses security protocol classes provided by SAP in SAP NetWeaver Developer Studio to carry out the authentication process. The imported data types are instantiated as order and order item objects and then filled with data.

Flow of the Java program

---

4 You can find the source code of the class it contains in the Appendix of this book. Alternatively, you can download it from the accompanying web site. At this point we will only describe the basic principles of the process within the program.

The method used for setting the corresponding fields was generated along with the data type classes. For example, you can set the material number using the generated method, **setMaterialNumber**. The corresponding **GET** methods are also available. Depending on the number of items used, the source code of this example can involve a lot of typing. This is because there are no input screens available that could be used here. So, it's up to you to decide how much further you want to extend the program.

Once the data is set, you must attach the items to and dispatch the order. Because the call used here is a synchronous call, the call's return value is assigned to an instance of the response format. If successful, the system displays the message "Purchase order **Purchase-Order-##** was successfully delivered". You must create the document number according to the schema, **PurchaseOrder-##**, because you will refer to it again in the following step of the case study. If the system displays a warning from the security protocol when you call the program, you can simply ignore it in this specific case.

Monitoring the
message path

The best way to monitor the delivery is to use SAP XI's message monitoring tool. However, this tool only allows you to monitor the delivery of the IDoc because the integration process was called by a synchronous call. In addition, you can use **Transaction SXMB_ MONI_BPE** if one of the process steps fails.

The proof that shows that the IDoc has been processed correctly can be found in **Transaction BD87** of business system A. If the IDoc is correctly received and processed, you can view the sales order in that transaction. Call **Transaction VA03** and open the input help of the **Order** input field. Select the search template, **Sales documents by customer**, and enter the purchase order number **PurchaseOrder-##** as the search criterion. Select your order from the list that displays by double-clicking on it. The purchase order number is then copied into the first screen and you can confirm your entries by pressing **Enter**. The system now displays a screen that looks similar to the one shown in Figure 5.63.

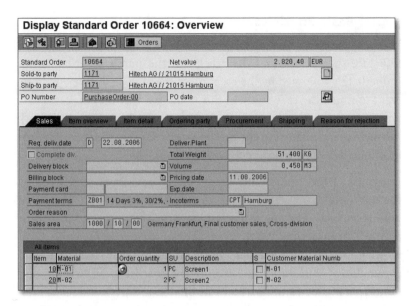

Figure 5.63 Display of the Sales Order

5.4 Delivering the Invoice

The final step in the case study involves delivering the invoice for the purchase order via email. This allows Hitech AG to enter incoming invoices into their system in real-time.

Flow of Step 4

The scenario is structured in such a way that SARIDIS automatically creates an IDoc with the invoice. This IDoc is sent to SAP XI where it is converted into an HTML document using XSLT. The HTML document is then sent to Hitech AG using the mail adapter.

Figure 5.64 illustrates the flow of this part of the scenario.

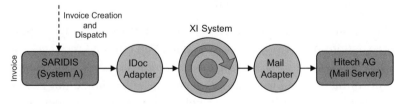

Figure 5.64 Flow of Step 4

5.4.1 Basic Principles

Realistic sales process

Those of you who have already edited sales processes in SAP R/3 or SAP ECC may know that the receipt of the purchase order is not immediately followed by the creation of the invoice. However, as we want to finish the case study in this book in a way that makes sense, we won't map the missing processes via SAP XI. You will work through them manually during the course of the scenario and, for example, deliver the ordered goods by yourself.

Maintaining the partner agreement

Integrating IDoc creation into the invoicing transaction is handled by the outbound parameters of the already existing partner agreement with Hitech AG. For this, you must login to System A as an instructor and call **Transaction WE20**. Navigate to partner agreement **1171**, which is located in the **Partner Type KU** folder. Create a new outbound parameter by clicking on the icon below the list of all existing outbound parameters, enter partner role **BP** (Bill-to party), and select message type **INVOIC** (Invoice/Billing document). To dispatch the IDoc, use the **XI_SYSTEM** receiver port which you created while preparing for the technical exercises. The IDocs are supposed to be transferred immediately. The basic type you will use for the invoice is **INVOIC01**. Figure 5.65 displays the settings to create the outbound parameter.

Go to the Message control tab. The system notifies you that the package size was set to 1. This means that IDoc packages are sent as soon as they contain one IDoc.

Add a new row by clicking on the corresponding icon below the list and select V3 (Billing) in the **Application** column (see Figure 5.66). Since the message type to be used is an invoice, enter **RD00** in the corresponding column. Because the invoice will be sent to a customer, you must select **SD09** as the only possible process code. Save the modified partner agreement.

Providing a mail server

The dispatch of emails from SAP XI does not require any specific preparations on the side of the XI system. You can send messages via SMTP and IMAP4 by specifying the relevant mail server. The "extension" of the training landscape with such a server should not pose a problem, especially because you will integrate mail providers that are generally accessible. As such, you do not need to operate a separate server for this scenario.

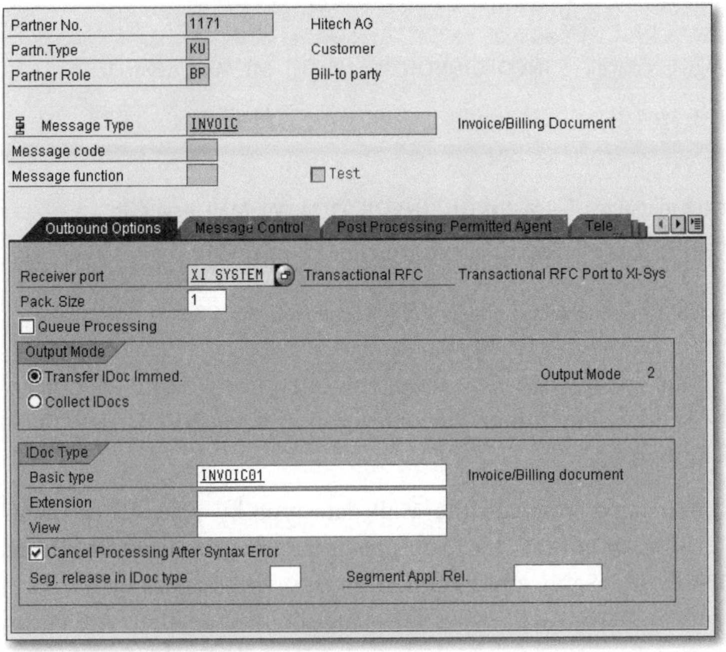

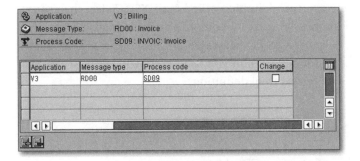

Figure 5.65 Creating the Outbound Parameter for Step 4

Figure 5.66 Setting Message Control for the Dispatch of the Invoice

5.4.2 Design

You will see that from the point of view of design objects, this scenario does not differ much from the other steps. The type and quantity of objects is comparable, but the sources of some objects are different from those used in other scenarios. For example, you will
obtain the data type for the email from SAP Service Marketplace, create the XSLT mapping externally, and import it at a later stage. Table
5.20 provides an overview of all design objects.

Overview of the
design objects

Type of object	Sender side	Receiver side
Message interface	**INCOIC.INVOIC01**	**MI_Mail_Async_In**
Message type		**Mail**
Data type		
Interface mapping	**IM_INVOIC_INVOIC01_to_MI_Mail_Async_In**	
Message mapping	**MM_INVOIC_INVOIC01_to_Mail**	

Table 5.20 Design Objects for Step 4 of the Case Study

Import the
IDoc interface

Due to the fact the IDocs are used, you can quickly create the objects on the sender side. Import the definition of IDoc **INVOIC.INVOIC01** from System A.

Creating the
objects on the
receiver side

You don't need to create the **Mail** data type by yourself; you can import it from an XSD file. You can obtain this file from **SAP Note 748024** in SAP Service Marketplace (*http://service.sap.com*). This file contains numerous data types for using the mail adapter. Appendix A contains a simplified version that contains only the Mail data type.

Go to the integration repository and navigate to your namespace to create a new external definition called **Mail_XSD**. Select the **xsd** category and import the corresponding file from your system (see Figure 5.67). If you go to the **Messages** tab now, you will see that—depending on the file version you use—it contains at least the Mail message. Save the external definition.

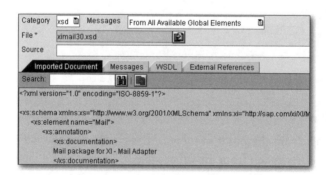

Figure 5.67 Importing Message Type "Mail"

Based on this message definition, create the message interface **MI_Mail_Async_In**, which uses the **Mail** message you just imported. The type of the interface is Inbound and is addressed in asynchronous mode. Save the message interface.

You won't create the message mapping for this scenario in the Integration Builder. Instead, import it as an XSLT file. You can find a template for this file in Appendix A and on the book's web sites, located at *http://www.sap-press.com* and *http://www.sap-press.de/1383*.

Creating the mapping objects

The mapping has the following effect: First, it contains the mail addresses for the sender and receiver. These addresses are firmly defined in our example, but you can, of course, also fill them dynamically. In addition, the Subject field of the mail is assigned the invoice number located in the IDoc. The mail content itself primarily consists of a table that displays the ordered objects, including some item data as well as the prices.

The XSLT file you created (or downloaded) must be included in an archive file. In this context, it doesn't make any difference if the archive file is a ZIP or a JAR file.

In the integration repository, navigate to your namespace and go to the **Mapping Objects • Imported Archives** directory; create a new object called **Mail_XSLT_Mapping** using the context menu. Select the archive that contains the XSLT file, **MM_INVOIC_INVOIC01_to_Mail.xsl** (see Figure 5.68), and save the archive object.

Figure 5.68 Selecting the XSL File

Next, create the interface mapping **IM_INVOIC_INVOIC01_to_MI_Mail_Async_In**. Its outbound message is IDoc type **INVOIC.INVOIC01**, while the target message interface is **MI_Mail_Async_In** (see Figure 5.69). Click the Read Interfaces button and change the mapping type to XSL in the list of mapping programs. Open the input help and select the message mapping **MM_INVOIC_INVOIC01_zu_Mail** from the archive, **Mail_XSLT_Mapping**.

Save and test the interface mapping. While doing this, you should create several duplicates of the source segment, **E1EDP01**. Although the display of the target message cannot show the finished HTML

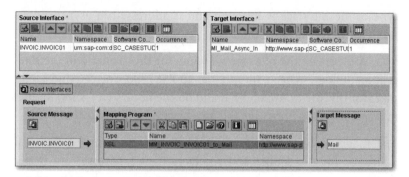

Figure 5.69 Interface Mapping for Step 4

document, you can nevertheless check whether the relevant fields are filled with data. If the test is successful, you should activate all new design objects using the change list.

5.4.3   Configuration

New configuration objects

A new element that you need for the configuration is a mail receiver channel for each student. In this channel, you must specify the SMTP or IMAP server as well as additional logon data.

At first glance, this step's configuration seems easy, as it can be quickly done using the wizard. While this is indeed the case, you must take into account the fact that presumably not all training participants use the same mail provider.

When the message is received by SAP XI, you can use the purchase order of the IDoc (**PurchaseOrder-##**) to determine which participant has sent the message. However, the question now is which receiver—and hence which communication channels—are available? The number of available business systems is not enough to provide a separate business system as a mail receiver for each student. To solve this problem, you'll need to create business services which allow every student to use a separate communication channel. By creating a separate business service for each student, you can specify separate recipients for the email. You already used this method in Step 2 of the case study although it wasn't necessary at that stage. Now we do need this object to obtain different targets and thus different communication channels in the receiver determination.

Table 5.21 provides an overview of all configuration objects used.

Type of object	Receiver side: System A	Sender side: Mail_Server_##
Communication channel		Mail_Receiver
Sender agreement	| SystemA | INVOIC.INVOIC01|*|*	
Receiver agreement		|SystemA||Mail_Server_ ##|MI_Mail_Async_In
Receiver determination	|SystemA|INVOIC.INVOIC01	
Interface determination	|SystemA|INVOIC.INVOIC01||Mail_Server_##	

Table 5.21 Elements in the Integration Directory of Step 4 in the Case Study

Login to the integration directory and navigate to your scenario, **XI_ CaseStudy_##**. Create business service **Mail_Server_##** and assign to it **MI_Mail_Async_In** from your namespace http://www.sap-press.com/ xi/casestudy/## as an Inbound interface. Save the new business service.

Creating a business service

Go to the **Service without Party · Business Services** directory and make sure that your new service is actually there. Create the **Mail_ Receiver** communication channel, set the **Mail** adapter type, and define the **Receiver** direction. Specify the **Transport Protocol** used by your mail server. In most cases, you can connect to a mail server via SMTP.

Creating the mail communication channel

For the **Message Protocol**, you can choose between **XIALL** and **XIPAYLOAD**. You can select the first option if the contents of the RFC822-compliant email are identical to the contents of the XI message. In that case, the XI message is a multipart MIME message whose first part contains the SOAP envelope. In the example, select the second option, **XIPAYLOAD** (see Figure 5.70), in which the email is used as the message payload.

Enter the URL for your mail server in the **Connection Parameters for Mail Server** section. If you use SMTP, the URL starts with the prefix **smtp://**, whereas if you use IMAP, it begins with **imap://**. If necessary, you can also select a user authentication by activating the corresponding option.

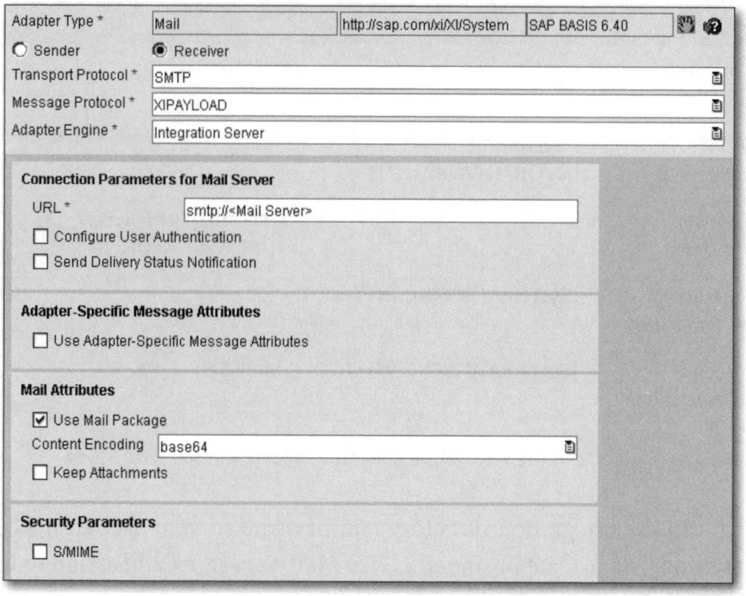

Figure 5.70 Settings for the Mail Receiver Channel

You must also make sure that the **Use Mail Package** option is activated in the **Mail Attributes** section. This setting is necessary so that
header data (such as the sender, receiver, and the message subject)
can also be read from the payload. Select content coding **base64** and
save the communication channel.

Calling the Config-
uration Wizard
Open the Configuration Wizard and create another **internal communication**. Specify **Business System A** as the sender and select the
IDoc adapter. The type of the dispatched IDoc is **INCOIC.INVOIC01**.
The receiver of the invoice is the **Mail_Server_##** business service
you just created. This business service can be reached via the only
configured interface, **MI_Mail_Async_In**. Communication is handled
by the **Mail** adapter. You should use communication channel **IDoc_
SenderChannel** of System A for the sender agreement.

Whereas the screen displayed only informational data during the
first creation of receiver determination **|SystemA|INVOIC.IN-
VOIC01**, all other students must now specify that they want to
extend the existing object. The interface determination **|Sys-
temA|INVOIC. INVOIC01||Mail_Server_##** should already display
the correct mapping to the inbound interface **MI_Mail_Async_In**.

Continue with the next step and select the only available communication channel of your business service, **Mail_Receiver**, for receiver agreement **|SystemA||Mail_Server_##|MI_Mail_Async_In**. Finally, add all objects to your scenario, **XI_CaseStudy_##**, and close the Wizard.

However, before you activate all of the objects, you must carry out one manual adjustment in the receiver determination: Depending on the number specified in the purchase order, we want the system to select the corresponding recipient of the invoice. This must be coordinated because the students will block each other in the following step.

Determining the email recipient based on the document number

For this, navigate to receiver determination **|SystemA| INVOIC.IN-VOIC01** and open it in editing mode. Go to the line that contains your business service, click in the **Condition** column, and open the input help to launch the Expression Editor. Select the IDoc field **INVOIC/ IDOC/E1EDK02/BELNR** as the left operand and set the right operand to the value, **PurchaseOrder-##**. Make sure that the operator being used is an equals sign (=). Insert a second condition by clicking on the corresponding icon. Here, you should select the IDoc field **/INVOIC01/ IDOC/E1EDK02/QUALF** for the left operand and set the value of the right operand to **001**. Figure 5.71 displays these settings.

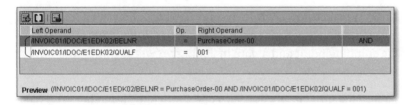

Figure 5.71 Settings in the Condition Editor

These two conditions ensure that the segment **E1EDK02** is evaluated for the delivery only if the instance of the segment contains the purchase order number due to the qualifier. The purchase order number, however, must contain a specific value.

Copy the condition and save the receiver determination. You can now activate all new configuration objects.

5.4.4 Process and Monitoring

The process of the scenario begins by creating the invoice on the basis of the sales order that has been received. Invoice creation presupposes that the goods have first been delivered. Moreover, you will track the message path once its dispatch has triggered and verify that it has been received as an email.

Flow of the Scenario

Creating an outbound delivery

To create an invoice that refers to the purchased order you received in the previous step, you must first carry out two additional steps that have not been implemented using SAP XI. These two steps consist of creating an outbound delivery and selecting a transfer order. The steps are necessary because, by default, you can only invoice orders that have been delivered.

> **Note**
>
> If you did not create a purchase order in Step 3 of the case study, you can manually enter a sales order via **Transaction VA01**. To do this, use the order type **OR** (Standard Order), sales organization **1000**, distribution channel **10**, and division **00**. Confirm your entries by pressing **Enter** and specify customer **1171** (Hitech AG) as the Sold-to and Ship-to party. Select purchase order number **PurchaseOrder-##** and fill the item list with items and quantities before saving your entries.

Go to **Transaction VL01N** in System A, which allows you to create an outbound delivery for a specific sales order. Enter **1200** (Dresden) as the shipping point and a date in about two weeks' time from now as the selection date.

To find the number of your sales order, open the input help and navigate to the search template, **Sales documents by customer**. Enter the **PurchaseOrder-##** in the purchase order number field and run the search. Double-click on your order in the list that displays. This copies the order number into the corresponding field, allowing you to confirm your entries. You can now check all the details for the last time before the dispatch is triggered (see Figure 5.72); save the document.

> **Note**
>
> Should you happen to lose the plot so that you don't remember which documents were created on the basis of your sales order, you can use **Transaction VA03** at any time to return to your order. If you select **Environment · Display document flow** from the menu, you can then view all the relevant documents.

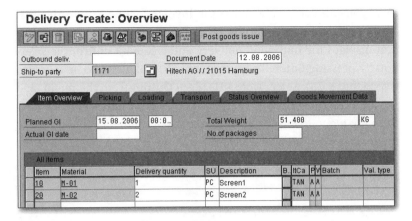

Figure 5.72 Creating an Outbound Delivery

The goods issue that has been triggered by the outbound delivery still requires a transfer order to be created before it can be completed. To do this, call **Transaction LT03**, which should already display the outbound delivery you just created. Set the warehouse number to **012** (Dresden) in the IDES system. Make sure that the **Activate Item** option is activated in the Control section (see Figure 5.73). Select **D Background** as Foreground/Backgrnd, which means that some transactions will be called and processed in the background. In addition, set Option 2 in the **Adopt pick.quantity** field to make sure that a goods issue is also posted automatically. Confirm your entries and wait until the system notifies you that a transfer order has been created.

Creating a transfer order for shipping

Create Transfer Order for Delivery Note: Initial Screen

Warehouse Number	012
Plant	
Delivery	80014043
Group	

Control
- ✓ Activate Item
- Foreground/Backgrnd — D Background
- Adopt pick.quantity — 2
- Adopt putaway qty
- Putaway TO proc.

Figure 5.73 Creating a Transfer Order for Shipping

Now you can eventually create the invoice for the sales order that has been delivered. To do this, go to **Transaction VF01**. The transaction displays the outbound delivery you created. Confirm the selection by pressing **Enter**. The system now lists all items to be invoiced (see Figure 5.74). Select **Goto • Header • Output** from the menu, and set the **6 EDI** medium for partner **1171**. Select **Edit • Further data** from the menu to ensure the message is sent immediately. Return to the message overview and save the invoice. As soon as you save the invoice, the IDoc is automatically dispatched and converted into an email.

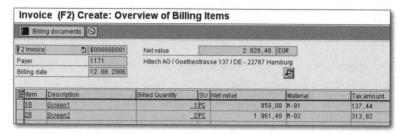

Figure 5.74 Creating the Invoice

Monitoring the Scenario

You should first call **Transaction BD87** in System A and check whether the IDoc was sent correctly. Verify that the messages of IDoc type **INVOIC.INVOIC01** are displayed in the outbox. If the system does not display any errors, you can move on to the next monitoring step, otherwise you must analyze the error message. Possible sources of an error at this stage are primarily incorrect partner agreements.

Due to the asynchronous send mode, the invoice IDoc can be monitored in the **Message Monitoring** module of the XI system. The message should go through without any significant interruptions or breaks. If errors occur, they result probably from the incorrect configuration of the mail adapter.

You can check the adapter by opening the **Adapter Monitoring** function in the Runtime Workbench and selecting the mail adapters. Unfortunately, you can only determine here whether or not the configuration is correct and whether messages have already been processed. The display is not as comprehensive as the display used for the file adapter, for instance.

The ultimate and most secure step when checking the successful dispatch of the invoice is to take a look into one's own mailbox. There you should have received an email that, depending on the email client, should look similar to the one shown in Figure 5.75.

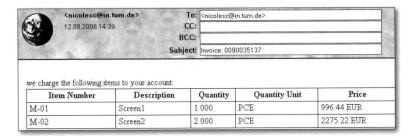

Figure 5.75 Invoice in the Inbox

This chapter discusses various concepts to enhance the case study and with the beer distribution game it provides a description of another extensive business process that includes different applications outside of SAP NetWeaver Exchange Infrastructure (XI). In addition, it sheds a light on the future development of SAP XI.

6 Enhancements and Outlook

Now that you have successfully completed the exercises and the case study for this book, the final step introduces you to some possible ways of how you can extend your knowledge in other, more complex scenarios. Our goal is to prepare you for future developments in the XI environment, as far as that is possible at the current stage. For this reason, the following sections deal with the status of SAP XI in the SOA environment and with the further development of the product itself.

6.1 Possible Enhancements of the Case Study

You have dealt with the case study in four different steps and certainly you will have thought at some stages that there is room for a more detailed consideration of specific aspects. The case study has been deliberately kept simple, that is to say, more simple than reality would be in such an environment. However, we now want to describe some concepts that enable you to extend the existing materials in such a way that you can go into further detail. For this purpose we can extend the case study in two different directions.

Distinction between two enhancement concepts

Extending the breadth of the case study

By "extending the breadth of the case study," we can examine the time before and after the process, or that we can take a look at the systems of the other companies.

Increasing the section under consideration

Here, the SARIDIS case study has only been used to a small extent and contains many processes and special cases that can be regarded as real challenges. For example, we could consider the purchasing processes, shift the material management aspect more into the focus of our interest, and so on. The sales and distribution process described in this book can also be modified, for instance, by carrying out a third-party business transaction.

The important factor here is that you can keep using the described sales and distribution process while discovering new scenarios. The process contains steps that are not supported by SAP XI. For example, the process can be complemented by the dispatch of an order confirmation or a shipping notification. In addition, it is not quite clear how SARIDIS controls and posts incoming payments. Furthermore, the practical sections in this book did not deal with the question as to which systems could be used on the side of Hitech AG or Sunny Electronics. Their applications may have some specific characteristics that require a modification of the processes. Those sections did not consider the question of what the scenario would look like if Sunny Electronics was assigned the order for the monitors.

Depending on your area of focus, you could, for example, also extend the Java application described in the third step in Chapter 5 to make it more user-friendly. Moreover, you could integrate the individual exercises, which are basically independent of the case study. As such, you could extend the material master record to create the items that will be ordered later by Hitech AG.

Another issue you could try to resolve is message exchange with other companies and partners. To keep a clear overview of the exercises and to avoid having to increase the system landscape any further, we decided not to consider message exchange with other landscapes or XI systems.

Extending the depth of the case study

Details of the described concepts
By extending the depth of the case study we mean the consideration of details of the described concepts and problems. One of these aspects is the issue of security. For example, many adapters allow you to make the corresponding security settings to attain a secure exchange of data, even across enterprise boundaries. Although we

described several adapters in the exercises, we did not got into further detail because the majority of other adapters require additional applications and servers whose integration into the overall concept would involve a considerable effort.

However, it is especially those additional systems that open new horizons to you and allow you to implement additional scenarios. For example, you could use the JDBC adapter if you used an appropriate database application. You could also use the JMS adapter for integration with other EAI applications.

One essential element that we have included in several cases in this book is business processes. These objects have such huge potential that you can, for instance, automate the entire case study with only two business processes that communicate with each other. That way, you can skip the manual steps carried out in the case study.

As you can see, you can develop many additional scenarios and variations based on the materials introduced in this book. However, because there are many other business processes that take place outside the SARIDIS case study, there are also many other ways to extend your knowledge of the SAP XI environment. Section 6.2 describes one possible example in this context: the beer distribution game.

6.2 Beer Distribution Game

The *beer distribution game* is a logistics simulation that was developed at the beginning of the 1960s at the Massachusetts Institute of Technology (MIT). It simulates a four-level supply chain that consists of a retailer, wholesaler, distributor, and a factory. You can find additional information on the beer distribution game, as well as a simulation of the game, at *http://www.beergame.lim.ethz.ch*.

Description

In its original version as a board game, each level is represented by a person who decides how much beer should be delivered to the previous level (in the case of the retailer the previous level is a customer who places weekly orders) and how much beer should be ordered from the subsequent level (in the case of the factory the subsequent level is the production department). The purpose of the game is to minimize the costs that occur along the entire supply chain. These costs consist of the following two components:

- ▶ Stockholding costs.

- ▶ Costs incurred by delivery delays.

Whiplash effect   The simulation illustrates the *whiplash effect* caused by time delays in the supply chain, and is characterized by strong fluctuations of the stock volumes at the individual levels (see Figure 6.1).

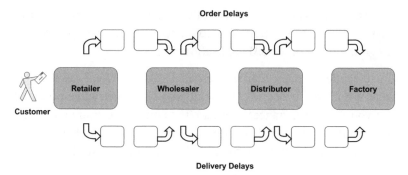

Figure 6.1 Supply Chain in the Beer Distribution Game

The following sections describe how you can implement simulation, and the associated business process, using SAP XI.

Business requirements   In the first step, we suggest for you to not map the processes of the individual supply chain levels via real ERP processes, but to use simplifying RFC modules instead. Each of these modules is assigned quantities to be ordered and delivered, respectively.

From a business point of view, the RFC modules contain a simple logic that decides on the quantity of beer to be ordered. Moreover, they place the actual orders, and receive and deliver goods. While two factories are being operated that receive the orders of the distributor on the basis of the available quantities of beer, there is only one retailer, one wholesaler, and one distributor. In SAP XI, the factories are selected with a BPEL process. Another task of SAP XI is to forward purchase orders to the subsequent levels and to dispatch shipping notifications to the previous levels. In addition, SAP XI logs all the steps involved in the program flow through the file adapter.

An external web service is used to register the stock volumes and open purchase orders to carry out a final evaluation of the overall costs of the supply chain. For this, the individual levels actively transfer their data to the web service. The individual levels are also

292

initiated (that is, the stock volumes are set) through a web service interface, which—in contrast to the previously mentioned web service—is provided by SAP XI. In other words, SAP XI acts as a server in this context.

To map the simulation, perform the following steps:

1. Map the individual supplay chain levels (retailer, wholesaler, distributor, factory) using the appropriate RFC modules and a message exchange between the supply chain levels via SAP XI.

2. Select the appropriate factory using a BPEL process.

3. Integrate an external logging service that logs all stock changes centrally using SAP XI's file adapter.

4. Integrate a monitoring service to evaluate the current stock volumes and the stock development during the course of the simulation.

5. Use a tool to initialize the individual supply chain levels (initial stock volumes, delays, and so on).

6.2.1   Predefined Software Components

The following description allows you to map the beer distribution game in SAP XI using the previously defined software components. In contrast to the detailed exercises in this book, this description represents a rough guide and should be considered as a gathering of ideas rather than instructions for a complete implementation. The predefined components are first described, and then we will continue with the design and solution concept.

In this exercise, we want to implement the individual supply chain levels in an SAP system. At the same time, however, those levels are treated in such a way that it is always possible to distribute them to several systems. The function modules used to implement the individual levels are created in a package.[1]

Function modules and supply chain levels

---

1 You can find a sample implementation at the following address: *http://eai.uni-lueneburg.de/sap-xi*.

There are six RFC-enabled function modules available for each supply chain level:

▸ Sending and receiving of purchase orders (the stock volumes are stored in a database table).

▸ Sending and receiving of goods deliveries.

▸ Initialization of stock volumes.

▸ Query of stock and purchase order data.

The factory represents an exception in this context: It receives purchase orders, but places production orders that are then carried out with a certain time delay.

Web services   The implementation of an external web service for monitoring purchase orders and stock volumes, as well as the web service client for initializing the stock volumes, is built on Apache Axis 1.3 (*http://ws.apache.org/axis*) and Jakarta Tomcat (*http://tomcat.apache.org*). You must deploy the web service on a publicly accessible server, which must meet the following requirements:

▸ Jakarta Tomcat 5.x and Apache Axis 1.3 or higher must be installed.

▸ The IP address of the server must be accessible from your SAP system.

▸ A relational database with JDBC driver must be available. (The sample implementation at *http://eai.uni-lueneburg.de/sap-xi* uses an Oracle database. Note, the database must be customized for your local environment.)

The most important operations of the web service are:

▸ addOrder(String senderName, int orderVolume), which is called when beer is ordered

▸ addDelivery(String supplierName, int deliveryVolume), which is called at the time of delivery.

Other methods are used to initialize a new game and to query the historical data for analysis in the beer analysis client.

6.2.2 Design and Implementation

SAP XI is used as an integration platform for exchanging messages and for flow logic (i.e., selection of the factory). In addition to the three interfaces for initialization, reporting, and logging, six additional interfaces are required for the retailer, wholesaler, and distributor. The factory does not need the interfaces for outbound purchase orders and inbound deliveries as these are mapped by the factory-internal production. Figure 6.2 illustrates the structure of this situation for one supply chain level.

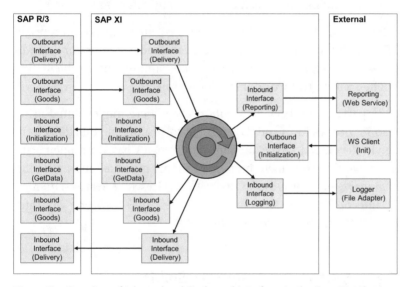

Figure 6.2 Overview of Inbound and Outbound Interfaces in the Beer Distribution Game

Once the individual supply chain level is initialized, the game starts with a customer request received by the retailer. The customer has only two functions: to place purchase orders and to receive deliveries.

If the requested quantity is in stock, the retailer delivers it to the customer. If the stock isn't available, the retailer directs a corresponding request to the wholesaler. The wholesaler sends a partial delivery to the retailer and places a purchase order with the distributor who, in turn, sends a corresponding purchase order to the factory. The factory produces the ordered quantity and sends a delivery to the distributor who forwards it to the wholesaler who forwards it to the retailer. Finally, the retailer can send the remaining quantity to the customer.

6.2.3　Options for Enhancement

In the second step, process of individual supply chain levels are mapped one after the other using real ERP processes. Instead of the RFC module used for inbound purchase orders we could, for instance, write an appropriate sales document using BAPIs or IDocs. We could also use a BPEL process to send purchase orders for the requested item to the superior supply chain level on the basis of the goods availability check. If access to different ERP systems is provided, it would also be interesting to map different supply chain levels on different ERP installations (perhaps even by different vendors).

Whereas the first stage of extension (i.e., mapping via appropriate RFC modules) represents a simulation under "laboratory conditions," the outlined extension contains almost any problem that might occur in real-world integration projects.

Only parts of the beer distribution game were implemented using web services as RFCs and IDocs. If the corresponding functions were newly developed today, modern technologies based on open standards would most likely be used. For this purpose, an application engineer would propose to use web services in a Service-Oriented Architecture (SOA). The next section describes how you can integrate SOA and web services with SAP XI.

6.3　SAP XI and Enterprise Services

SOA as a framework for independent services

The concept of an SOA is often discussed on the basis of technical aspects, such as web services. In this context, the term "SOA" refers to an architecture that describes the way in which software components interact with each other as independent services. Services have the characteristics described in Chapter 1 as they are, for instance, self-descriptive and self-contained.

SOAP-based web services are the most commonly used implementation of services in the sense of an SOA. Let's take a closer look at an online purchase order: If you select several individual goods from the catalog of an online store, the purchase order is mapped by a service that communicates with another service which queries the stock volume to determine whether or not the goods are available. The purchase order and delivery details are then transferred to another service that calculates the total and informs you about the delivery date. Moreover, a tracking number is generated to track the purchase order, and yet another service allows you to track the current whereabouts of the goods as they're shipped to your location.

This kind of architecture provides the flexibility to modify both the process flow and individual services. In this context, you must also consider aspects such as general security, transaction security, and compliance (for example, Sarbanes-Oxley compliance). Although positive effects on company development and the application landscape as such are often the objects of promises, the most convincing explanation missing is how these effects can be attained.

With its *Enterprise SOA* (formerly known as *Enterprise Services Architecture*), SAP clearly demonstrates the benefits for application development and the implementation of a corporate strategy based on service-orientation. To demonstrate the importance of the SAP NetWeaver Exchange Infrastructure within the Enterprise SOA, the following sections will examine *Composite Applications*, including the underlying architecture. You will see how the Enterprise SOA affects application development, which new application types can be developed, and how these applications can support and help you attain company goals. This has far-reaching consequences for IT, as it is no longer regarded as a bottleneck. However, it has a considerable share in the success of a business, provided the capabilities of the Enterprise SOA are used properly.

Effects on technology and business

6.3.1 Composite Applications

Today, most applications are no longer monolithic. As described earlier, end-to-end processes begin in an application and forward the control to another application, which is implemented by a third application. The actual application, which is referred to as a composite application, is now located right between the applications that provide the individual process steps.

These processes are not only about coupling the call sequence of the individual process steps in the connected systems of an integration platform with each other, but an application that's located between these systems must be able to store data by itself. In other words, it must contain a persistence layer of its own, or—as described in the

Composites are based on web service standards

invoice verification process in Chapter 1—access and update a cross-reference table.

Another requirement could be to provide new *user interfaces* (UI), since the called process steps themselves only contain user interfaces that have been developed for professional power users. In the new configuration, the UI must be designed for the role of an occasional user, which means the UI layout must be easier to use.

Figure 6.3 shows how composite applications represent a new type of application as they act as communicators between existing applications which enable new processes.

SAP positions composite applications as so-called *xApps*. As the "x" in xApps stands for "cross," this kind of spelling supports the idea of an application that runs crossways to existing applications.

Composite applications to separate processes and IT

An essential purpose of the composite applications is the separation of the process logic from underlying applications. This way, composite applications allow you to map new, innovative processes and increase user productivity without replacing already existing ERP, CRM, SRM, PLM, or legacy applications.

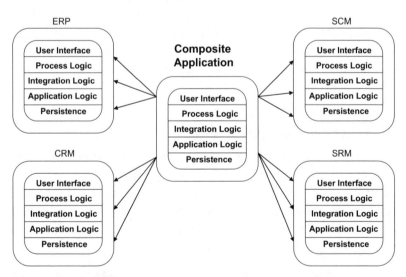

Figure 6.3 Composite Applications as New Applications Between Existing Applications (Source: Woods, Mattern)

SOA-based web services are not sufficient

To attain this, the existing applications must provide their functions as web services and store them in a directory. Using the Enterprise SOA, you can combine these services and, if necessary, together with newly developed web services they can be assembled to composite applications. Although these new combinations add considerable value, this does not yet meet the requirements of modern enterprise software. The existence of reusable components alone is not enough because the components themselves must already be developed with reusability in mind. Not only should web services be made available, they must rather be integrated into consistent, automated processes on the basis of an appropriate architecture.

This concept also requires the IT department to take on a new role. The IT department must build up more and more process knowledge and understanding; for instance, the able to answer questions such as which services can be provided as reusable web services.

Process knowledge is required to provide the right services

This means that the IT department must take on more responsibilities in complex projects to be able to identify the right services. This, in turn, requires that IT departments must complement their profound technical knowledge with knowledge of the interdependencies between the applications. In doing so, they can make their own suggestions regarding the improvement of processes, or the option of implementing new processes, based on existing and new technologies.

The IT department thus assumes a new role within the company. It is no longer a pure cost factor, but instead generates added value and has a positive effect on the corporate strategy. For example, the IT staff would be able to answer the following questions:

New role for IT department

- What is the optimal scope of a service?
- How can real applications and functions that are usually stateful be separated into stateless services?
- How can the increasing complexity be controlled with a growing number of integrated services?
- Where is persistence located if data is stored in distributed systems?
- Who decides which function should be used as a web service?
- How can a semantic integration between web services be ensured?
- How should access rights for these services be organized if the services are distributed across several systems?
- How can service level agreements be ensured?
- Which guidance and governance processes must be implemented?

Even though this book cannot answer all those questions, it should already have become obvious to you that the Enterprise SOA can be regarded as a convergence point between business and IT.

6.3.2   From Web Services to Enterprise Services

Within the enterprise services architecture, business content is encapsulated in enterprise services that represent an extension of web services.

Enterprise service as a useful business service   Let's look at the following scenario (see Figure 6.4): You have to carry out a credit standing review in the context of a sales order. In an "old world scenario" you would have developed a proprietary interface from your application to an external service provider (such as Dun & Bradstreet) to obtain the necessary information.

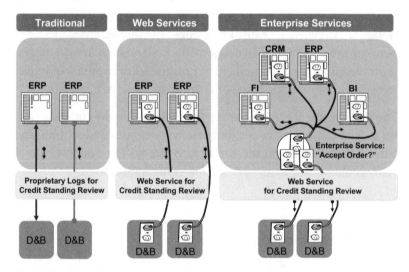

Figure 6.4 From Function Calls to Web Services and Enterprise Services

With the development of Internet technologies, new technical standards have established themselves that make it possible to replace the proprietary call with a web service. For example, a web service call is probably processed via HTTP and SOAP, while XML is used as a document exchange format. In particular, this means that the consumer of the service doesn't need to make any assumptions regarding the platform or implementation of the service. In addition, semantic standards have also emerged along with the web services. These standards define how the services are used and called, and also, how the processes themselves are organized; who assumes which role and takes on which responsibility.

But the actual question behind the service call is of a completely different nature, namely whether or not the sales order should be accepted. In this context, the credit standing review appears merely as one of several possible process steps. Prior to (or during) a credit standing review for an external provider, you may check the last incoming payment date of the customer in question in the accounting system. Alternatively, you might check the last sales order from this customer or their payment standing in the CRM system, you even want to refer to data warehousing reports for this customer.

The logic that determines how the credit standing review is interpreted, and what kind of information is needed, is implemented only once in an enterprise service and can be reused by each system that receives orders. Additional application logic that allows you to select a web service provider, or to store and compare data, is available as part of the enterprise service implementation.

For information on enterprise services that are currently being worked on and provided by SAP, you should refer to the SAP Developer Network (*http://sdn.sap.com*). In the **Enterprise SOA · ES Community** area, registered customers can develop and test client applications that use enterprise services.

Testing enterprise services

6.3.3 SAP XI as a Service Infrastructure

The SAP NetWeaver Exchange Infrastructure plays a major role in this overall concept. It is involved both in service enabling, which is the provisioning of functionality as services without having to re-implement these services as web services, and in the orchestrating services when it comes to combining existing and newly developed services into composite applications.

SAP XI to enable and orchestrate services

As you have seen in the practical examples of this book, the services in SAP XI are developed in the context of an outside-in model. In this model, the interfaces provided for integration are developed outside of the application in SAP XI and then made available within the applications by means of the proxy technology. Thus, SAP XI provides a uniform service infrastructure for a standardized definition, implementation, and use of services.

The modeling process itself allows process logic to be separated from the service implementation, and you can map new business processes much faster, particularly if (as shown in the previous example) encapsulated, reusable, higher-value enterprise services are being used.

6.4 Further Development of SAP XI

Up to this point, you have dealt with the architecture of the Enterprise SOA and the role of SAP XI in this overall concept. We now want to give you a final look at additional developments that can be expected.

6.4.1 SAP NetWeaver as a Business Process Platform

Development of the SAP NetWeaver Exchange Infrastructure in particular, and of SAP NetWeaver in general, described so far can be summarized, as shown in Figure 6.5. Up to this point, we have described the development of SAP technology as a transaction platform for SAP applications to an integration and composition platform in heterogeneous application landscapes. SAP NetWeaver now enables the step towards a business process platform.

Each new generation of SAP NetWeaver increased productivity, whether on the side of the end-user (by introducing intuitively usable screens), or on the entire process side (by implementing continuously improved, integrated, and consistent processes). At the same time, considerably improved technologies allowed companies to be more innovative.

At the times of the transaction platform, people used to think in terms of local applications, such as purchasing, sales, materials planning, and so on. And when talking of an integration platform people had in their mind technical aspects which is with which technology do you connect the applications. With a composite platform, however, people think in terms of cross-system processes, which is fostered by usage of a business process platform.

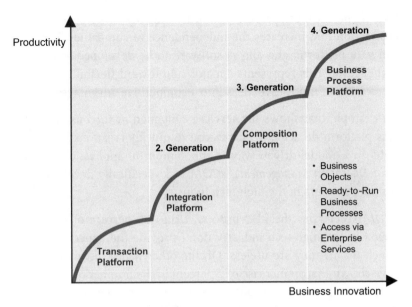

Figure 6.5 From Infrastructure to Applistructure

In addition to SAP NetWeaver as a technical software platform, the business process platform primarily contains the application platform that provides enterprise services whose metadata is stored in the *enterprise services repository* (ESR). This metadata can be combined into composite applications.

Abstraction and independence of the technical platform

In addition to services that originate from the business process platform itself, you can also describe services of external applications, or of legacy systems and proprietary developments in the ESR, and integrate those services with SAP services. Thus the added value of a business process platform consists of the "packaged" provisioning of functionality, which allows for specialized applications and business processes that use web service standards to be created easily. Not only are the service definitions stored in the ESR, but also the context and the process models.

In this context, tools such as SAP NetWeaver Visual Composer (which allows you to quickly create user interfaces based on existing services without having to write a single line of code) are used for model-driven development. Other useful toolsets are, for instance, ARIS (by IDS Scheer), which allows application developers to create high-level business process models, or Lifecycle Management in SAP Solution Manager for the implementation of processes in SAP applications.

Use of the business process platform generally involves a level of abstraction that increases the independence of companies from the software platform, and allows software to be developed at a much higher level. This represents a major step toward flexibility and the conversion of innovative ideas into a competitive advantage.

Model development

An example that shows the services contained in the business process platform do actually enable you to quickly create new applications in a model-driven way is the composite application, xCQM (*Cost Quotation Management*). xCQM was specifically developed for contract vendors in the high-tech industry.

xCQM accelerates the RFQ process. Up to 80 percent of the RFQs issued in the high-tech industry don't provide the expected result, which means they are useless. On the other hand, research studies have shown that an increase of 2 percent in the number of successful completions causes a profit increase of 10 percent. As such, it becomes self-evident how important it is to provide the responsible team with relevant information such as prices, certified and tested suppliers, or part numbers, to be able to respond to an RFQ. In real life, however, this data is distributed across different internal and external sales and distribution, product, and procurement systems. Services provided in the platform have made it possible to model and generate the entire xCQM application (see *http://www.sap.com/solutions/xapps/xcqm/index.epx*).

6.4.2 Enterprise Services Repository

As they exist today, the modeling options of the SAP XI Repository still contain traces of the original SAP concept to position SAP XI as an integration broker and business process management tool. The move toward a business process platform will increasingly shift to the fore the character of the business processes and the associated business objects, including the services they provide (which will inevitably result in extended modeling functions).

For this, the existing repository that primarily represents the technical view of services will be extended to provide enhanced options for the description of enterprise services as well as for designing, simulating, and fine-tuning business processes—and above all, for process execution. The SAP XI Repository thus develops into an *enterprise services repository* (ESR) whose essential components are illustrated in Figure 6.6.

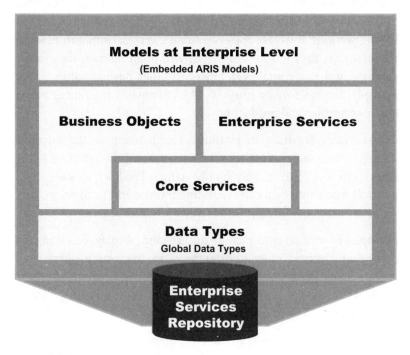

Figure 6.6 Enterprise Services Repository

To model business processes at the enterprise level, the ARIS modeling tool is integrated into the repository. This tool allows you to describe business architectures, and it helps you establish a methodical procedure and a uniform descriptive language. The design phase in which you use the tool consists of answering questions as to who does what and in which sequence, and what needs to be done by which applications. This phase is usually accompanied by a process analysis that is supposed to uncover organizational and structural weaknesses.

In Section 2.5, we already described the resulting potentials, particularly with regard to how you can derive an implementation from the models and later on the execution of the processes. To simplify the process integration, you can use tools that allow you to analyze currently running processes to determine which standard SAP processes are already being used by a company, and also to transfer these processes into ARIS as a basic model to start from. New models are created, based on the implemented processes.

Business objects and their services
Business processes are based on business objects, such as a sales order, a cost center, or an employee. For this reason, you must integrate those business objects in the enterprise services repository that provide the so-called *core services*, which will be described in the following sections. Business objects contain the actual application logic. Furthermore, they ensure the persistence of all relevant data in the database and also contain references to other business objects. For example, the sales order business object contains references to the business partner and product objects.

Core services
Core services are used to establish a connection to the business objects, which means the core services represent the interface to the objects. In this context, only highly standardized services are used, which is made sure by a corresponding framework. In addition, core services enable the interaction between business objects.

Examples of core services include the creation, display, deletion, and change of business objects, or services to run search queries for objects if key fields (such as the order number) are unknown. Core services can also be actions carried out on business objects, such as the rejection of a sales order.

A main use of core services is development of user interfaces. The standardization of services makes it possible to address objects in a uniform way so it won't create a problem to set up generic functions on the objects. Thus, the process of creating a user interface for a service has become much easier for an application developer (or for an occasional user) than it used to be.

Another area where core services are used is in the development of high-level services typically used for the separation of applications (A2A) and external (B2B) communication. In turn, business objects and enterprise services use global data types that define the same semantics for all objects and services.

The ESR whose profile is listed in Table 6.1 is used at the time of development and configuration. It represents the central storage location of business objects and their services to develop enterprise services used in enterprise models. The definitions in the ESR allow you to generate provider classes, interfaces, and proxies. Chapters 4 and 5 have described in great detail how the latter works at present on the basis of the currently available integration repository.

ESR Profile	
Tasks	The Enterprise Services Repository (ESR) is the design-time repository of service objects for the Enterprise Services Architecture.
Data	▶ Business objects (with associated objects) ▶ Service interfaces (with associated operations, message types, and data types) ▶ (ARIS) process models ▶ Business scenario and business process objects ▶ Mapping objects
Affected processes	▶ Design phase ▶ Configuration phase
Required Maintenance	During the design of enterprise services

Table 6.1 Enterprise Services Repository Profile

6.4.3 Modeling Next Practices from Best Practices

This way, a standardized development environment of business processes is created in which the design, modelling, and model-based configuration processes are carried out in an integrated solution. Thus, more than before, it is now possible to store business process knowledge in a central location, while the technical function of coupling new services or existing application functionality with each other allows you to create a service-oriented architecture, step-by-step.

Technically integrated solution

You can specify new, distinct processes ("Next Practices") at one business level and build them at a modeling level on the basis of existing applications ("Best Practices"), and their services, which operate on business objects and the application logic they contain. Process modeling methods and implementation tools allow a top-down specification of business processes. This is accompanied by transparency, homogeneity, and an easier adaptability to changing requirements — all of which result in a reduction of the total cost of ownership.

SAP also plans to integrate the ARIS toolset in an upcoming SAP NetWeaver release. This will allow you to navigate from the models created in ARIS to implementation content. Thus, if you double-click on the business object used in a model, you will be directly forwarded to its definition. This definition can, for instance, contain the structure of a sales order business object consisting of an order

ARIS for SAP NetWeaver

header and order item data, or it can display the relationship to the business partner object. In this context, the global data types used in these structures are also displayed:

Global data types define the attributes of business objects, such as an address or region as a global data type of the business partner object. Global data types are uniquely defined across the entire system and comply with the current Internet standard and other industry standards, such as UN/CEFACT. Figure 6.7 illustrates how you can navigate from the models into the definition and structure of business objects in the ESR.

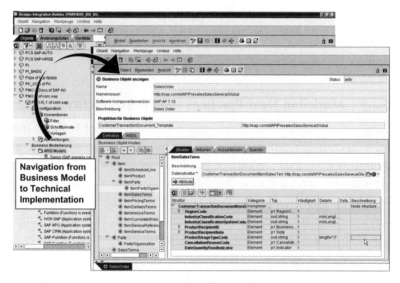

Figure 6.7 From the Business Model to the Implementation Details

6.4.4 Business Activity Monitoring

Monitoring process milestones

Other functions that will be made available in the future refer to topics such as *business activity monitoring* (BAM), which is used to monitor process milestones, among other things. It is supposed to allow the user to monitor and track the progress of a process, and to eventually use this monitoring data to analyze the efficiency of the process.

To make this possible, BAM itself goes deeper and provides new features, particularly with regard to the infrastructure. After all, this corresponds to an event enabling of the platform in that significant events are propagated beyond the boundaries of application systems.

Even today, the SAP system triggers 1,500 events from all possible applications. The events themselves are then processed by a workflow or a function module within the application. An application developer then makes sure that the events are forwarded as required.

However, in the future, this task will be handled by an event infrastructure that uses available services to forward local events provided by the business objects to external applications, such as a composite application or a BAM listener. In this scenario, the application developer does not model or code those relationships. If modelled in the right way, the event infrastructure "notices" that, for instance, a sales order was followed by a purchase order for necessary materials to fulfil the sales order. These relationships are illustrated in Figure 6.8.

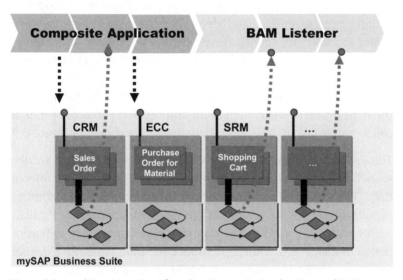

Figure 6.8 Local Events are Transferred to Composite Applications and BAM Listeners

Business activity monitoring describes a framework that provides users with the relevant context to respond with the appropriate actions to significant events. At the same time, users can monitor and measure the efficiency of business processes to identify weak points and improve the process.

The necessary event infrastructure is integrated in the SAP applications to collect, filter, and publish business events for use in other applications. For this, the events are transferred by relevant services to the so-called *milestone monitoring*.

Event infrastructure and milestone monitoring

Milestone monitoring consists of individual process steps that can be modelled using *Business Process Execution Language* (BPEL) tools. However, in contrast to other BPEL processes, they can only receive and transfer events as messages and trigger alerts. As scenario variants, applications can subscribe to events or milestone monitoring and respond to them accordingly. To analyze the process efficiency, the individual process instances tracked in milestone monitoring can be transferred to SAP BW, for instance, to evaluate the quality of the processes.

In a correspondingly modeled user interface (*Event Resolution Dashboard*), it is not only the alerts themselves that are presented in the case of exception and alert situations. The alerts are accompanied by the relevant context information as well as suggested solutions to eliminate the exceptions and alerts. The latter could be set up as a *guided procedure* for solving the problem. For example, if an agreed upon system availability falls short, a *service level agreement* could directly be offered, a notification to the customer could be created, or comparison reports for the recent months could be displayed. To solve the problem, the system could propose Best Practices or initiate collaborative tasks. These interrelationships are shown in Figure 6.9.

This is accompanied by relevant enhancements with regard to alert modeling and simplified options for the modeling of user interactions. Particularly with regard to user interaction and the definition of subprocesses in the context of the WS-BPEL standard, SAP collaborates with IBM on the development of an appropriate extension that is available as a whitepaper under the title, *WS-BPEL Extension for People* (BPEL4People) or *WS-BPEL Extension for Sub-Processes* (BPEL-SPE).

Modeling user interactions
Both, enhancement for user interactions and subprocesses, have become necessary because business processes go beyond activities that are implemented as web services. BPEL4People now proposes a common model for service orchestration and user integration. A direct requirement that results from this is that corresponding UIs (e.g., for alternative decisions) can be directly modeled and configured accordingly.

Modeling subprocesses
Subprocesses are used to decide how to divide large and complex business processes into module-based, reusable, and portable units. This way, it is intended to allow interoperable calls of subprocesses

on the basis of the infrastructures of different providers. For this, different call scenarios are described as well as the corresponding coordination protocols.

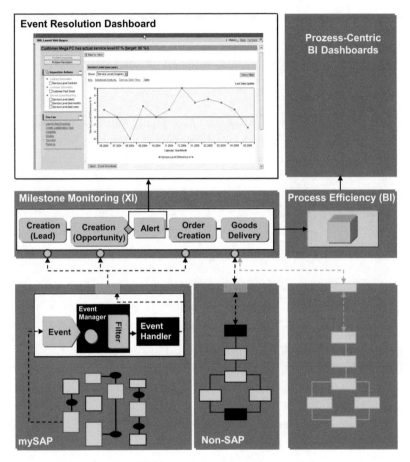

Figure 6.9 Architecture of Business Activity Monitoring (BAM)

Other extensions refer to the central management of alert categories used in service orchestration models. Alerts can be defined in terms of their quality and response times. Moreover, you can store long texts for users who have access to variables and finally, alerts can be integrated in the process, for example, as control steps.

Central alert management

Appendix

A   Exercise Materials

This part of the Appendix contains the source code and templates used for files used in the individual steps of the exercises and case study. Since long code listings are particularly prone to typos when entering them, you can download the respective files and SAP transports from the web sites that accompany this book, at: *http://www. sap-press.com* and *http://www.sap-press.de/1383*.

In some places, you can find date and time details that are to be considered merely as patterns for your own data.

A.1   Resources for Exercise 1 (RFC-to-File)

A.1.1   Function Module Z_RFM_MATERIALINPUT_##

```
FUNCTION Z_RFM_MATERIALINPUT_##.
*"----------------------------------------------------------
*"*"Local Interface:
*" IMPORTING
*"     VALUE(MATNR) TYPE  MATNR
*"     VALUE(MAKTX) TYPE  MAKTX
*"     VALUE(ERSDA) TYPE  ERSDA
*"     VALUE(ERNAM) TYPE  ERNAM
*"     VALUE(MTART) TYPE  MTART
*"     VALUE(MBRSH) TYPE  MBRSH
*"     VALUE(MATKL) TYPE  MATKL
*"     VALUE(MEINS) TYPE  MEINS
*"     VALUE(BRGEW) TYPE  BRGEW
*"     VALUE(GEWEI) TYPE  GEWEI
*"     VALUE(MTPOS_MARA) TYPE  MTPOS_MARA
*"----------------------------------------------------------
ENDFUNCTION.
```

A.1.2   Calling Program Z_PROG_MATERIALINPUT_##

```
*&---------------------------------------------------------*
*& Report   Z_PROG_MATERIALINPUT_##
*&---------------------------------------------------------*

REPORT  z_prog_materialinput_##.
```

```
PARAMETERS: pa_matnr TYPE matnr,
            pa_maktx TYPE maktx,
            pa_mtart TYPE mtart,
            pa_mbrsh TYPE mbrsh,
            pa_matkl TYPE matkl,
            pa_meins TYPE meins,
            pa_brgew TYPE brgew,
            pa_gewei TYPE gewei,
            pa_mtpos TYPE mtpos_mara.

START-OF-SELECTION.

  CALL FUNCTION 'Z_RFM_MATERIALINPUT_##'
    IN BACKGROUND TASK
    DESTINATION 'SystemA_Sender-##'
    EXPORTING
      matnr       = pa_matnr
      maktx       = pa_maktx
      ersda       = sy-datum
      ernam       = sy-uname
      mtart       = pa_mtart
      mbrsh       = pa_mbrsh
      matkl       = pa_matkl
      meins       = pa_meins
      brgew       = pa_brgew
      gewei       = pa_gewei
      mtpos_mara = pa_mtpos.
  COMMIT WORK.
  IF sy-subrc = 0.
    WRITE 'Call of function module was
          successful.'.
  ENDIF.
```

A.2   Resources for Exercise 2 (File-to-IDoc)

```xml
<?xml version="1.0" encoding="UTF-8"?>

<ns0:MT_Material xmlns:ns0=
"http://www.sap-press.com/xi/training/##">
  <MATNR>XI_BOOK-##</MATNR>
  <MAKTX>XI Book</MAKTX>
  <ERSDA>02082006</ERSDA>
  <ERNAM>sys_a-##</ERNAM>
  <MTART>FERT</MTART>
```

```
    <MBRSH>1</MBRSH>
    <MATKL>030</MATKL>
    <MEINS>ST</MEINS>
    <BRGEW>1,2</BRGEW>
    <NTGEW>1,0</NTGEW>
    <GEWEI>KGM</GEWEI>
    <MTPOS_MARA>NORM</MTPOS_MARA>
</ns0:MT_Material>
```

A.3   Resources for Exercise 3 (ABAP-Proxy-to-SOAP)

```
*&---------------------------------------------------------*
*& Report   Z_MATERIAL_EXISTENCECHECK_##
*&
*&---------------------------------------------------------*

REPORT   z_material_existencecheck_##.

PARAMETERS: p_mat TYPE BAPIMATALL-MATERIAL.
DATA : obj_ref
        TYPE REF TO zco_mi_abap_proxy_mat_exist_##,
        wa_output TYPE zmi_abap_proxy_mat_exist_##_in,
        wa_input  TYPE zmi_abap_proxy_mat_exist_##_ou,
        wa_return TYPE zmi_abap_proxy_mat_exist_##_re.

START-OF-SELECTION.

CREATE OBJECT obj_ref.

wa_output-material = p_mat.

CALL METHOD obj_ref->execute_synchronous
  EXPORTING
    output = wa_output
  IMPORTING
    input  = wa_input.

wa_return = wa_input-return.

WRITE: / wa_return-number, / wa_return-message.
```

A.4 Resources for Exercise 4 (Business Process Management)

A.4.1 Function Module Z_RFM_MATERIALINFO_##

```
FUNCTION Z_RFM_MATERIALINFO_##.
*"----------------------------------------------------------
*"*"Local Interface:
*"  IMPORTING
*"     VALUE(MATNR) TYPE   MATNR
*"     VALUE(ERSDA) TYPE   ERSDA
*"     VALUE(ERNAM) TYPE   ERNAM
*"----------------------------------------------------------

ENDFUNCTION.
```

A.4.2 Calling Program Z_PROG_MATERIALINFO_##

```
*&---------------------------------------------------------*
*& Report   Z_PROG_MATERIALINFO_##
*&
*&---------------------------------------------------------*

REPORT   z_prog_materialinfo_##.

PARAMETERS: pa_matnr TYPE matnr.

START-OF-SELECTION.

  CALL FUNCTION 'Z_RFM_MATERIALINFO_##'
    IN BACKGROUND TASK
    DESTINATION 'SystemA_Sender-##'
    EXPORTING
      matnr      = pa_matnr
      ersda      = sy-datum
      ernam      = sy-uname.
  COMMIT WORK.

  IF sy-subrc = 0.
    WRITE 'Call of function module was successful.'.
  ENDIF.
```

A.5   Resources for Step 1 of the Case Study (Request Creation)

```xml
<?xml version="1.0" encoding="UTF-8"?>
<ns0:MT_Inquiry xmlns:ns0="http://www.sap-press.com/xi/case-
study/##">
   <Customer>1171</Customer>
   <DocumentNumber>Inquiry-##</DocumentNumber>
   <CreationDate>20060806</CreationDate>
   <CreationTime>20:18:00</CreationTime>
   <CollectiveNumber>SUBMI_##</CollectiveNumber>
   <Vendor>SARIDIS</Vendor>
   <ValidTo>20060815</ValidTo>
   <InquiryItem>
      <ItemNumber>10</ItemNumber>
      <MaterialNumber>M-01</MaterialNumber>
      <Description>Screen1</Description>
      <Quantity>1</Quantity>
      <MaterialGroup>0207</MaterialGroup>
      <NetWeight>10</NetWeight>
      <GrossWeight>15</GrossWeight>
      <WeightUnit>KGM</WeightUnit>
      <DeliveryDate>20060820</DeliveryDate>
   </InquiryItem>
   <InquiryItem>
      <ItemNumber>20</ItemNumber>
      <MaterialNumber>M-02</MaterialNumber>
      <Description>Screen2</Description>
      <Quantity>2</Quantity>
      <MaterialGroup>0207</MaterialGroup>
      <NetWeight>10</NetWeight>
      <GrossWeight>15</GrossWeight>
      <WeightUnit>KGM</WeightUnit>
      <DeliveryDate>20060820</DeliveryDate>
   </InquiryItem>
</ns0:MT_Inquiry>
```

A.6   Resources for Step 2 of the Case Study (Quotation Process)

A.6.1   Creating the ZQUOT_ITEM Structure

Call **Transaction SE11** in business system B and select the **Data type** option. Enter the name **ZQUOT_ITEM** in the field to the right of the option, click the **Create button, and then select the Structure** option. Create the items in the **Components tab, as shown in** Figure A.1.

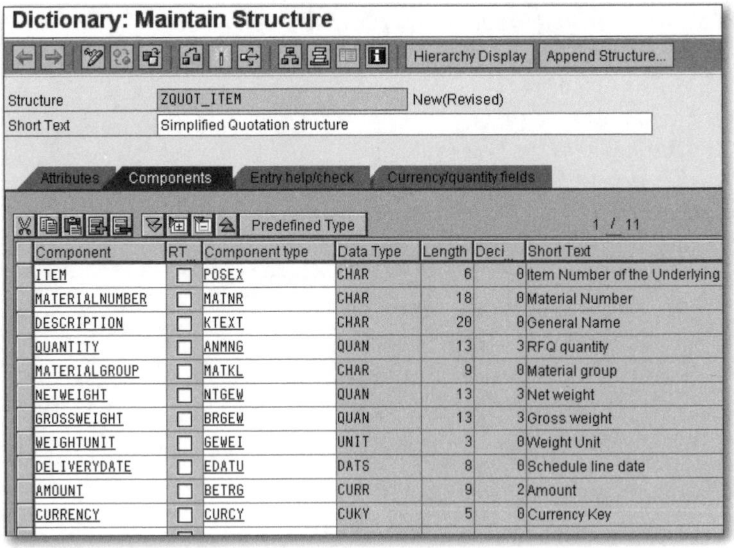

Dictionary: Maintain Structure

Structure	ZQUOT_ITEM		New(Revised)			
Short Text	Simplified Quotation structure					

Attributes | Components | Entry help/check | Currency/quantity fields

Predefined Type   1 / 11

Component	RT	Component type	Data Type	Length	Deci	Short Text
ITEM	☐	POSEX	CHAR	6	0	Item Number of the Underlying
MATERIALNUMBER	☐	MATNR	CHAR	18	0	Material Number
DESCRIPTION	☐	KTEXT	CHAR	20	0	General Name
QUANTITY	☐	ANMNG	QUAN	13	3	RFQ quantity
MATERIALGROUP	☐	MATKL	CHAR	9	0	Material group
NETWEIGHT	☐	NTGEW	QUAN	13	3	Net weight
GROSSWEIGHT	☐	BRGEW	QUAN	13	3	Gross weight
WEIGHTUNIT	☐	GEWEI	UNIT	3	0	Weight Unit
DELIVERYDATE	☐	EDATU	DATS	8	0	Schedule line date
AMOUNT	☐	BETRG	CURR	9	2	Amount
CURRENCY	☐	CURCY	CUKY	5	0	Currency Key

Figure A.1 Components of Structure ZQUOT_ITEM

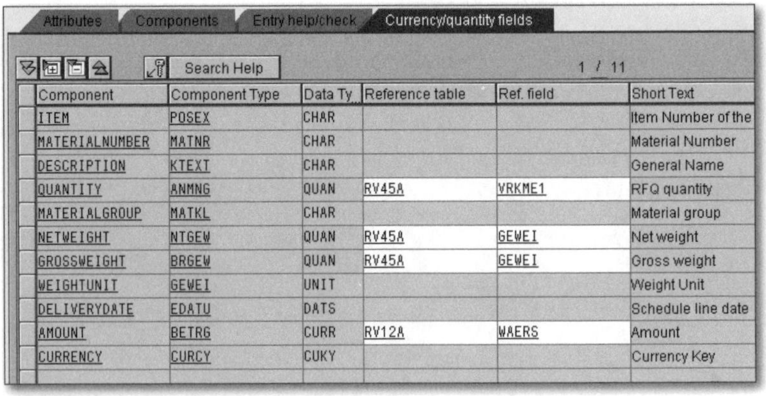

Attributes | Components | Entry help/check | Currency/quantity fields

Search Help   1 / 11

Component	Component Type	Data Ty	Reference table	Ref. field	Short Text
ITEM	POSEX	CHAR			Item Number of the
MATERIALNUMBER	MATNR	CHAR			Material Number
DESCRIPTION	KTEXT	CHAR			General Name
QUANTITY	ANMNG	QUAN	RV45A	VRKME1	RFQ quantity
MATERIALGROUP	MATKL	CHAR			Material group
NETWEIGHT	NTGEW	QUAN	RV45A	GEWEI	Net weight
GROSSWEIGHT	BRGEW	QUAN	RV45A	GEWEI	Gross weight
WEIGHTUNIT	GEWEI	UNIT			Weight Unit
DELIVERYDATE	EDATU	DATS			Schedule line date
AMOUNT	BETRG	CURR	RV12A	WAERS	Amount
CURRENCY	CURCY	CUKY			Currency Key

Figure A.2 Maintaining the Currency and Quantity Fields

Then go to the **Currency/quantity fields** tab and maintain the fields, **QUANTITY**, **NETWEIGHT**, **GROSSWEIGHT**, and **AMOUNT**, as shown in Figure A.2. Save the structure. The menu path **Structure • Check • Check** and **Structure • Activate** allows you to check and activate the object first.

A.6.2 Structuring Web Service Z_SUNNY_QUOTATION

```
FUNCTION z_sunny_quotation.
*"----------------------------------------------------------------
*"*"Local Interface:
*"  IMPORTING
*"     VALUE(IM_COLLECTIVENUMBER) TYPE  SUBMI
*"     VALUE(IM_VENDOR) TYPE  ELIFN
*"     VALUE(IM_CUSTOMER) TYPE  CHAR40
*"  EXPORTING
*"     VALUE(QUOTATIONDATE) TYPE  ANGAB
*"     VALUE(VALIDTO) TYPE  BNDDT
*"     VALUE(CURRENCY) TYPE  KOEIN
*"     VALUE(VENDOR) TYPE  ELIFN
*"     VALUE(NETPRICE) TYPE  NETPR
*"     VALUE(COLLECTIVENUMBER) TYPE  SUBMI
*"     VALUE(DOCUMENTNUMBER) TYPE  VBELN
*"     VALUE(CUSTOMER) TYPE  CHAR40
*"     VALUE(TAXRATE) TYPE  MSATZ
*"     VALUE(TAXAMOUNT) TYPE  MWSBP
*"  TABLES
*"      ITEMS STRUCTURE  ZQUOT_ITEM
*"----------------------------------------------------------------

  DATA wa_item TYPE zquot_item.

  quotationdate = sy-datum.
  validto = sy-datum + 7.
  currency = 'EUR'.
  vendor = 'Sunny Electronics'.
  collectivenumber = im_collectivenumber.
  documentnumber = 'Sunny_Web'.
  customer = im_customer.
  taxrate = 16.

  netprice = 0.

  LOOP AT items INTO wa_item.
    TRANSLATE wa_item-materialnumber TO UPPER CASE.
```

321

```
      CASE wa_item-materialnumber.
        WHEN 'M-00'.wa_item-amount = 859  * wa_item-quantity.
        WHEN 'M-01'.wa_item-amount = 859  * wa_item-quantity.
        WHEN 'M-02'.wa_item-amount = 980  * wa_item-quantity.
        WHEN 'M-03'.wa_item-amount = 944  * wa_item-quantity.
        WHEN 'M-04'.wa_item-amount = 1016 * wa_item-quantity.
        WHEN 'M-05'.wa_item-amount = 449  * wa_item-quantity.
        WHEN 'M-06'.wa_item-amount = 859  * wa_item-quantity.
        WHEN 'M-07'.wa_item-amount = 716  * wa_item-quantity.
        WHEN 'M-08'.wa_item-amount = 1123 * wa_item-quantity.
        WHEN 'M-09'.wa_item-amount = 1202 * wa_item-quantity.
        WHEN 'M-10'.wa_item-amount = 1267 * wa_item-quantity.
        WHEN 'M-11'.wa_item-amount = 1345 * wa_item-quantity.
        WHEN 'M-12'.wa_item-amount = 787  * wa_item-quantity.
        WHEN 'M-13'.wa_item-amount = 828  * wa_item-quantity.
        WHEN 'M-14'.wa_item-amount = 868  * wa_item-quantity.
        WHEN 'M-15'.wa_item-amount = 1095 * wa_item-quantity.
        WHEN 'M-16'.wa_item-amount = 1295 * wa_item-quantity.
        WHEN 'M-17'.wa_item-amount = 1441 * wa_item-quantity.
        WHEN 'M-18'.wa_item-amount = 718  * wa_item-quantity.
        WHEN 'M-19'.wa_item-amount = 863  * wa_item-quantity.
        WHEN 'M-20'.wa_item-amount = 889  * wa_item-quantity.
      ENDCASE.
      wa_item-amount = wa_item-amount / 10 * 11.
      wa_item-currency = 'EUR'.
      MODIFY items FROM wa_item.
      netprice = netprice + wa_item-amount.
    ENDLOOP.

    taxamount = netprice / 100 * taxrate.

ENDFUNCTION.
```

A.7 Resources for Step 3 of the Case Study (Entering a Sales Order)

```
package sap.press.com.xi;

import sap.press.com.xi.types.DT_SalesOrder;
import sap.press.com.xi.types.DT_SalesOrderItem;
import sap.press.com.xi.types.DT_Response;

import java.math.BigDecimal;
import java.rmi.Remote;
```

```
import java.util.Calendar;

import
  com.sap.security.core.client.ws.
  AuthenticationContext;
import
  com.sap.security.core.client.ws.
  SecurityProtocol;

public class SendJavaProxy
{
public static void main(String[] args)
{
try
{
MI_SalesOrderSyncOut##ServiceImpl jsaImpl = new
              MI_SalesOrderSyncOut##ServiceImpl();
Remote remote =
jsaImpl.getLogicalPort(MI_SalesOrderSyncOut##.class);
MI_SalesOrderSyncOut##BindingStub stub =
(MI_SalesOrderSyncOut##BindingStub) remote;

//Authentification
SecurityProtocol securityProtocol =
  (SecurityProtocol)stub._getGlobalProtocols().
  getProtocol("SecurityProtocol");
AuthenticationContext ac =
  securityProtocol.getAuthenticationContext();
String user = "user";
String password = "password";
ac.setUsername(user);
ac.setPassword(password);

DT_SalesOrderItem SOItem1 = new DT_SalesOrderItem();
DT_SalesOrderItem SOItem2 = new DT_SalesOrderItem();
DT_SalesOrder SalesOrder = new DT_SalesOrder();

//SalesOrderItem 1
SOItem1.setItemNumber("0010");
SOItem1.setMaterialNumber("M-01");
SOItem1.setDescription("Screen1");
BigDecimal quantity1 = new BigDecimal("1");
SOItem1.setQuantity(quantity1);
SOItem1.setMaterialGroup("0207");
BigDecimal netweight1 = new BigDecimal("10");
```

```
SOItem1.setNetWeight(netweight1);
BigDecimal grossweight1 = new BigDecimal("12");
SOItem1.setGrossWeight(grossweight1);
SOItem1.setWeightUnit("KGM");
Calendar deliverydate1 = Calendar.getInstance();
deliverydate1.set(2006, 05, 20);
SOItem1.setDeliveryDate(deliverydate1);

//SalesOrderItem 2
SOItem2.setItemNumber("0020");
SOItem2.setMaterialNumber("M-02");
SOItem2.setDescription("Screen2");
BigDecimal quantity2 = new BigDecimal("2");
SOItem2.setQuantity(quantity2);
SOItem2.setMaterialGroup("0207");
BigDecimal netweight2 = new BigDecimal("12");
SOItem2.setNetWeight(netweight2);
BigDecimal grossweight2 = new BigDecimal("14");
SOItem2.setGrossWeight(grossweight2);
SOItem2.setWeightUnit("KGM");
Calendar deliverydate2 = Calendar.getInstance();
deliverydate2.set(2006, 05, 25);
SOItem2.setDeliveryDate(deliverydate2);

//Fill Itemlist
DT_SalesOrderItem[] SalesOrderItems = {SOItem1,
  SOItem2};
SalesOrder.setSalesOrderItem(SalesOrderItems);

//Fill Header
SalesOrder.setCustomer("1171");
Calendar validto = Calendar.getInstance();
validto.set(2006, 05, 25);
SalesOrder.setValidTo(validto);
SalesOrder.setDocumentNumber("PurchaseOrder-##");
SalesOrder.setVendor("SARIDIS");
Calendar cdate = Calendar.getInstance();
SalesOrder.setCreationDate(cdate);
SalesOrder.setCreationTime(cdate);
SalesOrder.setCollectiveNumber("SUBMI_##");

//Send Data
DT_Response Response = stub.MI_SalesOrderSyncOut##(Sales-
Order);
```

```
System.out.println("Type: "+Response.getType()+ ",
  Message: "+Response.getMessage());

}
catch (Exception e)
{
e.printStackTrace();
}
}
}
```

A.8   Resources for Step 4 of the Case Study (Invoice Delivery)

A.8.1   External Mail Definition (from SAP Note 748024)

```xml
<?xml version="1.0" encoding="utf-8" ?>

<xs:schema
  targetNamespace="http://sap.com/xi/XI/Mail/30"
  xmlns:xi="http://sap.com/xi/XI/Mail/30"
  xmlns:xs="http://www.w3.org/2001/XMLSchema">

<!--
  * Mail
  -->
  <xs:element name="Mail">
    <xs:annotation>
      <xs:documentation>Mail package for XI - Mail
        Adapter</xs:documentation>
    </xs:annotation>
    <xs:complexType>
      <xs:sequence>
        <xs:element name="Subject" type="xs:string"
          minOccurs="0">
        </xs:element>
        <xs:element name="From" type="xs:string"
          minOccurs="0">
        </xs:element>
        <xs:element name="To" type="xs:string"
          minOccurs="0">
        </xs:element>
        <xs:element name="Reply_To" type="xs:string"
```

```
                    minOccurs="0">
        </xs:element>
        <xs:element name="Content_Type"
          type="xs:string" minOccurs="0">
        </xs:element>
        <xs:element name="Content_Description"
          type="xs:string" minOccurs="0">
        </xs:element>
        <xs:element name="Content_Disposition"
          type="xs:string" minOccurs="0">
        </xs:element>
        <xs:element name="Date" type="xs:dateTime"
          minOccurs="0">
        </xs:element>
        <xs:element name="Message_ID" type="xs:string"
          minOccurs="0">
        </xs:element>
        <xs:element name="X_Mailer" type="xs:string"
          minOccurs="0">
        </xs:element>
        <xs:element name="Content" minOccurs="0">
          <xs:annotation>
            <xs:documentation>any mixed content
              type</xs:documentation>
          </xs:annotation>
        </xs:element>
      </xs:sequence>
      <xs:attribute name="encoding" type="xs:string">
          <xs:annotation>
            <xs:documentation>
              optional encoding name (base64,
              quoted-printable)
            </xs:documentation>
          </xs:annotation>
      </xs:attribute>
    </xs:complexType>
  </xs:element>
</xs:schema>
```

A.8.2   XSD File for Message Mapping

```
<xsl:stylesheet
xmlns:xsl="http://www.w3.org/1999/XSL/Transform"
version="1.0"
```

```
xmlns:ns0="urn:sap-com:document:sap:rfc:functions"
xmlns:ns="http://sap.com/xi/XI/Mail/30">

<xsl:output method="xml" encoding="utf-8"
  indent="yes" />

<xsl:template match="/">
              <xsl:apply-templates select="INVOIC01"/>
</xsl:template>

<xsl:template match="INVOIC01">
 <ns:Mail>
   <Subject>
     <xsl:text>Invoice: </xsl:text>
     <xsl:value-of select="IDOC/E1EDK01/BELNR" />
   </Subject>
   <From>
     <xsl:text>Sender Mail Address</xsl:text>
   </From>
   <To>
     <xsl:text>Receiver Mail Address</xsl:text>
   </To>
   <Content_Type>
     <xsl:text>text/html</xsl:text>
   </Content_Type>
   <Content>
     <html>
       <head>
         <meta content="text/html;charset=ISO-8859-1"
         http-equiv="Content-Type" />
       </head>
       <body>
         <xsl:text>We charge the items to your
             account:</xsl:text>
         <br/><br/>
         <table border="1" cellPadding="1"
           cellSpacing="1" width="60%">
           <tr>
             <th>Item Nummer</th>
             <th>Description</th>
             <th>Quantity</th>
             <th>Quantity Unit</th>
             <th>Price</th>
           </tr>
           <xsl:apply-templates select="IDOC/E1EDP01" />
```

```
        </table>
      </body>
    </html>
  </Content>
 </ns:Mail>
</xsl:template>

<xsl:template match="IDOC/E1EDP01">
 <tr>
   <td>
     <xsl:value-of select="E1EDP19[QUALF=002]/IDTNR" />
   </td>
   <td>
     <xsl:value-of select="E1EDP19[QUALF=002]/KTEXT" />
   </td>
   <td><xsl:value-of select="MENGE" /></td>
   <td><xsl:value-of select="MENEE" /></td>
   <td>
     <xsl:value-of select="E1EDP26[QUALF=004]/BETRG" />
     <xsl:text> EUR</xsl:text>
   </td>
 </tr>
</xsl:template>

</xsl:stylesheet>
```

B   Bibliography

This bibliography provides an overview of the literature that is explicitly mentioned in this book. The list is not exhaustive and is rather intended to enable you to get familiar with the subject of integrating IT systems.

▶ Aleksy, Markus; Korthaus, Axel; Schader, Martin: *Implementing Distributed Systems with Java and CORBA*. Springer, 2005.

This comprehensive work describes the concepts of CORBA (including interface definition language) and object request brokers, and it demonstrates how you can develop distributed systems using Java and CORBA.

▶ Alonso, Gustavo; Casati, Fabio; Kuno, Harumi; Machiraju, Vijay: *Web Services*. Springer, 2004.

This book stands out among the numerous other books on the subject of web services by focusing on the description of the essential concepts including service composition.

▶ Conrad, Stefan: *Föderierte Datenbanksysteme*. Springer, 1997.

This textbook provides a complete description of the concepts of data integration using federated database systems and it also treats the subjects of semantical integrity and transaction management.

▶ Conrad, Stefan; Hasselbring, Wilhelm; Koschel, Arne; Tritsch, Roland: *Enterprise Application Integration*. Spektrum, 2005.

This profound, up-to-date book on the subject of integrating IT systems describes the basic principles as well as concepts and design patterns on the basis of practical examples.

▶ Erl, Thomas: *Service-Oriented Architecture*. Prentice Hall, 2006.

An introduction to SOA: What are the specific features of services? How can services be modeled and implemented using web services?

▶ Grosso, William: *Java RMI*. O'Reilly, 2001.

A very technical book. After an introduction to the general networking technologies it provides a very detailed description of how to use the Java Remote Method Invocation including the requirements, implementation, and underlying protocols.

▸ Keller, Wolfgang: *Enterprise Application Integration*. dpunkt, 2002.

This book contains an easy-to-understand description of the subject of EAI that is based on real-life examples. In addition, it provides a checklist containing questions on using and selecting EAI products.

▸ Juric, Matjaz B.; Sarang, Poornachandra; Mathew, Benny: *Business Process Execution Language for Web Services*. Packt Publishing, 2nd edition 2006.

This is one of the few currently available books that primarily focus on the structure and application of BPEL.

▸ Mertens, Peter: *Integrierte Informationsverarbeitung 1*. Gabler, 2005.

One of the standard books used in teaching information management. It focuses on the integration of IT systems.

▸ Scheckenbach, Rainer: *Semantische Geschäftsprozeßintegration*. Deutscher Universitätsverlag, 1997.

This thesis casts a light on the technical and organizational issues raised by a cross-company integration of IT systems.

▸ Sharma, Rahul; Stearns, Beth; Ng, Tony: *J2EE Connector Architecture and Enterprise Application Integration*. Addison-Wesley, 2002.

This book provides a detailed introduction into the Java Connector Architecture that's used a s a basis for the extension of SAP XI.

▸ Woods, Dan; Mattern, Thomas: *Enterprise SOA: Designing IT for Business Innovation*. O'Reilly, 2006.

The book by Dan Woods and Thomas Mattern is currently the most up-to-date book on the subject of Enterprise SOA. It uses questions and answers to describe the nature of a service-oriented architecture, how such an architecture is implemented by SAP, and how customers can migrate from their current architecture to Enterprise SOA. The book is intended for a large target audience, from business analysts to enterprise architects that are planning to familiarize themselves with the potentials of an SOA architecture.

C   The Authors

Valentin Nicolescu studied Economics at the University of Hohenheim, Germany. Since 2003, he has been technical head of the *SAP Hochschul Competence Center* (SAP University Competence Center, SAP HCC) at the Technische Universität München. His responsibilities in this role include operating SAP training systems for third-level institutions throughout Germany, and providing SAP training to third-level lecturers.

His focus areas are the products in the SAP NetWeaver platform and teaching classic ERP with SAP R/3 and mySAP ERP. He is a certified SAP Technology and Development Consultant for SAP XI and a Technology Consultant for Web AS and Enterprise Portal.

Professor Burkhardt Funk studied physics and information technology at the universities of Kiel, Würzburg and Stony Brook (USA). After obtaining his PhD degree, he began work in 1997 at McKinsey & Company, where he was a consultant in the areas of retail banking and e-business for international banking institutions. In 2000, he founded his own company.

Today, Burkhardt Funk is Professor of Information Management at the University of Lüneburg, Germany. At the Institute for Electronic Business Processes, his areas of work include the business process-oriented integration of business IT systems and the application of web service-based technologies. He is also a managing partner of the *Gesellschaft für Wirtschaftsinformatik Lüneburg mbH* (Lüneburg Society for Information Management (GWIL)), the main activity of which is carrying out development-intensive projects in the SAP area.

Professor Peter Niemeyer studied mathematics at the University of Ulm and the Technical University of Berlin, Germany. He began work at SAP AG after obtaining his PhD degree in 1996. Initially, he spent many years as an application developer in the Financials area of SAP, and then became a Software Consultant, handling several development-oriented projects for national and international companies.

Today, Peter Niemeyer is Professor of Information Management at the University of Lüneburg, Germany. At the Institute for Electronic Business Processes, his areas of work include application development on the basis of ERP systems, and the business process-oriented integration of business IT systems. He is also a managing partner of the *Gesellschaft für Wirtschaftsinformatik Lüneburg mbH* (Lüneburg Society for Information Management (GWIL)), the main activity of which is carrying out development-intensive projects in the SAP area.

Matthias Heiler holds a degree in physics and is a Solution Sales Executive at SAP AG in Walldorf, Germany. After his studies, he worked as a mainframe application developer in the aviation industry, and then as a project manager on international projects in the areas of banking and automotive for a US consulting firm. He has worked at SAP since 1995, first as a trainer in the area of SAP Basis (R/2 and R/3), and then switched to the Sales area in 1999.

Today, his focus area is service-oriented architectures, particularly integration platforms and business process management. He also lectures in business processes with SAP systems at the International University of Bruchsal, Germany.

Dr. Holger Wittges obtained his PhD degree from the University of Hohenheim, Germany, under the supervision of Professor Krcmar and with the topic "Connecting Business Process Modeling and Workflow Implementation". He then worked for three years as an IT project leader with debitel AG in Stuttgart, Germany.

Since 2004, he has been operations head of the SAP Hochschul Competence Center (*SAP University Competence Center* (SAP HCC)) at Technische Universität München. His current research areas are standard software, service-oriented architectures, and performance metrics in ERP systems. He is also a certified Technology Consultant for SAP NetWeaver—Enterprise Portal & Knowledge Management.

Thomas Morandell studied information technology, with mathematics as his minor subject, at Technische Universität München. During his studies he worked at a number of companies, including OSRAM GmbH. He is now a Development Consultant at SPV AG, and focuses mainly on products of the SAP NetWeaver platform.

Florian Visintin studied information technology, with economics as his minor subject, at Technische Universität München. He is now a Development Consultant working mainly in the area of SAP NetWeaver. During his studies, he worked in a number of companies including Pentos AG in the area of Lotus Notes, focusing on the SAP NetWeaver Exchange Infrastructure.

Benedikt Kleine Stegemann studied information management at the University of Lüneburg, Germany. During his studies, he also worked for a number of companies, including Infracor GmbH (Degussa group) and Airbus Deutschland GmbH in Hamburg. He is now a Development Consultant with GWIL GmbH and works mainly on development projects in the SAP area.

Index

Whiplash effect   292
Wholesaler   291
Work area   187
Work item   194, 254
Workflow   27
Workgroup   117
Write mode   137
WS-BPEL   310
WSDL   34, 35, 162
WSDL interface   163

X

xApps   298
xCQM   304
XI format   55
XI service   96

XI tools   107
XIALL   281
XIISUSER   98
XIPAYLOAD   281
XIRWBUSER   99
XML document   232
XML file   232
XML message   143
XSD document   56
XSD file   278
XSLT file   279
XSLT mapping   74, 277

Z

ZIP   279
Zip code area   55

Completely new, 3rd edition of the benchmark ABAP resource

New chapters on Web Dynpro, Shared Objects, ABAP & XML, regular expressions, dynamic programming, and more

Up-tp-date for SAP NetWeaver 2004s (ABAP release 7.0)

approx. 1050 pp., 3. edition, with DVD 5
79,95 Euro / US$ 79.95
ISBN 1-59229-079-5, Feb 2007

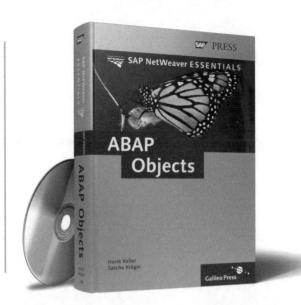

ABAP Objects

www.sap-press.com

H. Keller, S. Krüger

ABAP Objects

ABAP Programming in SAP NetWeaver

This completely revised third edition introduces you to ABAP programming with SAP NetWeaver. All concepts of modern ABAP (up to release 7.0) are covered in detail. New topics include ABAP and Unicode, Shared Objects, exception handling, Web Dynpro for ABAP, Object Services, and of course ABAP and XML. Bonus: All readers will also receive a complimentary copy of the newest Mini SAP System.

**Practical Examples for all
NetWeaver and .NET
Integration Levels**

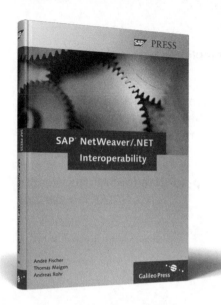

approx. 400 pp., 69,95 Euro / US$ 69.95
ISBN 978-1-59229-088-8, Jan 2007

SAP NetWeaver/ .NET Interoperability

www.sap-press.com

A. Rohr, T. Meigen, A. Fischer

SAP NetWeaver/.NET Interoperability

This comprehensive book is focused on heterogeneous system landscapes built using SAP and
Microsoft components, and quickly teaches readers
about the vast integration capabilities within all
levels of the NetWeaver stack. Developers,
consultants, and IT managers will benefit from
practical examples of all components: interface
technologies like BAPI and RFC, process integration
with XI and BizTalk, information integration with BW
and MS BI, as well as user integration with SAP
NetWeaver Portal, SharePoint, and Office (including
a preview on Duet, formerly known as Project
Medocino).

Interested in reading more?

Please visit our Web site for all
new book releases from SAP PRESS.

www.sap-press.com